TWILIGHT OF EMPIRE:
Responses to Occupation

TWILIGHT OF EMPIRE: RESPONSES TO OCCUPATION

ISBN 0-9763009-0-7

2nd Printing

Published by Perceval Press
1223 Wilshire Blvd., Suite F
Santa Monica, CA 90403
www.percevalpress.com

"Seeking Honesty in U.S. Policy" by Joseph Wilson, reprinted with permission of the *San Jose Mercury News*.

"Stretched Thin, Lied to, and Mistreated" by Christian Parenti, reprinted with permission of *The Nation*.

"Veiled and Worried in Baghdad" by Lauren Sandler, reprinted with permission of the *New York Times*.

"Every Morning the War Gets Up from Sleep," by Fadhil al-Azzawi, reprinted with permission from the author and Boa Editions, Ltd.

Editors: Mark LeVine, Viggo Mortensen, Pilar Perez
Design: Michele Perez
Copy Editor: Sherri Schottlaender

Printed in Spain at Jomagar, S/A

Cover image: An American soldier from the First Cavalry Division hits women with a stick as he tries to maintain order during a propane distribution. LYNSEY ADDARIO/CORBIS 2003

TWILIGHT OF EMPIRE:
Responses to Occupation

PERCEVAL PRESS

CONTENTS

All photographs by Lynsey Addario

EDITOR'S NOTE

The more progress we make on the ground, the more free Iraqis become, the more electricity is available, the more jobs are available, the more kids that are going to school, the more desperate these killers become because they can't stand the thought of a free society.
　　　　　　　　　　　—President George W. Bush

This is the first time that I have seen a parallel to Vietnam, in terms of information that the administration is putting out versus the actual situation on the ground.
　　　　　　　　　　　—Senator John McCain

The glaring contradiction between "the actual situation on the ground" and what often seems to be a deliberately misleading picture painted for public consumption by the Bush administration has created an informational void that a largely cajoled and co-opted mainstream media has shown little or no interest in filling. The dangerous gap between what we are told and what can readily be observed in places like U.S.-occupied Iraq and Afghanistan makes the firsthand information and reasoned assessments offered in books like this one indispensable.

While *Twilight of Empire: Responses to Occupation* does not claim to provide an exhaustive overview of motivations for, or consequences of recent U.S.-led invasions and occupations, it does provide significant new pieces of the evolving puzzle. If "truth is found where contradictions meet," as writer Lindsay Clarke put it, then this book can serve to guide those who would try to find that meeting place. It is, in fact, dedicated to all people, whether they be from the United States, Afghanistan, Iraq, or elsewhere, who strive to keep an open mind and work for peace.

Haitham Hashim, 26, a police officer in the Kazimiya Police force, holds a girl's sandal that he found amidst the destruction of an explosion in Baghdad. LYNSEY ADDARIO/CORBIS 2004

PREVIOUS SPREAD: An Iraqi woman walks through a plume of smoke rising from a massive fire at a liquid gas factory as she searches for her husband in the vicinity of the fire in Basra. LYNSEY ADDARIO/CORBIS 2003

FOREWORD

It has been a year since *Twilight of Empire* was first published, with its extraordinary collection of firsthand accounts, incisive essays, and poetry presenting the war in Iraq with a vivid intensity rarely matched in the literature on that war. Tragically, the picture it presented of Iraq under United States occupation has not changed—it is in fact reinforced by what we read in news accounts every day.

As I write this in the fall of 2004, the number of dead U.S. soldiers has exceeded one thousand, and every day there are more killed and wounded. When Medea Benjamin wrote from Baghdad in early 2003 that "the clock is ticking and patience is wearing thin," she was describing a phenomenon applicable to both Americans and Iraqis, who are still enduring death and suffering long after President Bush triumphantly declared "Mission Accomplished."

The Bush Administration has made strenuous attempts to conceal from the public photos of bodies being returned to the U.S., as well as information about the thousands of wounded soldiers. Nevertheless, those stories have emerged, even if only sporadically, in the mainstream press. A story in the *New York Times* on December 30, 2003, told of a young man who, after months in Iraq, came home blinded. His mother, visiting him in the hospital, saw a young female soldier crawling along the floor, her legs gone, her three-year-old son trailing behind her.

On September 22, 2004, war correspondent Chris Hedges related the story of Sue Niederer, whose only son had been killed in Iraq: Niederer showed up at a Republican gathering in her New Jersey town to confront Laura Bush with a sign that read, "President Bush killed my son," and shouting, "Why don't your children serve?" She was arrested and handcuffed before being released.

Sue Niederer's outburst is a reflection of an increasing anger against the war among families who have lost loved ones. Another mother, Ruth Aitken, whose son was killed in fighting around Baghdad, told a reporter, "It makes me mad that this whole war was sold to the American public and to the soldier as something it wasn't." A number of these outraged parents have formed a group called Military Families Against the War. One of the group's leading members is the father of Marine Lance Corporal Jesus Suarez del Solar, who has said that his son died for "Bush's oil."

Although the casualty toll among U.S. soldiers has been played down by the government and has not been emphasized by the media, the grim news nevertheless has eroded the public's patience with the war. By mid-2004 polls showed that more than half of the American people felt that the war is not worth its cost in human suffering.

The word "impatience" is wholly inadequate to describe the Iraqi reaction to the U.S. military presence. Profound sadness at the fate of their country, grief at the death of family and friends, fury at the occupiers—those are the dominant reactions of the Iraqi people as reported by observers on the ground. As an example, Jodie Evans quotes an Iraqi in this volume: "Are the Americans doing this to destroy us?"

The Iraqi victims of this war have been largely invisible in the American press, which has obsequiously followed the lead of the Pentagon. The Pentagon itself says again and again that it does not keep track of Iraqi casualties. I recall the statement of General Colin Powell at the end of the first Gulf War in 1991, when he boasted about the small number of U.S. casualties; when asked about Iraqi casualties in this war, he replied, "That is a matter I am not terribly concerned with."

Also in this book, Kristina Borjesson, an independent journalist, speaking with her interviewer about the control of information on American television, states that the reality of human suffering is hidden from the public. As I write this in September of 2004, a Knight Ridder report of statistics compiled by the Iraqi health ministry (like other Iraqi ministries, it is under the authority of the occupying forces) says that in just the five previous months, 3,487 Iraqis have died, most of them civilians, and many of them children.

Statistics, no matter how shocking, are cold and inadequate. In the same news report, Dr. Mumtz Jaber, a vascular surgeon in Baghdad, told of his sister and brother-in-law, who did not stop fast enough at an American checkpoint; their three-year-old son was shot and killed when soldiers opened fire. At the morgue in Baghdad, the physician there said he saw a family of eight brought in—three women, three men, two children—who were sleeping on their roof (it was too hot inside) when a military helicopter shot and killed them all.

One would have to multiply such individual stories by the thousands to grasp the reality of a military operation that claims only to be fighting against "terrorists." You will find in this book, in the piece by journalist Eman Ahmed Khammas, a Sunni Muslim who lives in Baghdad, figures from Iraq Body Count. This group of British and U.S. researchers reports that during the war (that is, in the several weeks of "shock and awe" before the occupation itself) close to 8,000 Iraqis were killed, with 20,000 injured.

And what of those Iraqis—perhaps 10,000 or more—who have been seized from their homes or off the streets to be put into indefinite detention, simply on "suspicion," with no hearings, no right to attorneys, no charges filed. Some of these people will be released months later, without any explanation. The treatment suffered by these detainees may range from ordinary humiliation to the sexual abuse and torture inflicted by U.S. forces in Abu Ghraib prison.

A February 2004 report by the International Committee of the Red Cross (ICRC) said about these detainees: "In almost all instances . . . arresting authorities provided no information about who they were . . . nor did they explain the cause of arrest. . . . Certain military intelligence officers told the ICRC that in their estimate, between 80 percent and 90 percent of the persons deprived of their liberty in Iraq had been arrested by mistake."

And what about the lives of those Iraqis who escape death, mutilation, or imprisonment? How do they live day by day? They live, for the most part, without clean water or electricity or adequate health care or sewage disposal, and they live in a state of constant fear. What the U.S. government has called the "reconstruction" of Iraq has become a sorry joke—it is really a story of profiteering and corruption. A Reuters dispatch in August 2004 reported that an official U.S. audit found that more than $8 billion given to Iraqi ministries by the former U.S.-led authority could not be accounted for.

Naomi Klein's piece in this volume provides a clue to the reasons for this disaster: the U.S. government, with its utter devotion to the capitalist ethic of greed, has in effect turned the Iraqi economy over to multinational corporations who have swarmed all over the country with only one thought in mind—profit. When the profit motive is primary, human needs are left behind.

Klein finds in Iraq a microcosm of what has been happening all over the world—the power of the United States and the World Bank and the International Monetary Fund has been used to turn public enterprises over to private corporations, and this insistence on deregulation has had calamitous results for ordinary people. While the press shows photos of poor people looting stores, Klein gives us a larger picture, revealing the "economic looting" of Iraq by the multinationals.

Perhaps it's no wonder that someone has painted the following phrase in English under the new statue that has replaced the dismantled statue of Saddam Hussein in Baghdad: "All done. Go home."

It is refreshing to find in the pages of this book the thoughts and the feelings of Muslims opposed to the American occupation who believe in nonviolent solutions. Americans need to be acquainted with such sentiments in order to reject the ideas put forth by some intellectuals in the United States who speak about "Muslim fanaticism" and a "clash of civilizations."

I have no doubt that the reason so many Americans still support the Iraq war is that they remain mostly ignorant of history due to what Studs Terkel has called "our national amnesia." This ignorance begins in school and is perpetuated by the mass media and the political leadership of the nation. If there were some sense of history among Americans, they would immediately connect the word "occupation" with the second World War, when we became familiar with the phrases "occupied France," "occupied Denmark," "occupied Europe." The word "occupation" suggests a shocking connection between Hitler's invasion of other countries—he also claimed to be "liberating" them—and the unprovoked U.S. invasion of Iraq. And then, perhaps recalling the "resistance movements" in France and elsewhere in Europe, people might begin to understand why the Iraqis are violently resisting the American presence in their country.

Most Americans do not know the history of the Middle East, and Mike Davis reminds us in these pages about the brutal British conquest of the very same lands now occupied by American and British forces. Does Prime Minister Tony Blair not feel a twinge of shame at the thought that he is engaging in a pitiful re-creation of those years after World War I when English planes bombed helpless villagers and Winston Churchill proposed the use of poison gas against the resisting Arabs? Davis reminds us that the "aerial terror" tactics we have become accustomed to since Ethiopia, the Spanish Civil War, and World War II—since Addis Ababa, Madrid, Dresden, Tokyo, Hiroshima, Nagasaki—began in the Middle East with the bombing of Libya. And yes, the British Empire was "victorious," but at what horrific cost to the people of in the region? And did that victory not end ultimately in ignominy?

Is that not the fate of arrogant empires, and will that not be our own fate, sooner or later? Have we forgotten that in Vietnam, the longest of American wars, even with our enormous, frightening military machine with its B-52 bombers, its chemical weapons, its unsurpassed technology, we eventually had to exit that destroyed land even as our leaders insisted all the while that we must "stay the course?"

Books like this one help spread the truth, which has a power greater than guns. Empires topple because human beings can only take so much of tyranny, whether it comes from inside or from abroad. Through all the haze of violence and suffering, we may be seeing the twilight of empire.

An Iraqi man detained by soldiers with the 4th Infantry Division, 3rd Brigade, from the 1st Battalion–68th Armored Regiment, stands bound against a wall in a compound. LYNSEY ADDARIO/CORBIS 2003

INTRODUCTION

Twilight of Empire: Responses to Occupation offers an incisive and moving collection of perspectives in these increasingly dangerous times. Written at a moment when a president who was not popularly elected is declaring endless war, the essays, interviews, and reports in this book are each a critical piece of the arguments that need to be heard now more than ever.

On September 11, 2001, we were broadcasting *Democracy Now!* from our studio in the garret of a nineteenth-century firehouse in New York City's Chinatown. Blocks away, the first jet had hit the north tower of the World Trade Center. At 9:03 A.M., the second plane hit the second tower. We heard a faint boom, but from within our studios it sounded like a common sound of the city. We soon got word of the horror and destruction that was occurring just blocks away from us at what was to become known as Ground Zero. We finished the show but kept our line open to the satellite uplink at Pacifica station KPFA in Berkeley, and we continued broadcasting throughout the day. Our colleagues at Downtown Community Television, the non-profit television production and training facility that owns the firehouse, opened the doors and offered the people streaming up the road water and use of telephones. We brought people upstairs to broadcast their eyewitness accounts. At 5 P.M. we witnessed the collapse of Building Seven, most likely as a result of Rudolph Giuliani's ill-placed Emergency Command Center's massive diesel fuel depot within.

An evacuation zone was established at Canal Street, two blocks to the north of us, so the *Democracy Now!* crew decided to stay in the firehouse so we could continue to broadcast over the coming days. We slept on the floor for three nights as the military occupied Lower Manhattan. Early in the morning of Friday, September 14, I went out with another *Democracy Now!* producer, and we walked toward Ground Zero. The streets were empty: buildings and abandoned cars were completely covered with dust that has since been proven to be highly toxic. There were Humvees and portable klieg lights closer to Ground Zero, parked at intersections filled with pallets of bottled water and exhausted-looking members of the National Guard. As we navigated as close as we could, we witnessed the smoldering ruins, saw the fires still raging undergound, and watched the heavy traffic of trucks hauling away load after load of steel beams piled like fallen logs.

Turned back at a security gate, we rounded back to Church Street, past Wall Street, and on to Battery Park, at Manhattan's southernmost tip, which had become a bustling military camp. Olive-green vehicles of all sizes circled the park. Signs had been hung with billeting instructions and security detachment schedules, all in the military's inscrutable jargon. It was still hours before dawn, but hundreds were awake and at work. We encountered a woman in green camouflage fatigues. She was from upstate New York and was a helicopter pilot in the National Guard. We asked her what she thought. She had just arrived and was likely going to be assigned to guard duty, protecting access to Ground Zero. She said that she was horrified at the scene of devastation a block away. She then said something that was both unexpected, but not altogether surprising: she said she hoped that there wouldn't be a military response, that as a mother she didn't want to see more death come out of this act of terrorism. She declined to speak on camera, even anonymously, but her words stayed with me.

Soon after, the Bush administration announced the color-coded Terror Alert System, with colors designating the government's publicly pronounced assessment of the threat of a terrorist attack. Since that time, all of New York City has remained on Orange Alert, with green-camouflaged soldiers from the National Guard with machine guns at the ready standing out amidst the white paint and concrete of our subway stations. NYPD Commandos in body armor, also with machine guns, patrol the sidewalks and Starbucks of Manhattan. President Bush appointed Tom Ridge, the governor of Pennsylvania, to be the Secretary of Homeland Security: he created havoc nationally by encouraging people to cover their windows with plastic sheeting and duct tape.

In response to this color scheme—widely held to be a convenient public relations tool to manipulate people with fear when the Bush administration needed to distract the public from genuine issues—a group of women got together and formed Code Pink: Women for Peace. Bedecked in brilliant pink clothing, with pink feather boas and pink umbrellas, these women started networking to oppose war and to unify people against the use of 9/11 for cynical political goals. They protested, they maintained a continuous vigil outside the White House, and they networked through traditional means and via the Internet.

The global peace movement was unable to prevent the bombing of Afghanistan, in which thousands of civilians were killed—these deaths were referred to collectively by the Pentagon and their supportive press corps as "collateral damage." As U.S. Secretary of State Colin Powell says, "We don't count enemy dead." And so it was up to civil society, to journalists and activists from Code Pink and allied organizations, to go to Afghanistan and investigate and document the civilian casualties of the U.S.-led invasion. The stories were horrible and common: entire extended families were wiped out; U.S. helicopter gunships hovered over villages with no connection to the Taliban government or Al-Qaeda and rained bullets down on women and children. At *Democracy Now!* we followed these delegations, kept in touch with independent journalists like Robert Fisk and John Pilger, and broadcast this different picture of a bloody invasion that was ignored by the mainstream media.

By September 2002, with Osama bin Laden still at large and U.S. corporations enmeshed in an accelerating cascade of corporate scandals, the Bush administration, facing its most serious criticisms since 9/11, seemed strangely quiet. We were soon to find out why. I was just about to speak at the Power to the Peaceful Rally in San Francisco, organized by the great hip-hop artist Michael Franti, when Code Pink co-founder Medea Benjamin came over to me. "Did you hear what Andrew Card just said?" she asked. (Andrew Card is George W. Bush's Chief of Staff, and the former chief lobbyist for General Motors.) "From a marketing standpoint, you don't roll out a new product in August," Card said. Bush was just finishing up one of his many vacations, waiting for the proper moment to launch his new fall line with Tony Blair. On September 7, the two men held a joint press conference at Camp David and announced that Saddam Hussein was an imminent threat to the safety of the U.S. and Britain.

Thus began the six-month marketing blitz that led to the massive and violent implementation of the Bush Doctrine of preemptive war, with the now sadly familiar consequences: uncountable civilian casualties and continually mounting U.S. troop casualties. The occupation is causing a deepening crisis for the president and the British prime minister as it becomes costly, violent, and unpopular in Iraq and at home, even as the stated reasons for war remain unproven and have essentially been cast aside. At the time of this writing, more than 164,000 members of the National Guard and military reservists are on active duty, the majority of them having had their assignments lengthened. What for many soldiers was likely a way to supplement family income—as suggested in the recruitment slogan of "One weekend a month and two weeks a year"—has now become a living hell as they are stationed in cramped quarters in Iraq, in 120-degree weather, facing dangerous assignments and daily attacks from an invisible enemy.

The administration's chief weapons inspector, David Kay, returned from three months in Iraq with 1,200 inspectors, having spent $300 million. Number of weapons of mass destruction found: zero. He claims he needs $600 million more and asks for an additional six to nine more months. The timeline is not lost on anyone watching the presidential election cycle. The Republican Party very carefully chose New York as its convention city; the gathering will take place one week before September 11, 2004, and most regard this as both a grotesque politicization of the mass murder that occurred at Ground Zero and another carefully orchestrated roll-out of a new product timed to coincide with the presidential campaign season.

With so much at stake, we each must take responsibility for the health of our democracy. We must hold those in power accountable, and we need to pressure the media to do its job of challenging those in power rather than acting as their stenographers. We need a society in which dissent is commonplace, so that when someone at work takes a break by the water cooler and hears someone else criticize those in power, it is not shocking. The major media in the U.S. must also be held accountable. It is not only Pacifica Radio, NPR, and PBS that use the public airwaves: ABC, CBS, and NBC all use them as well, and they are required by law to serve the public interest, which they fail to do with increasing audacity.

For the water-cooler dissenters, or for the many millions who once supported the government's actions but now have serious questions, this book will serve as an invaluable resource. Its pages are filled with eloquent firsthand accounts, reports from award-winning journalists, and expert analysis from people who are virtually excluded from the narrowly defined sound-bite exchanges that the mainstream media allow on their infotainment news programs.

Read this book, share this book, and engage in informed and frequent discussion on the topics within: Empire, Occupation, War, Peace. Regardless of your position on the issues, make debate and dissent commonplace, for debate and dissent are at the core of any strong, healthy democracy. Together we can break the sound barrier.

BAGHDAD JOURNAL #1

Medea Benjamin and I brought a group of fourteen people to Iraq in February 2003. About six months before that we had founded Code Pink: Women for Peace, a response to the Bush Administration's color-coded terrorist weather watch. Code Pink called on women and men to "wage peace" through proactive, creative protest and nonviolent direct action. Our February visit to Iraq was intended as a "preemptive strike" for peace—specifically, we tried to establish person-to-person contacts with Iraqi women and also report on what we saw and heard without the filter of corporate media. We returned to Iraq in July to witness the occupation.

"Is it better before or after the invasion?" I ask Faruk, who had cared for us so generously on our first trip to Baghdad in February.

"It was better during the bombing," he explains, with a look that says, can't you see for yourself? Later I learn that his house was bombed and he was still in the process of fixing it.

"Before, we had one Saddam. Now we have one hundred. Are the Americans doing this to destroy us?"

How can I answer this question? It is similar to the question I was asked during my February visit: "Why does Mr. Bush want to bomb us?"

In the aftermath of the U.S. invasion, we felt the need to return to Baghdad. We needed to see the people we had met on our previous trip, friends we thought of daily as we watched the fire and smoke of "shock and awe." We needed to learn how they had fared through the American invasion. We had also received funding and support to lay the groundwork for setting up the International Occupation Watch Center (IOWC), a project of United for Peace and Justice and a coalition of other international peace groups. The IOWC is intended to

be an independent organization that will monitor the activities of the coalition military forces and foreign corporations, thus providing the international community with reliable, independent information; the IOWC also supports local efforts to improve the lives of the Iraqi people in order to help them rebuild their country and move toward self-rule.

Our delegation consisted of me, Reverend Patricia Ackerman, and Gael Murphy, all from Code Pink; Medea Benjamin of Global Exchange, the co-founder of Code Pink; Ted Lewis of Global Exchange; and documentary filmmakers Gerard Ungerman and Audrey Brohy.

As before, we flew to Amman, Jordan, to arrange the overland caravan crossing to Baghdad. In February the trip across the desert cost us 39 U.S. dollars; now the bidding was between $150 and $500. We settled on $175—as I wondered if the extra $25 would save us from the dangers on the road, I knew in my gut that it didn't really matter. We'd already surrendered to the fates in deciding to come here.

One encounters "Ali Baba" crime—a description used by Iraqis—when trying to cross the desert from Amman to

Baghdad. About twenty cars a day are held up going through Fallouja, though the "Ali Babas" do let the occupants live. Actually, a GI at the border told us that these Ali Babas were kind, in general: last week they had taken a truck and all its contents but left the Jordanian driver by the side of the road with thirty dollars and his shirt so that he wouldn't be totally stranded.

To cross the desert and make the border in time for the caravan, we left our hotel at 1:30 in the morning. By the time we reached the border, the intense rose light of dawn spread across the desert. On the Jordanian side, hundreds of trucks waited to cross over, laden with merchandise of all sorts: packaged goods, computers, tires, plywood, machine parts, replacements for things either worn out from years of sanctions, destroyed in the bombing, or carried off by looters; most of this material is intended for the use of the occupying forces, because most Iraqis are without jobs or the money for such things. We met two Jordanians who were taking in a load of beer and alcohol. On our February trip it had been impossible to find a drink except in the high-rent district of Baghdad. Later, in Baghdad I would see drunken men roaming the streets, something I had never encountered before the war.

Some borders make sense, at least in terms of geography. The Jordanian side is relatively cool, with rolling hills and even evergreen trees. Crossing into Iraq one enters the desert, a vast, empty scrub done in various shades of dirt which goes on forever, unbroken save for the occasional little clump of cement-block buildings that constitute the villages in this region. The heat is all-encompassing, inescapable, filtered through the gray dust that hangs in the air and coats every

surface. You are almost always thirsty, and everyone obsesses about water: where to get it, how much to carry.

It had taken three hours to enter Iraq in February—now it took minutes. We saw our first mutilated image of Saddam, its tiles scratched and gouged. A GI sat atop his dusty tank looking hot and bored, like all the other GIs around the border, their guns strapped to their legs and machine guns thrown over their shoulders.

We were conducted to a cinderblock structure built on a cement slab, a contrast to the inviting and comfortable living room where we'd been greeted in February and taught a few words of Arabic as we were served chai.

"That sucks!" someone shouted as we entered the small room.

The speaker was a young GI from Colorado named Rick, who was not much more than eighteen years old. He was visibly distraught, jittery, pacing around the bare dirty room as if his body could not contain his nerves. He could not seem to stop talking. Another slightly older GI sat silently in a corner, his face expressionless, a machine gun on his lap.

We gave our passports to the bored Iraqi man behind the window. He barely looked at our documents as he stamped them (no visas required)—we could have been anyone. Paul Bremer declared that with the exception of weapons and drugs, anything could be brought into the country, duty-free, for a period of three months; though we could have been smuggling kilos of heroin and Uzis, no one bothered to open our bags.

Anyone, it seemed, could now get into Iraq, and everyone was: Jordanians, Palestinians, all coming in waves from the surrounding Arab countries. There were businessmen from Europe and Japan in silly-looking black suits, and American men from the South. All were

Heaps of trash and sewage line the streets of Baghdad. LYNSEY ADDARIO/CORBIS 2003

looking to profit from the new Wild West, the Iraqi Gold Rush, where there are few rules and little authority to get in the way of profits.

Our friend Amal would tell us later as we sat in her garden: "We are a wounded animal in the forest; everyone is coming to take their piece of our flesh."

After the perfunctory ritual of having our passports stamped, we talked a while with the GIs stationed in the room. The younger of the two, the anxious eighteen-year-old from Colorado, was upset because he had tried to call his girlfriend on a cell phone borrowed from a Danish businessman, and just as he had finally made the connection, the phone died. He hadn't spoken to her in more than a month, and he was sure she was about to dump him. "She's gonna leave me," he repeated, "I know she's gonna: I'm gonna get that Dear John letter, I can tell"—that is, when the mail finally arrived. The soldiers' living conditions, we quickly discovered, were miserable: erratic mail, bad meals, uncomfortable beds, hellish heat, and no idea when they'd be going home.

"You missed the caravan," Rick informed us. "They took off a half hour ago." He suggested that we wait for another but had no idea when that might be. A look of concern crossed his face when we voted to go it alone.

Hassan, our driver, wasn't too concerned. "Don't worry," he told us. "Before we get to Fallouja, I will stop at my friend's grocery store and pick up a machine gun. We'll put it in the middle of the front seat and the Ali Babas won't bother us."

The road out from the border crossing area is gone; we have to make our way across the desert. Looking to the side we see a crater of concrete and steel ripped and peeled back by a missile. It reminds Patricia and me of Amriya, the bomb shelter we visited in February where more than four hundred women and children were killed by American missiles in 1991. A thick silence filled the car.

Our six-hour drive through "Ali Baba land" (our driver's expression) was uneventful. We sped down the highway past the debris of battle: the carcasses of tanks, Humvees, overturned buses, exploded shells, and bomb craters, along with the occasional shepherd and his flock picking their way through the rubble.

We passed the skeleton of a burnt-out red Ferrari.

"Uday's," our driver informed us.

I have no way of knowing if that was true or not, and I don't think it matters. It's the truth that people tell themselves, the story that they've created to make some sense of the chaos: Here is the wreckage of Uday's Ferrari, the ruined remains of Saddam's regime.

The Baghdad that greeted us in July was not the Baghdad we'd left in February. Most of the taller buildings have been destroyed or damaged, leaving crumpled steel frames, burnt-out shells, walls full of holes and scarred by flames. Rolls of razor wire lined the streets. The air was a haze of dust weighed down by heat. As we crossed the bridge that leads to the street where our apartment was, we could see the destruction along the banks of the Tigris, where nearly every building appeared to be damaged. The United Nations Development Program was an empty husk with black scorch marks rising from the windows, as if the flames had left their shadows behind. On the Tigris side, all the restaurants were abandoned and wrecked, either from the bombing or the looting.

Tanks blocked opposing traffic about halfway to our hotel, so cars came straight at us as they made left turns; we were salmon swimming upstream against the current of cars, with no traffic lights or controls of any sort. This was our first experience of life without electricity.

Earlier we had passed long lines of parked cars as we drove through the streets; we later learned that they were waiting for gas. Without electricity, the gas pumps don't work properly. To avoid the lines, some men arrive on foot with cans to fill by hand. Similar lines exist for kerosene and gas for cooking, because the gas isn't being delivered to people's homes. All of this has created a very dangerous situation. The hospitals are full of burn cases.

We again stayed in the Andaluz Apartments, across the street from the Palestine Hotel, where the Al-Jazeera reporter was killed by American tank fire. The owners and staff greeted us with hugs and celebration. We had all grown close during the tense days of our February stay, and it was a great relief to find that our friends had made it through the bombing. The staff of the Andaluz Apartments is in many ways typical of places that service foreigners: they are, in general, highly educated professionals who speak excellent English; many were engineers and English literature majors. They are doing jobs for which they are overqualified, but in a country under sanctions, the jobs for which they were trained frequently do not exist, and positions involving interaction with foreigners provide higher salaries and good tips.

Continued . . .

A U.S. soldier stands guard as a building burns behind him following a grenade attack on a Humvee in August
2003. LYNSEY ADDARIO/CORBIS 2003

THE UNGRATEFUL VOLCANO

Does the Pentagon have a "bureau of history"? Is there a room somewhere in that vast labyrinth where monkish researchers toil over the ancient archives of power, exhuming the lessons of colonies won and lost, empires risen and fallen?

I doubt it. The Pentagon's interest in history is probably the same as the Swiss passion for surfing or the Saudi Arabian enthusiasm for ice hockey: rather oxymoronic.

Too bad. A great deal of carnage might have been avoided if Donald Rumsfeld—or for that matter, Tony Blair—had bothered to read the letters of Gertrude Bell and the diaries of Winston Churchill. Gertie and Winnie knew the land between the rivers terribly well. After all, they were the ones who transformed three prosperous and ethnically distinct provinces of the Ottoman empire into an unhappy British client state.

"Iraq?" Been there and done it, old boy. Our turn was bloody tragedy; now you Yanks get the apocalyptic farce. Odd how history repeats itself on the banks of the Euphrates, isn't it? Cheerio.

Let us imagine what kind of memo these old imperials might have passed along to their cowboy descendants, a precis, as it were, of the previous occupation.

It wouldn't really be a "cautionary tale"—after all, we are already far too far up river in the heart of darkness. Caution and humanity have already been stuffed into body bags. But the British precedent might indicate a general trajectory for imperial hubris. They too started out expecting hugs and kisses and ended up giving back bombs and genocide.

I. MISS BELL'S TEA PARTY

What Woodrow Wilson would later denounce as the "whole disgusting scramble" for the Middle East began when the British invaded "Mesopotamia" in 1914. The War Office already knew that the twentieth century would be powered by petroleum, and officially the British were only protecting their oil properties in neighboring Persia from untoward Turkish or German attentions; unofficially, they were also prospecting for oil around Basra.

The conquest of Mesopotamia was supposed to be a triumphal procession in the face of desultory Turkish resistance. In actuality, it was a singularly unhappy hike that involved a lot of heat, dust, thirst, and dying. The British advance first turned into an ignominious retreat, and then a catastrophe at Kut-al-Amara in 1916. The British were forced to organize a second, far larger expedition. In 1917 the redcoats finally fought their way into Baghdad and allowed Miss Bell to take her tea on the banks of the Tigris.

The general presumption was that now that the bad Turks were gone, the rest of the population would shower love upon the British. "It's a wonderful thing to feel the affection and confidence of a whole people around you," Bell enthused in the early months of the occupation. Officially the Oriental Secretary (that is to say, the resident expert on the "Arab mind") in the British administration, the erudite and adventurous Miss Bell was Paul Wolfowitz *avant l'lettre:* the optimistic ideologue of the happy occupation.

Her blueprint was not dissimilar to the plan unveiled by the United States Deputy Secretary of Defense in winter 2003. The occupation of Iraq, according to Bell, would be strictly pay-as-you-go, with oil exploration—now doubled with the illegal British annexation in 1918 of the Mosul region—reimbursing the hard-pressed Exchequer, while Iraqis (although they were not yet called that) policed themselves under British supervision. Liberated from the iron heel of Ottoman rule, the locals would be slowly tutored in democratic values, even though the new dispensation was, in fact, based on arrogant English sahibs ruling in partnership with a handful of Sunni notables while Kurdish sheiks were arrested, Shia clerics persecuted, and tribal oil lands confiscated.

The population drew unfavorable comparisons between Turkish rule, with its comfortable quotient of local self-government, and British occupation, with its ruthless drive for efficiency, especially in the collection of taxes. Despite growing restiveness, Miss Bell was still camped on a cloud. "On the whole," she wrote in 1918, "the country is being opened up, and on the whole the people like it. . . . Basra is under peace conditions, and we have had almost no trouble in Baghdad." Her boss and Paul Bremer's predecessor, Sir Arnold Wilson, was equally optimistic: "The average Arab, as opposed to the handful of amateur politicians of Baghdad, sees the future as one of fair dealing and material and moral progress under the aegis of GB [Great Britain]."

The next year at Versailles, the broader Arab national cause—in whose service Bell and her colleague, Colonel T. E. Lawrence, had insinuated themselves early in the war—was comprehensively betrayed by the Anglo-French division of the Middle East which gave Zionism its beachhead in Palestine and turned Syria over to France. Mesopotamia, meanwhile, was the object of a fierce intramural struggle inside the government of Lloyd George. On one side were the "Indianists," who wanted an old-fashioned colony with lots of permanent sinecures for unemployed British aristocrats; on the other side were "Arabists" like Bell, who desperately wanted a throne to assuage the Hashemite dynasty just evicted by the Foreign Legion in Damascus. ("You will understand," one British official wrote to another, "that what is wanted is a King who will be content to reign but not govern.")

There was little concern about what the ordinary population thought about colonial satraps or foreign monarchs. The Kurds were especially impatient, and in May 1919 they rose up against the British and were crushed. Bell and others in Baghdad thought that was the end of the affair, while in London those in power were more worried about the Americans and Standard Oil's demands for a piece of Mesopotamia.

2. THE CHURCHILL DOCTRINE

At the same time, some of the most brilliant minds in London were concentrating on how to reduce the soaring costs of the occupation. Winston Churchill, who was both Secretary of State for War and for Air, wrote to Royal Air Force head Hugh Trenchard in February 1920 wondering if Britain couldn't economize by replacing troops with planes. He expressed interest in chemical weapons, like the mustard gas bombs that the RAF had used against the Bolsheviks. Trenchard was enthusiastic, and in March he responded with a detailed plan for air force control of Mesopotamia. It came just in time.

On May Day 1920, the Treaty of San Remo established Iraq as a British Mandate. Three weeks later, four British soldiers were killed at Tel Afar, near Mosul, after the arrest of a local sheik. An armored car squadron was dispatched to restore order but was ambushed and annihilated by local rebels. It was the beginning of a general uprising—such as the United States may yet face—by Miss Bell's "affectionate" subjects.

Later Churchill would cynically marvel in private over his government's success in uniting the Iraqis against them. "It is an extraordinary thing that the British civil administration should have succeeded in such a short time in alienating the whole country to such an extent that the Arabs have laid aside the blood feuds they have nursed for centuries and that the Suni [sic] and Shiah [sic] tribes are working together. We have been advised locally that the best way to get our supplies up the river would be to fly the Turkish flag. . . ."

The leadership of the rebellion was drawn both from the purged cadre of the old regime (ex-Ottoman officers and officials) and from the angry Shia majority in the south. (Sound familiar?) By the middle of July fighting had spread throughout the lower Euphrates. Brigadier Coningham lost thirty-five men storming the insurgent citadel of Rumaitha only to find that rebels had moved on to seize the town of Kifl. While marching on Kifl, the Manchester Regiment was surprised in its camp and almost massacred. Major General Leslie lost 180 men with another 160 captured. There was near panic.

But the Cabinet in London was distracted by the guerrilla war in Ireland as well as by the counterrevolution in Russia. After all the glowing reports from Baghdad by Miss Bell and other "Arabists," there was disbelief that 130,000 locals were actually in arms against Britain. The crisis worsened in August as the uprising reached the upper Euphrates and the outskirts of Baghdad; outbreaks in the Kurdish north soon followed. Rebels cut off rail links to Persia and captured a number of key towns, including Baquba and Shahraban, killing every English official they could lay their hands on.

Churchill pressed the RAF to proceed with work on gas bombs ("especially mustard gas") but was finally forced to break the budget by calling in Indian reserves. The tide began to turn against the insurgents. The British Army set a barbaric precedent by using poison gas shells, while the RAF dropped bombs, and according to historian David Omissi, "machine-gunned women and children as they fled from their homes." The slaughter was indiscriminate and coincided with the hanging of political prisoners in Baghdad.

In September T. E. Lawrence wrote a letter to the Sunday *Times* protesting the savagery of Britain's "friendly occupation gone wrong." It might well be republished in the *New York Times* today.

> Our government is worse than the old Turkish system. They kept 14,000 local conscripts embodied, and killed a yearly average of 200 Arabs in maintaining peace. We keep 90,000 men, with aeroplanes, armoured cars, gunboats, and armoured trains. We have killed about 10,000 Arabs in this rising this summer. . . . How long will we permit millions of pounds, thousands of Imperial troops, and tens of thousands of Arabs to be sacrificed on behalf of a colonial administration which can benefit nobody but its administrators?

3. THE DEVIL'S LABORATORY

Thanks to bombers, poison gas, and armored cars, the British finally regained control of the country in September 1920. Tough Indian Office types enforced a Carthaginian peace. Through Christmas, expeditions ranged across the rebel zones burning villages, executing suspects, confiscating livestock, and enforcing punitive fines.

Churchill, soon to be promoted to Colonial Secretary, continued to advocate aerial terror as the cheapest and most effective way of ruling "ungrateful volcanoes" like Iraq and other Muslim colonies. In March 1921 the RAF put the finishing touches to an "air control" plan that envisioned eight squadrons of aircraft (including two of bombers) plus six RAF armored car companies taking the place of most of the regular Army divisions.

The essence of the strategy, explained Wing Commander Chamier, was that retaliation should never be halfhearted. The RAF must inspire absolute terror. "All available aircraft must be collected; the attack with bombs and machine guns must be relentless and unremitting and carried on continuously by day and night, on houses, inhabitants, crops and cattle."

Miss Bell herself, along with Arab notables, attended a thrilling RAF demonstration of the new incendiary weapons it proposed to use on delinquent villages and recalcitrant tribes.

> It was even more remarkable than the one we saw last at the Air Force show because it was more real. They had made an imaginary village about a quarter of a mile from where we sat on the Kiala dyke and the two first bombs dropped from three thousand feet went straight into the middle of it and set it alight. It was wonderful and horrible. Then they dropped bombs all round it, as if to catch the fugitives, and finally fire bombs which even in the brightest sunlight made flares of bright flame in the desert. They burn through metal, and water won't extinguish them. At the end the armoured cars went out to round up the fugitives with machine guns.

Fiery death from the air, moreover, became punishment not only for armed rebellion, but even more commonly, for failure to pay taxes. As one of Churchill's biographers gently put it, in early June 1921 an "aerial action had been taken on the Lower Euphrates, not to suppress a riot, but to pressure certain villages to pay their taxes." When Churchill queried the appropriateness of using bombers to collect taxes, Sir Percy Cox replied that he was merely implementing the Churchill doctrine and rhetorically asked if the Secretary for War and Air really wanted "to stifle the growing infant" of airpower. Churchill immediately avowed, "I am a great believer in airpower and will help it forward in every way."

Bombing and strafing, as a result, became fiscal and administrative, as well as military, policy. Iraq, so to speak, became the devil's laboratory for the Colonial Office's new experiment in using airpower to control colonial populations. As Jonathan Glancey reminded readers of *The Guardian* last April: "Terror bombing, night bombing, heavy bombers, delayed action bombs (particularly lethal against children) were all developed during raids on mud, stone and reed villages during Britain's League of Nation's mandate."

From his new and higher perch in the Colonial Office in late 1921, Churchill observed with satisfaction that "aeroplanes are now really feared." He continued to lobby for use of poison gas in Iraq and elsewhere. When a Colonel Meinertzhagen, familiar with the horror of gas attacks on the Western Front, challenged the application of this "barbarous method of warfare" to Arab civilian populations, he was harshly rebuked by Churchill, who replied, "I am ready to authorize the construction of such bombs at once."

Air control remained official policy through the 1920s, under Labour as well as Tory governments. One of the worst atrocities occurred in the late autumn and winter of 1923–24, when the Bani Huchaim tribal group in the Samawa area of Iraq was unable to pay its taxes. On the verge of starvation amidst a severe water shortage, the Bani Huchaim pleaded destitution. As one historian emphasizes, "There was no suggestion that there had been any serious unruliness or disorder in the area." Nonetheless, they were given a forty-eight-hour ultimatum and then were set upon with bombers. The RAF officially recorded the slaughter of 144 people, including women and children.

Although occasional opponents at home, like George Landsbury, denounced "this Hunnish and barbarous method of warfare against unarmed people," it was the foundation of the puppet throne upon which the British employed the foreign Hashemite prince, Faisal, in 1921. His election, by 96 percent of his new subjects—the triumph of Miss Bell's "Arabist" cause—was a rigged plebiscite orchestrated by the corrupt sheiks and notables and patrolled by the RAF. The real winner was the Iraq Petroleum Company and its London shareholders.

As one world-weary veteran of empire would observe in 1925: "If the writ of King Faisal runs effectively throughout his kingdom it is entirely due to British aeroplanes. If the aeroplanes were removed tomorrow, the whole structure would inevitably fall to pieces."

This history, probably unknown to most members of Congress—Democrat as well as Republican—who endorsed the U.S. attack on Iraq, remains, of course, a poisonous memory to all Iraqis. More broadly, ordinary people in the Muslim world recall that they were the original guinea pigs upon whom the European colonial powers, starting in Libya in 1911–12, perfected the terror bombing of civilian populations. The road to Guernica, Warsaw, Dresden, and Hiroshima began on the banks of the Euphrates and the flanks of the Atlas. In addition to Iraq, the RAF inflicted the "Churchill Doctrine" on civilian Egyptians, Palestinians, Somalis, Sudanese, Yemenis (Aden), and Afghanis in the 1920s. In the same decade, the Spanish and the French bombed and gassed the rebel villages of the Morrocan Rif. Who were the "terrorists" then?

OVERLEAF: Major David Long of Civil Affairs 352 tests out a chair in a warehouse full of Uday Hussein's belongings in the Republican Palace compound. LYNSEY ADDARIO/CORBIS 2003

REGARDING HOW TO GO ABOUT COMBATING BOMBER JETS, GUIDED MISSILES, AND OTHER ULTRAMODERN TECHNOLOGICAL INSTRUMENTS OF MASS DESTRUCTION

This text was written just a few days before the "Coalition" bombing and the subsequent colonizing campaign (or maybe it is more correct to say "privatizing campaign") began. Rereading the text I wrote then, I cannot overcome the sadness that comes from knowing that a certain reality has been stolen. The U.S. did invade and now controls Iraq and its natural resources. The U.S. is trying by all means to divide the Iraqi population by ethnic and religious factions in order to better dominate them. Nonetheless, something tells me that the Muslim teacher is still teaching with the same dedication as always; the boy with the enormous ears still yawns in the morning; the man who sells dried fruit still opens his stand . . . but who knows, any one of them could be one of the more than 10,000 "collateral damage" Iraqi lives that this war has claimed. The only thing that I know for certain—which is confirmed by the news that I hear every day about the resistance—is that the war machine is, and forever will be, incapable of stealing from people and nations their most powerful weapons: hopes and dreams. Let this text testify to that conviction.

MARCH, 2003

While walking the streets of Baghdad, one tends to forget that one is in a city on the brink of war. Here children scurry in the dust, men attend to their business, young women dressed in tight velvet skirts laugh, talk, and flirt, their hair covered with shawls that give them the seductiveness of mystery. The faces of Iraqi women still must be counted among the most beautiful in the world.

One cannot help thinking that danger should be most tangible in the neighborhoods and along the avenues of a city over which looms the menacing presence of hundreds of thousands of soldiers and Marines armed with the most sophisticated killing equipment ever created. One might think that panic would be widespread and constant in the face of a seemingly imminent "conventional" bombardment that may have results not so different from those of the not-so-conventional bombs that fell on Hiroshima and Nagasaki. One might think such things, but one would be mistaken. In Baghdad, life continues as if there were no evident danger. University students arrive on time for their Spanish-language classes, and as they talk with us, the Spanish and Latin-American human shields, they seem more surprised by the idea that there are Muslims on the other side of the world than by the possibility that in a few days Baghdad may be demolished, as it was in the times of the Mongolian invasions. Teenagers play soccer in the cluttered alleys that characterize the poor neighborhoods of this river city. Shias celebrate the Day of the Massacre in the same way they have done since the first time the Umma was divided with blood, less than a century after the death of the Prophet[1] (s.a.w.s).[2]

It's not that people have no concept of the magnitude of the threat, but rather, under the deterministic view that characterizes the Islamic vision of life, *"insallah"* (if God wishes) is the key phrase. *Insallah* we will defeat the Americans. *Insallah* we will live, and of course, *insallah* we will die.

Because of this, it seems, the people most worried by the consequences of a bombardment are not those city inhabitants over whom hovers the sword, but rather the hundreds of foreigners, coming from all the trenches of the planet, who daily connect to the Internet and read the online versions of the *New York Times, The Guardian, El País,* and even *La Jornada* with something similar to the morbid feeling of someone who attends a horror movie in order to experience the adrenaline rush created by fear. For them, every announcement of war seems a villain more terrible than Jason from *Friday the 13th,* and each glimpse of peace a benevolent hero coming to the rescue. The locals, however, are not so misled. Perhaps *insallah* is in reality the only certainty that we can grasp: *insallah* that the gathering of the Horsemen of the Apocalypse in the Azores (Bush, Blair, and Aznar) is not the first trumpet; *insallah* that the United Nations will end its criminal embargo and that children in the Saddam Hussein Pediatric Hospital will get antibiotics and other basic medicines; *insallah* that the highly educated archeologist-turned-tour-guide with whom I met in Babylon will be able to return to his excavations and also fulfill his dream of visiting our Mayan ruins. *Insallah, insallah, insallah.*

Day to day, big and small *insallahs* come to pass: Allah grants us life for another day. A man waters the plants in front of his house. A Sunni teacher hurries to get to the El-Iptijar junior high school where she teaches girls, Sunnis as well as Christian and Shia students. A sleepy boy with a pair of enormous ears rubs his eyes and yawns as he boards the bus that will take him to grade school.

And this is the way to fight against bomber jets, guided missiles, and other ultramodern technological instruments of mass destruction: Living through every day, loving, studying, working, uprooting the nightmare of invasion from our sleep. As we were told by the man in charge at one of the many grain and dried fruit supply centers that exist in this town: If the Americans bomb, he still plans to open his business at the regular time, from ten in the morning to twelve at night, because what Bush wants is to paralyze the Iraqi people, terrorize them, and in the face of a people who bow only to *taqwa* (awe of God), a successful invasion may be a very hard thing to accomplish. *Insallah.*

1. The Day of the Massacre is the day in which al-Husayn, descendent of Muhammad (s.a.w s.), was killed over differences about who was the rightful successor as Khalif. From this quarrel emerged the Shiites, who represent a large part of the Iraqi Muslim population.
2. The abbreviation "s.a.w.s." stands for "Salialahu alehi wa salaam," which means "May peace be upon him." As a Muslim, when I mention the name of the Prophet (s.a.w.s.), I say, write, or at least, think "Salialahu alehi wa salaam," for he brought salvation to humankind and we thank him thus.

United States Ambassador Paul Bremer during a meeting in his office in the Republican Palace.
LYNSEY ADDARIO/CORBIS 2003

BOMB BEFORE YOU BUY:
THE ECONOMICS OF WAR

This text is adapted from a speech delivered at McGill University in Montreal on October 25, 2003.

A couple of days after September 11, the *National Post* newspaper ran a story with the headline "Globalization Is So Yesterday." No one was interested in talking about the ravages of capitalism, we were told. The world was now focused on an entirely new set of issues: war, terror, and the clash of civilizations. Everything we thought we knew before September 11 no longer applied.

It was nonsense, of course. But it is true that many of us in the globalization movement were caught somewhat flat-footed by the military upsurge of these last two years. Yes, many of us instinctively made the transition from trade issues to antiwar activism, but we were not able, at first, to fully connect how warfare is used to enforce the very economic policies we had been fighting against.

The antiwar movement, for its part, faced a similar problem making these connections. The mainstream of the antiwar movement in North America focused almost exclusively on the visible atrocities of war: the violence, the human rights abuses, the broken international laws. When explaining *why* these wars were erupting, rarely did we surpass pat answers like, "It's about the oil." Some even argued that analyzing the economic model that sees war and occupation as market opportunities was "too divisive." Activists were urged to stay on message, to focus on the effects of war rather than its underlying causes.

I believe that this failure to marry the economic analysis of the globalization movement with the moral outcry of antiwar activism ended up hurting both movements. By failing to see the lengths to which capital will go to crack open new markets, the globalization movement seemed soft and naive. So did the antiwar movement: attempting to stop a war without directly confronting the economic system behind it is like trying to stop a bomb after it has already been dropped. In this context, peace never had a chance.

Fortunately, these artificial divisions are beginning to break down, because now that the war in Iraq is "over," the economic project behind the attack has emerged fully formed.

What is that economic program? It's the familiar one we in the globalization movement have been fighting against, enforced by the North American Free Trade Agreement (NAFTA), the World Trade Organization (WTO), the International Monetary Fund (IMF), the World Bank. It's a model that is sometimes called "globalization" but which the Latin Americans call "neoliberalism" and the French call "Savage Capitalism." For my purposes here, I am going to call it "McGovernment," because it is a kind of economic franchise, a globally enforced set of policies designed to make the world safe for multinational corporations.

McGovernment has three key components:

- Mass downsizing of the public sector. This makes sure that investors enjoy low taxes and low wages from a "flexible" workforce. It also starves the public sector, making it seem useless and inefficient and thus primed for . . .
- Mass privatizations. Privatizations give multinationals infinite investment opportunities to buy up public services and natural resources.
- Mass deregulation. This falls into two categories: The first form of deregulation is designed to eliminate the supports that protect local businesses, such as subsidies and restrictions on foreign ownership, thus eliminating the local competition for multinationals. The second form of deregulation is designed to remove all restrictions on the mobility of foreign capital, such as rules that require companies to keep some of their profits in the country where they made them.

So there you have it: the universal recipe for McGovernment—downsize, privatize, and deregulate. The result of all this corporate lubrication can be seen around the world in the commodification of ever more parts of the public sphere, from schools and hospitals to seeds and water.

In rich countries like ours, these economic policies are introduced relatively gradually. In poor countries they are introduced quickly, enforced by the International Monetary Fund in exchange for loans. When these policies were introduced in Argentina in the 1990s, the transformation of society was so rapid and so devastating that President Carlos Menem called the reforms "surgery without anesthetic." In Chile, when the reforms were introduced under Pinochet, they were called "shock treatment." In Russia, the IMF called it "shock therapy."

What is going on in Iraq right now makes those reforms look like spa treatments. Radical economic reforms that are usually spread out over decades are being rammed through in six months. Iraq's shock therapy has been implemented through "shock and awe" military force.

Iraq, as we all know, is a rich country. It has an embarrassment of natural resources and public services that have yet to be privatized; this is true for much of the Arab world. Oil wealth has kept Arab countries relatively outside the world trade system. Even in U.S. ally nations like Saudi Arabia and Kuwait, the oil companies, along with much else, are still owned by the government.

The growth represented by these untapped markets has become irresistibly tantalizing. Why? Because capitalism functions like a drug addict, and its drug of choice is growth; without a fix, it dies. And fixes are hard to come by these days. It's not just that the stock market hasn't recovered since its pre-9/11 bust. It's also that some of the market's most reliable suppliers of the growth drug have, of late, been holding out.

From the U.S. and European perspective, it used to be that if there was one thing you could count on in matters of international trade, it was the desperation of the poor. No matter how bad the deal, it was always better than nothing. But all of a sudden, poor countries are banding together and busting up trade rounds, standing up to the International Monetary Fund, and even turning down foreign investment.

Across Latin America, privatizations are being stopped in their tracks; oil pipelines are being resisted by local populations from Nigeria to Colombia; gold and copper mines are being rejected because their ecological cost is greater than their economic benefits. Center-left candidates have come to power in Brazil and Ecuador, promising to govern in the interest of the poor. In Argentina, popular protests pushed out the neoliberal government of Fernando de la Rua. Meanwhile, Hugo Chavez has held on in Venezuela despite the most dogged attempts by the elites in that country and in the U.S. to throw him out. And just last week in Bolivia, massive political protests forced president Gonzalo Sanchez de Lozada to resign. The uprising was sparked by an unpopular plan to sell the country's natural gas to the United States. The Free Trade Area of the Americas (FTAA) is hugely unpopular across Latin America, and the World Trade Organization talks just collapsed in Cancún. Poor countries are saying, we have tried these policies and they made us poorer, hollowed out our collective wealth—we don't want more of the same.

Free Trade Lite, which wrestles market access through backroom bullying during trade negotiations, isn't working anymore. That's why the market is getting desperate. That's why the Bush crew has stopped asking and started grabbing, upgrading Free Trade Lite to Free Trade Reloaded, which seizes new markets on the battlefields of war.

And that is precisely what the Iraq attack has been about. Bush has openly said that he wants a Free Trade Zone in the Middle East within a decade. It's the next project after the creation of the FTAA, and it all starts with Iraq. Iraq is the foothold, the wedge into an entire region that represents a massive new market opportunity. Senator John McCain put it well: Iraq, he said, is "a huge pot of honey that's attracting a lot of flies."

The "honey" isn't just the oil. It's also the water, the phones, the roads, the schools, the media, the trains, the planes, the jails, and anything else that can be turned into a commodity and sold for profit. The flies are named Bechtel, Halliburton, MCI, ExxonMobil, Wackenhut, TimeWarner, Wal-Mart, Boeing, NewsCorp, DynCorp, and on and on.

But before I go any further, let's make one thing absolutely clear: the United States government must compensate the Iraqi people so they can rebuild their country. The U.S. owes Iraq huge war reparations; it is a moral duty and it must be met. The problem is that the vast majority of the money for Iraq isn't going to the Iraqi people for reparations, for them to spend however they decide. It is being parceled out to U.S. firms selected by the Bush administration, for something called "reconstruction."

When you hear the word "reconstruction," it sounds perfectly benign. What could be wrong with Americans going to Iraq to rebuild bombed-out bridges and hospitals? It sounds like the Peace Corps. Only these companies aren't going to Iraq just to rebuild it—they are going there to buy it. As we speak, the country is being transformed into a giant shopping mall for U.S. (and a few British) multinationals.

It's the sale of the century: "Bomb Before You Buy."

Immediately after the war began, we started hearing about huge reconstruction contracts being handed out by the United States Agency for International Development (USAID). They were handed out in secret, without open bidding, to a handful of U.S. firms. And there was something new going on: Contracts to rebuild schools and hospitals which used to go to UNICEF or the Red Cross (nonprofit humanitarian agencies) were going to private education and health care corporations, companies that push privatization in the U.S. and Canada and see schools and hospitals as market opportunities.

And then there's Bechtel. Bechtel has a contract now worth more than $1 billion to oversee the rebuilding of roads, bridges, the electricity grid, and more. Many Iraqi entrepreneurs are angry that these jobs, which could help them get their economy running again, are going to Americans. The answer from Washington: Iraqi reconstruction is our booty—we bombed it, we bought it.

Anger at Bechtel is also mounting in Iraq because they aren't doing a very good job. According to a recent article in *The Economist*, in five months Bechtel has managed to rebuild a one-mile road bypass. Of the forty-nine bridges damaged during the attack, rebuilding work has only begun on three. Half of Baghdad's phone lines are still out.

And of course we have to talk about Halliburton, where Vice President Dick Cheney used to work as CEO. Cheney still retains Halliburton stock options and has been paid more than $350,000 in deferred compensation since taking office, but he nevertheless accuses anyone who calls that a conflict of interest of taking "cheap shots."

Allow me to be cheap: Halliburton has so far been paid $1.4 billion for its work in Iraq (its contracts can go as high as $7 billion). What is important to understand is how badly Halliburton needed this cash injection. Last year the company looked as if it was about to go the way of Enron. It was mired in accounting scandals and lawsuits; indeed, Halliburton posted a $500 million loss last year. One of its subsidiaries, Kellogg Brown and Root, was on the verge of filing for bankruptcy. Now Halliburton's share price is up 77 percent—not bad for a market slump—and it posted a $26 million profit last quarter.

The bottom line is that, as CEO, Dick Cheney got Halliburton into all kinds of trouble, but as Vice President, he saved Halliburton's butt—that's no exaggeration.

So what is Halliburton doing for the money? It is playing two key roles, and both of them have to do with privatization. The first is protecting Iraq's oil supply—putting out oil fires and repairing pipelines—so it can eventually be privatized. The second involves the rapid privatization of the U.S. Army. George W. Bush has decided that the Army's "core competency" is combat and that everything outside out that can be farmed out to temps. Halliburton has become the U.S. military's temp agency. Its temp soldiers build the army bases, cook the food, clean the latrines, do the soldiers' laundry, and cut their hair, all at cheaper salaries, of course, with the profits going back to Halliburton. One-third of the Iraqi mission is subcontracted to private companies.

So let's recap. The U.S. government, looking for new investment opportunities for its ailing firms, waged an unprovoked war with a partially privatized army, cleaning up afterwards using many of the same for-profit companies. But here's the kicker: When everything is cleaned up, America is going to sell Iraq off in pieces to these very same companies. I wish I could say that it was going to sell Iraq off to the highest bidder, but it's actually selling the embattled country off to the highest Bush-Cheney campaign donor.

The reconstruction of Iraq has already begun to seamlessly segue into the privatization of Iraq.

The real goal is now clear: The U.S government aims not just to rebuild Iraq's roads, but to turn them into privately owned and operated highways. It aims to not simply reconstruct the bombed-out water system, but to sell it to a company that will charge highly profitable rates for access. It aims to not just put out the oil fires and fix the oil pipelines, but to sell them entirely.

Bush, Donald Rumsfeld, and Paul Bremer now openly admit that they envision the "reconstruction" of Iraq as a remaking of it into a deregulated free-market economy. As journalist Robert Fisk pointed out, Bremer's choice of clothing says it all: a business suit with combat boots. In August Bremer wrote a memo containing policy instructions to the Iraqi Council—a body he hand-picked—in which he complained that Iraq's economy was too "protectionist" and dominated by "socialist economic dogma." He stated that Iraq must "pry open" most of its "industries for foreign investment." Sure enough, on September 19, 2003, two hundred Iraqi state firms were put up for privatization. Reconstruction has turned into the auctioning off of an entire country—someone else's country.

And according to new laws introduced by Bremer, U.S. firms can retain 100 percent ownership of banks, mines, and factories of all kinds. The only exception is oil, but this too will come. And who is going to buy all these Iraqi companies? The same U.S. firms that took part in the reconstruction.

Let's look at Bechtel again. On the global stage, Bechtel is one of the most aggressive proponents of the privatization agenda; one of its primary businesses is convincing foreign governments to sell off their water systems. Indeed, Bechtel was thrown out of Bolivia because, after it privatized the water in Chochabamba, prices escalated by 50 percent. Bechtel even deemed it illegal to collect rainwater (which it claimed was unfair competition). But in Iraq, Bechtel doesn't have to convince foreign governments to sell them the water, because there is no foreign government, just the U.S. government selling to U.S. corporations in foreign countries.

It's quite an amazing feat: they have actually managed to cut out the middleman.

What is going on in Iraq has never been about reconstruction—it has always been about privatization disguised as reconstruction, mass robbery masquerading as reparations.

A new company called New Bridge Strategies has been launched by Joe Albaugh, Bush's former campaign manager. It specializes in helping U.S. companies take advantage of Iraq's "unprecedented opportunities." One of the company's partners described the opportunities this way: "Getting the rights to distribute Procter and Gamble products can be a gold mine. One well-stocked 7-Eleven could knock out thirty Iraqi stores; a Wal-Mart could take over the country." There it is, the economic project behind this war: a massive new market, bombed into being.

But before Iraq can be turned into a free-market Mecca, a few more things have to happen. I talked earlier about McGovernment, but McGovernment isn't just about privatization; it also has to be about downsizing and deregulation.

Rest assured that Bremer is moving full steam ahead on both those fronts. Regarding downsizing, in his first month in Iraq Bremer fired more than 400,000 Iraqis without pensions or re-employment programs. He called these mass layoffs of state employees "de-Baathification"—the purging of Saddam Hussein's party officials from government. Of course, some of that was necessary in order to clean out Saddam Hussein's henchmen and propagandists, but Bremer's layoffs went much further. Low-level civil servants with no ties to the party have been fired en masse. In the name of "de-Baathification" he launched a full-scale attack on the public sector. Why? For the same reason the public sector is attacked here at home: to create opportunities for privatization, to create a flexible workforce willing to work for less, and to lower the tax burden.

So with privatization and downsizing taken care of, what's needed to finish the McGovernment package is deregulation. When Bremer and Bush talk about bringing "the free market to Iraq," it sounds like Iraqi businesses are going to have all sorts of wonderful new opportunities. Yet we know that hasn't been the case during reconstruction (now jokingly referred to in Iraq as "the full-Halliburton employment program").

United States troops from the 101st Airborne Division work out of the battle command center of the Division Main Headquarters in one of Saddam Hussein's former palaces. LYNSEY ADDARIO/CORBIS 2003

But there are other ways that Iraqi businesses are being pushed out. When Bremer arrived, Iraqi-owned companies were obviously in rough shape; they had been pummeled by almost thirteen years of sanctions and two months of looting, not to mention two wars. So it would have made sense—if the U.S. were serious about rebuilding Iraq's economy—to concentrate on getting the electricity and phones operational, as well as providing the parts and materials needed for Iraq's damaged factories. But that's not what Paul Bremer did. Instead, just twenty-six days after the war was declared "over," with the lights and phones still off in Baghdad, Bremer flung open Iraq's borders to foreign multinationals; overnight, the market was flooded with cheap TVs, food, and clothes. What happened next was entirely predictable—hundreds of Iraqi companies were wiped out.

Once again, Iraq isn't being rebuilt; it is being erased. First by war, then sanctions, then war again, then looting, and now by absurdly unfair foreign competition which never gave Iraq's industries a chance to survive. Why? Well, the erasure of Iraqi firms is good news for foreign multinationals wanting a piece of Iraq's action; it's easier to get your Wal-Mart or 7-Eleven if the local competition has already been helpfully decimated.

Bremer has given these foreign investors other goodies too. On the same day that he put those two hundred state companies up for sale, he also announced that foreign firms doing business in Iraq would get tax breaks—from 15 to 45 percent—even more generous than those Bush has been handing out at home. He also removed all restrictions on taking profits out of the country.

From a foreign investor's perspective, Iraq is a dream come true. Everything that these companies lobby for at home but never receive in their entirety—because of this pesky thing called democracy—has been generously handed to them in Iraq. The country is a blank slate on which the most ideological Washington neoconservatives are designing their dream economy: fully privatized, downsized, deregulated, and open for business. Donald Rumsfeld said recently that "Iraq will have some of the most enlightened and inviting tax and investment laws in the free world."

But there's just one catch, and it's a big one: Iraq isn't part of the free world, because it isn't free.

In fact, it's under occupation, which means that the decisions about Iraqi society's core nature—how much foreign ownership of its economy will be allowed, whether it will have a public or private health-care system, how it will make use of its oil revenues—are being made without the consent of its people. Why? Because once the Iraqis have their own government, they might decide that they don't want to sell their country to Bechtel and Halliburton. But once the contracts are signed, it's all over. If the Iraqi people, once they have democracy, decide they want to change course, it will mean breaking signed contracts, expropriating assets, changing the terms of agreements, and the U.S. will not stand for that.

In the name of democracy, the Iraqi people are being robbed of the most basic democratic principle: the right of sovereign people to govern themselves and decide their collective destiny. Just as Iraq entered the so-called free market in the dark, they will now enter democracy handcuffed to key economic decisions already made for them. Then they will be told to hurry up and vote for their new leaders, just in time for Bush's reelection campaign.

As we all know, it's too late to stop the war. But if we act now, there is just enough time to deprive Iraq's invaders of the myriad economic prizes that are the *reason* they went to war in the first place. And this is the task faced by both the globalization and the antiwar movements: to try to stop the economic looting of Iraq.

BAGHDAD JOURNAL #2

Our first stop is the Iraq Assistance Center, where we found the public affairs office and picked up our free cell phones from MCI, courtesy of the U.S. taxpayers. It was Friday afternoon, the Muslim Sabbath; Baghdad felt like a ghost town. Beyond the ruined buildings, garbage was heaped in the streets, razor wire everywhere. The sense that we journeyed through an abandoned city increased when we reached the compound. Tumbleweeds drifted across the dirty street and caught on the razor wire.

The Iraq Assistance Center was originally a convention center used primarily by those close to Saddam, and most Baghdad residents had never been inside it. Now it sits surrounded by three sets of barriers and is guarded by tanks and GIs wilting in the heat. After five sets of checkpoints, we got inside, leaving behind us at the gate Iraqi men and women pleading for answers about missing sons and husbands. We weren't Iraqi and did not need assistance, so we could enter.

Inside the compound it was nearly deserted; we were told by the woman at the MCI trailer it was because of the Fourth of July. Later I remembered it was also Friday, always a quiet day in Iraq. After a stop in the lovely air-conditioned trailer provided by MCI which serves as a communication center, we passed through the security checkpoint—this time there was a body search, so a woman GI was called inside to attend us. We entered into the great hall and climbed the grand staircase to the second floor, where we were greeted by friendly reservist Mark Ingram from Oklahoma, a sixties

holdout who laughingly complained that his toe rings were digging the daylights out of him. He joked as he handed us a form that "you too can play army and be embedded with a unit," adding that it was safer to do so during the invasion. Like most of the soldiers we spoke to, he wanted a real bed and three hot meals instead of a hard, wooden, bug-infested cot and barely edible Meals, Ready-to-Eat (MREs). All of the Bush administration's talk of "supporting the troops" is exposed as empty rhetoric when you see how these soldiers are actually living, overstretched and undersupplied in an attempt to prove that America can fight a war on the cheap. When we had left the states, the administration was planning to cut the troops' hazard pay, even though more U.S. soldiers are being killed and injured per day than during the period of "major combat" that Bush proclaimed over on May 1.

One of our objectives was to meet with Margaret Bhadi, Paul Bremer's advisor on gender affairs, to apply whatever pressure we could on the Coalition Provisional Authority (CPSA) to include a representative number of women on the Iraqi Governing Council that would supposedly serve as a transitional parliament on Iraq's road to democracy. To arrange the meeting we needed to go to the palace where the CPA had its headquarters. Sergeant Ingram pointed us to the shuttle bus that ran to the palace.

You meet the most interesting people waiting for that shuttle: CPA employees looking as if they'd just stepped off a golf course; GIs; businessmen; evangelists from Florida and Georgia here to bring humanitarian aid and the salvation of Jesus. The majority of Americans we met were from the South, including most of the GIs and the CPA employees. I strike up a conversation with one of them, who tells me he is "running operations" in Baghdad. He is a friendly fellow, a bit flirtatious, so I play along: "Will you take me on a tour of Baghdad?"

Sure, he says, now that they've gotten everything "back to normalcy" here.

"Normalcy—what does that mean to you?" I ask.

"You should have been here a few weeks ago," he says to me with a smile. "We have things running now."

I ask him if he's making fun of me. I tell him that I've just arrived to a sort of hell outside these walls and that this is far from normal. I was here in February, I tell him, and this is not what "normal" looks like. The playfulness ends and he goes back to talking to the men gathered with him.

I press on, ask him his qualifications for this job. "I was on the Atlanta police force for thirty years and have taken classes in management," he responds.

Again I think he's pulling my leg, but as I continue to question him, I realize that he's serious. I ask if they see much of the city, and he tells me no: "It's not safe out there."

The rundown shuttle that takes us to the palace is driven by a Kellogg Brown and Root employee from Savannah, Georgia, who was a trucker back home, but the money is better here. Regardless, he tells me he can't wait to get back home.

"Why can't the Iraqis drive this bus?" I ask.

"No one trusts them," he replies. "The only jobs the Iraqis have at the Assistance Center are menial or as translators, but they might be let go," he

informs me. "They've been seen pacing through the compound, and the fear is that they might be giving target information to the 'terrorists' and 'remnants of Saddam's regime' who are attacking American targets." He is sweating and tired of the back and forth.

The palace is the exercise in excess that you would expect from contemporary accounts of Saddam's regime: it's dripping with gold and velvet, all ostentation and stupidity. Bremer's offices are arranged around a huge rotunda with marble walls, a gold dome, and stained-glass windows; it's protected by a security system like those at an airport, with green lights flashing up and down the side, flanked by green marble columns. We nickname his office "Oz." We can hardly believe that the CPA has chosen to make its home in this place, this symbol of oppression and corruption. I remember a quote from General Tommy Franks during the invasion about how we aren't bombing the palace because we will soon own it.

United States Ambassador Paul Bremer walks through the Republican Palace after a meeting with the Ministry of Finance.
LYNSEY ADDARIO/CORBIS 2003

We notice a flyer on a partition by Bremer's meeting room for a Fourth of July party. It promises fresh lobster tails and shrimp, a visit from the "Original

A U.S. soldier jumps off a high diving board at a Fourth of July celebration at one of Saddam Hussein's main palaces in Baghdad. LYNSEY ADDARIO/CORBIS 2003

Terminator," Arnold Schwarzenegger, and across the flyer is printed "Hasta La Vista, Baby"—"beer and barbeque at Saddam's pool at 5:00 pm."

It's just five o'clock, so we decide to find the party.

Outside we see GIs heading toward a line of palm trees. We pass a trailer and stop to ask a female GI for directions. "What's in the trailer?" we ask.

"The laundry," she responds. "The NGOs and higher-ups in the CPA drop off their dry cleaning here and it gets sent to Kuwait to be done."

I ask, given the 65 percent jobless rate in Iraq, whether it wouldn't make sense to do the laundry here.

The GI shrugs her shoulders and says, "Nothing makes sense to me these days," and points us to the entrance of the pool area.

We could hear the laughter, the splashing, and the music before we entered, but we were not prepared for what we saw.

The pool area, supposedly favored by Saddam's wife, looks like the back of an elegant hotel. It's landscaped with vast manicured lawns and rows of tall palms, and the centerpiece is an enormous tiled pool with a fountain in the middle with synchronized jets of water; there's also a huge high dive that holds up to ten people. As we entered, groups of GIs did cannon-balls together off the platform. Bagpipe music played over a PA system. Tables are decorated in red-white-and-blue bunting, barbeques grill hot dogs and burgers, and tubs are full of beer, but I do not see the promised lobster tails and shrimp.

Not many people were in the pool. I asked one female GI why she wasn't swimming. "Who thought to bring a swimsuit?" she replied. A few women ventured into the shallow water in sports tops and shorts. Everyone gathered together in sort of self-segregated clumps: white, black, gay, and occasionally men mingling with women, all having their first beers since their deployment.

Most of the people who are courageous enough to approach us are businessmen, most of whom are from the South. I look around, hoping to find a new story in the crowd, and I see someone who looks intellectual, slightly Southern Californian, has a ponytail, and keeps his distance from the crowd. I introduce myself and learn from him that before coming to Baghdad he had taught religion and political philosophy at a private, conservative college in Southern California. "I'm Bremer's intelligence advisor on the Shiites," he tells me. He talks about the reports he prepares for Bremer each day which determine how the CPA should respond to the Muhajedeen who are trying to find their place in the new power structure. I ask a question about fundamentalists, and he tells me the people here are extremists—everyone is a fundamentalist. I am shocked by his arrogance and his banter, which is Machiavellian at best. He misses Southern California, he tells me, and has sent home for his roller blades. "I'm only here for six months; I can take it. The work we do here is extremely important," he wants me to know.

"We're going to take a page from Saddam's book," he says with an insider's confidence. "Fear is the founda-tion of any government. If you make a dog hungry, he'll follow you anywhere."

I find myself too uncomfortable with what he is saying, so I ask for his number and where he is staying to try again with him later. The sun has started to set behind the palace. Bremer was to have addressed the party, but he's been delayed by some bad news: an audiotape purportedly by Saddam has surfaced. We get this information from a man who says that he is Bremer's valet and the organizer of this event. Currently he's fretting about securing a karaoke machine for tomorrow's entertainment. He invites us to join him for a tour of the sex toys and wild animals at Uday's palace. We decline. It's getting late, and we are in the middle of a compound with no clear way to get back to the Andaluz—and we've been warned to be inside by 8 P.M. The DJ starts to play the Rolling Stones: "You Can't Always Get What You Want." We notice the Iraqi men in blue sailor outfits circulating through the grounds, empty-ing the trash.

The valet gets on his walkie-talkie and arranges for a Humvee and two lieutenants to take us to the back gate, where we can get a taxi. We feel the fear as we stand on a Baghdad street at dusk and hail a cab.

Continued . . .

AMERICAN MUSLIMS AND IRAQ

... It's getting cold in California
I guess I'll be leaving soon
Daylight fading
Come and waste another year
All the anger and the eloquence are bleeding into fear ...
—Counting Crows, "Daylight Fading," from *Recovering the Satellites* (1996)

I am a Canadian Muslim and also an academic who studies Islam. My doctoral dissertation was on Muslim communities in Toronto, and my own work is on Muslim communities in North America. Since 1997 I have been living in the United States while teaching in the Department of Religious Studies at California State University, Northridge. With the terrorist attacks on September 11, 2001, Islam and violence became synonymous in the minds of many people. More than twenty years earlier, the Iranian revolution (and its aftermath) first alerted many people in North America to the role of violence in the contemporary Muslim world. While many people consider Islam to be a religion of violence, many Muslims consider Islam to be a religion of peace. Clearly, anyone teaching courses in the study of Islam has to be aware that he or she cannot criticize, promote, or be objective about Islam and Muslims without taking a political stand.[1]

After the war on Afghanistan, when it became clear that Iraq would be the next target, a number of us did what we could to assert our opposition to that upcoming war. At my university the following letter (incorporating passages from a letter circulated by the Fellowship of Reconciliation) was drafted and signed by a large number of faculty and staff in the fall of 2002:

> We, the undersigned members of the academic community at California State University, Northridge, are opposed to an invasion of Iraq by the United States. We remember the words of the Reverend Dr. Martin Luther King Jr., who on April 4, 1967, during the Vietnam war said: "Some of us who have already begun to break the silence of the night have found that the calling to speak is often a vocation of agony, but we must speak. We must speak with all the humility that is appropriate to our limited vision, but we must speak."
>
> We are opposed to U.S. military aggression against Iraq. It is as simple as that. As educators, we do not want our children, grandchildren, or students to go to war. We have not been attacked by Iraq. We have, however, since the end of the Gulf War, punished the Iraqi people through a comprehensive program of sanctions. A million Iraqis have died in the past decade, and now we threaten them with war. Contrary to the rhetoric of President Bush, we do not live in fear, but we understand that much of the world lives in fear of us.
>
> International law, the United Nations charter, and the clear testimony of

most nations of the world all forbid invading another land to control its leadership, or to confront a hypothetical future threat.

Indeed, in the case of the Iraqi threat, it is all hypothetical. Last May, the U.S. State Department published a compilation of terrorist activity across the globe. There was no mention of Iraq in it and no evidence of Iraqi involvement in the awful September 11 attacks.

"No" is the word that must now be whispered in the soul, shouted from the rooftops, declared to our groups and contacts, proclaimed from our places of worship, taught in our schools, colleges, and universities, and find its way into the media even if many others would rather rush to conform.

We ask all persons of conscience to resist this unjust war. It will not be fought in our name. Now is the moment to say "NO."

At my university a peace and justice group was created in response to the impending war.[2] What was heartening to me as a Muslim was that I wasn't in any way the driving force behind this group. Our university has a large number of Central American students, a new Central American Studies program, and one of the oldest Chicano/a Studies programs in the country. Many of our students from countries like Nicaragua or El Salvador have experienced in their bodies the effects of American foreign policy. And for more than three decades our Chicano/a Studies faculty and students have spoken the truth to power.

When the war against Iraq inevitably came, the widespread opposition to the war came as a relief for Muslims in America. Many of us had worked tirelessly since the attacks on 9/11 to educate the public about Islam. We, as Muslims, were horrified by and condemned the attacks, and our sympathies and prayers were with the victims and not with the terrorists. In the year after the attacks, many of us grieved for this country—our country—and the loss of the very civil liberties that made it such a wonderful example for the rule of law.

The line that I have been repeating over and over to myself comes from a song by the local California band Counting Crows: "All the anger and the eloquence are bleeding into fear." We fear for our country—our home—and what will become of it. The Patriot Act erodes all of our freedoms, and its latest iteration promises to be much worse. More than 1,000 people are still detained without cause. Brave people, most notably Japanese Americans who have firsthand experience of where that particular road leads, have spoken out against the detentions. The artist Garry Trudeau has, with his usual brilliance, addressed the issue of the detainees in his Doonesbury comic strip.

We who are Muslim need your help. To borrow a line from the poet Langston Hughes, we too are America. There is so much that needs to be done for healing and reconciliation in this country. We praise God and rejoice in the number of people who are willing to do the hard work that lies ahead for all of us.

---

1. Tazim R. Kassam has written an excellent essay on the issues of teaching Islam post-9/11: "On Being a Scholar of Islam: Risks and Responsibilities," in *Progressive Muslims: On Justice, Gender, and Pluralism*, ed. Omid Safi (Oxford: Oneworld Publications, 2003), pp. 128–44.

2. The Web page for the group is http://www.csun.edu/~csunupj/.

Though United States officials, including United States President George W. Bush, declared the deaths of Saddam's sons definite, Iraqis still had doubts and demanded proof of their deaths. LYNSEY ADDARIO/CORBIS 2003

"WHATEVER YOU SELL CAN BE BOUGHT": AN INTERVIEW WITH KRISTINA BORJESSON

Kristina Borjesson, Emmy Award–winning journalist and editor of *Into the Buzzsaw: Leading Journalists Expose the Myth of a Free Press,* knows what it's like to be on either end of an intimidated news media. After a diligent investigation of the TWA Flight 800 tragedy led Borjesson to conclude that the doomed plane was downed by arms fire, the decorated journalist was summarily dismissed from CBS and nearly excommunicated from mainstream media altogether.

Such dangerous—sometimes deliberate—friction promises to obfuscate the picture of what is truly happening on the ground in Iraq for those turning to CBS, Fox, CNN, or other like-minded outlets. If anything, Borjesson would argue that conventional American media is the last place one should search for the truth about why we are in this quagmire, who is responsible, how it is ravaging lives on all sides, and what the future holds for Iraq's continually oppressed citizenry.

Sandra Fu: SF   *Kristina Borjesson:* KB

SF: *What do you think of the news media's handling of the Iraq situation?*

KB: I don't think the news media is handling it. First, let's go back to before the war and look at something very interesting. The mainstream media, whether it's radio, cable, or network TV, reaches a critical mass of people, and if information doesn't reach that critical mass, it basically doesn't exist. And most of the media's news sources were military people, Bush administration officials, and the pundits who agreed with them. Interestingly, at the same time Colin Powell was trying to sell the war to the UN using information that we now know was false, his son Michael Powell at the FCC was deciding whether or not the same media conglomerates that control the stations his father was using to sell the war could own more TV and radio outlets and establish an even larger presence in the market. What better time to sell a war when you have the mass media by the bottom line? Once we went to war, information was controlled through embedded journalists—there were very few voices emerging with real reportage. You didn't see the devastation, you didn't see thousands of civilians dead in the streets or their homes. And now in the postwar stage, we still really have no idea about what's going on, except from the soldiers, who are now apparently writing letters home to their parents, which in turn causes their parents to come forth and say, "Hey, our media isn't really telling us what's going on." Now citizens are doing the job for journalists! War is an extreme activity; billions of dollars are being spent to maintain this occupation, and for what purpose? Was it really to liberate the Iraqi people, which was the big selling point? Look at

· 4 7 ·

the current cabinet—the vice president, national security advisor, our secretary of state—these are people involved in the oil and arms industries. If you look at the chessboard and the pieces, it is very clear.

SF: *Did you notice a distinction between print media and broadcast media in the war/occupation coverage?*

KB: There was more analysis and in-depth coverage in print; this is always the case, for fundamental reasons. First of all, there's the nature of TV. As an audiovisual medium, TV conveys information more powerfully, but print is much better for providing detailed background information and analysis. There's been some good print coverage of the war and occupation, but compared to television reporting it didn't have much impact. Only TV has access to enough people at the same time to reach the mass public consciousness. Case in point: The *Christian Science Monitor* reported that right after 9/11, polling data showed that only 3 percent of Americans who were asked open-ended questions about who was behind the attacks mentioned Iraq or Hussein. But by January of this year [2003], 44 percent of Americans believed that "that either 'most' or 'some' of the September 11 hijackers were Iraqi citizens." This happened because "legitimate news sources," consisting primarily of Bush administration members, regularly went on TV and linked the Iraqis with 9/11. The fact that many reputable print outlets reported that Hussein wasn't connected to 9/11 didn't matter. There was a lot of good independent radio coverage on this too, but again, nothing hit the mass public consciousness; mainstream radio coverage basically mirrored mainstream TV.

Because TV is more powerful, the information it conveys about major events is more highly controlled. TV's primary purpose is marketing, not conveying information, so anything that's going to affect its marketing function—like reporting on controversial subjects, or reporting facts that aren't good for business or the administration in power—just won't happen. Mainstream print outlets are subject to marketing constraints too, but they still have more wiggle room than mainstream TV. Also, there are lots of independent print outlets as well as numerous Internet sites (which I consider print media, unless they have audiovisual components to them) which provide coverage that their bigger counterparts won't. Independent TV outlets providing coverage of major events like the war/occupation are practically nonexistent.

SF: *So many people seem to need to have the dots connected for them.*

KB: And the reason why is because the information given to them isn't coverage of anything specific. Tell us what's going on: Why can't somebody ask people who are directly involved? It's Reporting 101—if you have a problem, then you go to the people who have their hands on the problem. Mainstream media never does that.

SF: *Perception is reality, as advertisers say.*

KB: Exactly. Pundits come on the air and tell you what the American military has done that day, who got shot and where. They give you vignettes bereft of context.

SF: *Where should people turn for news that actually informs?*

KB: Foreign news sources, because they are more free to report on what the U.S. is doing than U.S. reporters are. People can go to the BBC. I happen to like *AsiaTimes* online; I think they do a great job of reporting in context. I think the Center for Public Integrity has a really good website. But people have got to make the effort. At this point, they actually have to seek good coverage, because they're not going to get it from network television. And it's annoying—why do you have to go to the Internet to get decent reporting? Shouldn't you be able to expect it from the networks? No, because there are conflicts between their business interests and the public service mandate.

SF: *Meanwhile, the truth about what's happening on the ground in Iraq gets lost along the way.*

KB: The truth rings true. You just have to go to firsthand news sources. If all of your journalists are nicely tucked away in tanks, then they're not going to be crossing to the other side where the missiles have fallen, where the bombs have exploded. They aren't going to record the devastation that America has caused, not so much to the opposing military, but to the people. America doesn't truly engage in hand-to-hand combat anymore; we're safe and comfortable while it is the civilians being killed instead of the opposing soldiers.

SF: *When CNN war correspondent Christiane Amanpour appeared on* Topic A With Tina Brown *on CNBC, she commented, "I think the press was muzzled, and I think the press self-muzzled. I'm sorry to say, but certainly television, and perhaps to a certain extent my station, was intimidated by the administration and its foot soldiers at Fox News. And it did, in fact, put a climate of fear and self-censorship, in my view, in terms of the kind of broadcast work we did." What do you think of Amanpour's statement, and what is the significance of it?*

KB: I salute Amanpour for speaking out. It is a very big deal that she did. I'm fascinated that she talked about the "administration and its foot soldiers at Fox News" creating a climate of fear at CNN. How, specifically, did they do that? She didn't really answer the question. She talked about questions not being asked and "disinformation . . . at the highest levels," but she didn't specifically address how the administration and Fox cowed reporters at CNN.

As CNN's crown jewel correspondent, Amanpour can get away with making a statement about the press muzzling itself, but don't expect a rash of journalists to follow with their views on slanted reporting and muzzling. Other journalists don't have the immunity from punishment that Amanpour enjoys by virtue of her star status. The others will come out when—if ever—it's safe to do so.

SF: *What does this mean for the American public?*

KB: The Amanpour interview? Speaking optimistically, it means another brick in the wall was taken out to give the American people a glimpse of what's really going on—actually, since we're talking about Amanpour, maybe two bricks. But there's still a lot of wall to tear down.

SF: *What about integrating the information coming from the countless Iraqi newspapers? Would that give us a more accurate view?*

KB: Absolutely, if news sources would do that. But the U.S. has a profound problem: we live as if we're the only nation on the planet. We don't care about what's going on in other countries. We don't care what happens to the populations that supply us with cheap shoes and shirts. We don't care who gets killed in Iraq—we want our cheap oil. America is extremely provincial; we know nothing about what our government or our businesses are doing in Iraq. We've lived with blinders on, and that's why 9/11 was such a shock. Saudi money was pumped into that tragedy, and yet they've suffered no consequences. But in Iraq, there's a dictator who, by the way, was our friend a few years ago.

SF: *People don't seem to care about that part.*

KB: When you say to them, "If you don't care about that, then how can you be horrified about 9/11?," then they say, "You're not patriotic." They don't seem to understand that we all have to live on this planet. It's full of countries, and we're in each and every one of them doing things that we wouldn't accept if any of them came here and tried the same. Look at Noriega—he was our man in Panama, yet when [George Herbert Walker] Bush needs to disassociate himself from the drug dealing he knew was occurring, what does he do? Turns Panama into a military operation and kills several thousand people. What if other countries came and did that here? Americans don't consider this; it's as if the people in those countries are less than human, as if their lives don't count. And if you don't care, that's fine, but be ready to pay the price. I'm from Haiti, and we have an expression there: "Pluck the chicken but don't make it scream." Well, the planet is America's chicken, we've been plucking it to death, and it's finally screaming at us. We're losing friends left, right, and center.

SF: *All of this seems to be a comment on the dangers of using just the government or military to supply you with crucial information.*

KB: Well, they can trust the mass media to put out what they say, no questions asked. Consider the poll that asked Americans if they believed Saddam Hussein was directly involved in 9/11. People answered yes, even though it was false. Why? Because that's what the administration was disseminating to the media and from there it sank into the national consciousness. This was a way for the administration to get to Iraq.

SF: *Fear is a tool of control.*

KB: The administration didn't care what the American people wanted; they disagreed with protesters and they disagreed with the UN. They used anything that suited their mission to sell this war, because anything they disseminated would be broadcast on national television—and in the case of Fox News— ardently defended. CNN used the same sources and floated what I call the "Bill Hemmer" or "Paula Zahn" questions, that is, nothing that would put the administration's feet to the fire. Whatever the administration had to throw at the people to get them to keep quiet, they did it. Think about it: If you're making money in arms and oil, you're going to make money on the war and the reconstruction. How much money have these people already made? How are the deals and accounts set up? Halliburton and Bechtel get no-bid contracts— how does that get kicked back? Why is Halliburton getting a no-bid clause? Who's working there? How is this working? Follow the money.

SF: *Meanwhile, the people in Iraq, especially the women, are being robbed of life's necessities.*

KB: Particularly outside of the United States, women are robbed of something as fundamental as an education. It's a huge issue, because what you have in many countries are societies where literally half the population has no viability beyond breeding. I'm wondering what would happen if there were real movements, real efforts to empower women, especially in those countries where it is culturally unacceptable. And when I say empower them, I mean educate them so they can become economically independent. It's hugely political, educating women, because then they have influence over the men they rear—that might make a difference. It's actually an avenue that's not explored enough, because not enough women care or pay attention.

SF: *Why do major media outlets ignore the women in these countries?*

KB: Women aren't the power centers. They have no power. In those countries, the crowds and leaders, almost always men, get the coverage.

SF: *It's alarming that women's issues aren't getting more coverage, given the fact that America cited women's hardships—in Afghanistan at least—as a chief reason why such countries need to be liberated in the first place.*

KB: You always have to keep this in mind: Whatever you sell can be bought, and if it turns out to be false, oh well. With Iraq, it was not just nuclear but also chemical weapons of mass destruction. It really doesn't matter if women aren't liberated once you actually get into Afghanistan, just as it won't eventually matter if weapons of mass destruction are found in Iraq. It's the Orwellian Ministry of Truth factor—the very opposite of what is true today could be reported tomorrow. Meanwhile, the other truth has disappeared, as if it didn't exist.

IRAQ, OR THE LAST PIECE OF THE MASK

I am a woman Islamist, an intellectual, and a citizen of the world. As a consequence, my reaction to the Iraqi tragedy—a tragedy occurring at a Dante-esque scale—is three-dimensional.

I am a woman, a human being naturally destined to give life and dispense love, not to wage war and partake in chaos. What's more, however, because I am an Arab-Muslim woman, what happens in Iraq and throughout the Third World only adds to the numerous and extremely painful bruises that my culture, and thus I, have experienced. It undermines my will to continue working to see this world, God willing, one day living in peace, "*as-salam.*" This Arabic word, "*as-salam,*" not only means "peace," but it also refers to one of the names of God. And God chose this word for my Muslim brothers and sisters to use as a daily greeting: "*Assalamu alaykum,*" which means "May peace cover you."

From the mouth of a Muslim woman, such a greeting has not always been commonplace. In our society power has been usurped by cruel dictators like Saddam Hussein. As the outside world began to notice how Muslim women have experienced the repercussions of tyranny—in their societies, in their homes, and on their bodies—the assumption was made that Islam was and is our torturer. The perverted version of Islam that enslaves and oppresses Muslim women is not the Islam that God destined as a universal message of equity and spirituality. This false Islam is the sort that a man like Saddam Hussein adds to Iraqi nationalism in order to play on the emotions of the Muslim world.

Considering the sad state of affairs in Iraq, I would love to have been able to believe in the idea of the Good Samaritan country—be it the United States, England, or any other seemingly well-intentioned nation—coming to save us from the tyranny that the country had become mired in. My fellow sisters and I, who would have been the main beneficiaries of any truly liberating action from outside, looked forward to a meaningfully changed society where they could hope to find in men real and equal partners within the family structure or in the community as a whole. The fall of Saddam should have made me happy.

I would have loved to have believed the American propaganda, the promise of democracy and absolute Good defeating tyranny and absolute Evil. As one of many Islamic women struggling to regain my original rights granted by God, such a gift from Heaven would have pleased my soul.

I am saddened by the clear-eyed knowledge I now have that President Bush did not go to war for Good, or even against Evil, but for oil and in order to satisfy an appetite for domination which America no longer attempts to hide from the world. In the wake of the invasion and occupation, we are farther from democracy than ever before.

From my perspective as an Arab and Muslim woman and as a citizen of the world, the American system seems to serve primarily as a vehicle for the President to manipulate the people of the U.S. Cynicism has always been the hallmark of any

Realpolitik, but no power in the history of humanity has combined such will for domination with such a destructive arsenal as the United States today. While President Bush still makes a minimal effort to justify his actions in speeches and by superficial propriety, I fear that what has happened in Iraq will be the final unveiling of hypocrisy. When this happens, neither Americans nor any of the world's citizens will have the luxury of fooling themselves and ignoring the obvious any longer.

As a member of a movement that for thirty years has resisted the absurd policies of despotism with nonviolence, a glimmer of hope is seen each time we discover on the Internet, in a publication, or in a declaration, that other citizens of the world have as much desire as we do to bring common sense and humanity to government and society. It is good to know that there are truly virtuous people like Noam Chomsky, John Esposito, Scott Ritter, John Entelis, Richard Crane, José Bové, and hundreds of others who know how to say "no," who truly care about the ideas behind a global community. Their words and actions correspond perfectly to the spirit of Islam as referred to by Omar, valuable Companion of the Prophet, when he instructed his fellow citizens: "Do learn how to say 'no' [to injustice], loudly and with your whole being."

America has become the mirror of our absolute misfortune, but we must always remember that hope is the most basic necessity for political action, regardless of how tempting it is to react to irresponsible violence with irresponsible violence, to meet hatred with hatred. In the current situation it is our job as women, men, and Muslims to respond not through suicidal actions springing from unthinking anger, but rather in the most well-considered and socially aware manner possible.

Nahla Juwad waits for her sister outside of the Baquba Children's Hospital after an attack against American soldiers on the hospital grounds, mid-morning, July 26, 2003. LYNSEY ADDARIO/CORBIS 2003

A soldier with the 4th Infantry Division, 3rd Brigade, from the 1st Battalion–68th Armored Regiment, stands guard over detained Iraqis. LYNSEY ADDARIO/CORBIS 2003

THE CHANGING FACE OF OCCUPATION:
WHAT NUMBERS CANNOT TELL

On April 10, 2003, the morning after Saddam's statue fell in one of Baghdad's central squares, an American soldier, chewing gum and blowing bubbles, sat atop his tank near the square and watched a young Iraqi man pushing a carriage full of medical equipment, computers, and an air-conditioner, all looted from the nearby al-Sadoon Hospital. Another soldier was standing on the roadside preventing people from approaching the square by holding up both hands and repeating "Go back, go back." There were no Iraqis in the square behind him, only American tanks and vehicles. This small scene tells a lot about the presence of the occupation forces in Iraq from the very beginning.

However, after six months of war and occupation, an essential change has occurred in the small scene described above. The soldier on the tank will no longer expose himself to danger in the streets; instead he has pulled back into hidden corners and surrounded himself with high sandbags and barbed wire. Baghdad's main streets are now filled with ugly barracks, checkpoints, and high walls at the entrance to public buildings, which block the traffic and create many problems. Entering these buildings now takes longer and is more difficult.

The other soldier will no longer use bare hands to prevent people from passing, nor will he shout in a monotone, "Go back." Instead he stands grim-faced, aiming his gun at passing Iraqis and using it unhesitatingly whenever someone fails to understand the message. Today there have been hundreds of casualties in mistaken, random, and indiscriminate shootings; many of them are women and children. The most flagrant was the killing of ten Iraqi policemen by American fire a week ago—this was the third time that U.S. soldiers killed a policemen.

Baghdad today is another city—everything has changed. The streets, buildings, and squares are almost deserted after 6 P.M., and they are devoid of women, whether at the money-changing tables lining the main streets, among the homeless children and families squatting in public buildings, with the camera-and-notebook-laden foreigners looking for the next story, or at the fuel queues snaking out of the petrol stations. However, the most significant change can be read on the Iraqi faces that articulate mounting bewilderment and shock.

The last six months in Baghdad have been too long—an age. For a nation that has been patient for decades and has undergone three wars, thirteen years of sanctions, political repression, and continual outside threats, six months has been too long to wait for relief, too long to wait for positive changes.

Given the casualties of war, the mass deaths inflicted by bombing, the chaos of looting, the immolation of public buildings, the shock of the rapid fall of the state, people now understand the real face of the occupation and its true meaning: negligence, lies, arrogance, and humiliation. In no time Iraqis have discovered that all the promises have led only to more empty promises projected into some unforeseeable future.

The problems of daily life, exacerbated by the existence of the occupying forces, lie heavily on the Iraqi people: insecurity; the absence of effective Iraqi authority; unemployment and accompanying fear of the future; constant shootings; stories of indiscriminate firing upon civilians; thousands of haphazard arrests for unknown reasons, with detainees taken to unknown places for undefined periods of time. These new conditions have been added to the existing realities of a deeply divided and impoverished Iraq.

In the midst of the current devastation, accurate statistics and numbers are illusive because the occupying forces deliberately attempt to conceal negative facts wherever possible, and significant events or trends are not systematically documented.

Iraq Body Count, a volunteer group of British and U.S. academics and researchers, has stated that 7,798 Iraqis were killed during the war (2,356 in Baghdad alone), and 20,000 were injured (8,000 in Baghdad). There are no statistics on the number of civilian casualties in Baghdad since May 1, 2003, the day President Bush declared the official end of the war, but Dr. Faiq, the director of Baghdad's forensic hospital, has said that based on bodies brought to the morgue, the average number of people killed daily is twenty to thirty. In July, for example, 720 people were killed, 470 of them shot. This is a 47 percent increase from July 2002. *Guardian* journalist Peter Beaumont, writing on September 14, 2003, put shooting-related deaths at 400 a month.

The occupying authorities, officially known as the Coalition Provisional Authority (CPA), bear the responsibility for this dramatic rise in murders, even if some of the killings were not by their forces. According to the 4th Geneva Convention, these authorities are fully responsible for the protection of the civilian population.

Although the first order of the occupying authorities was to provide for local authority, insecurity is the most important problem facing Iraqis. This insecurity has many causes, including the absence of real local authority; the inefficiency of the new Iraqi police, who lack weapons; the terrifying midnight raids mounted on Iraqis; and the occupier's negligence, withholding of logistical information and authority, unwillingness to jeopardize their soldiers' lives, and refusal to apply Iraqi law to the occupying countries' citizens.

Lately, many new kinds of crimes—killings in broad daylight, armed robberies, kidnappings, rapes, and car hijackings—have appeared. Mr. Abdul-Razaq Al-Ani, a judge at the New Baghdad court, says that in the space of two weeks there were 50 killings, 176 car thefts, 4 robberies accompanied by killings, and 2 kidnappings for ransom. The occupying authorities deal with the issue by focusing on the need for their soldiers' security. When Colin Powell was asked about security during a September 14 press conference in Baghdad, he spoke only of the personal security of U.S. soldiers. To him and other occupiers, security means eliminating armed resistance and nothing else.

Another pressing problem facing Iraqis is the occupation forces' power of arbitrary arrest. Often those arrested are unaware of exactly why they were arrested, and their families know neither where their loved ones are nor how long they will be held. According to Amnesty International, there are approximately thirty Iraqi prisons, with Baghdad Airport, Bucca in Basrah, and Tesfiraht the three largest prison camps. The official detainee population stands at 10,000, according to the occupation authorities, but the CPA lists do not necessarily represent all detainees, because these lists are updated infrequently and dozens of people are arrested daily. From former prisoners, stories of torture, bad treatment, and the denial of human rights are prevalent.

The country's devastated economic situation creates the ideal conditions for crime to flourish. The World Food Program report of June 6, 2003, stated that one-fifth of Iraqis suffer chronic poverty. The Iraqi Union of the Unemployed says there are currently ten million people (approximately 60 percent of the working-age population) unemployed in Iraq.

This year's war has added misery to the already suffering classes. In the Al-Thawra (now Al-Sadr) district of three million inhabitants—mostly farmers who immigrated to the capital over the last fifty years—four out of five families live in a house measuring, on average, two hundred square meters. Most of them are newly unemployed, widows, or disabled; the majority are ex–prisoners of war or soldiers released from service when the Iraqi army was dissolved after the war. Many families are homeless or squatting in deserted public buildings or schools. The schools in deprived areas are in inadequate buildings, basically large barracks without any furniture. There are 18 families (120 individuals) inhabiting a school with no running water and no private sanitation in section 37 of Al-Thawra, while section 76 practically floats over a sewage lake. Some families live in garbage. These places have become key centers of

An Iraqi woman pleads with U.S. troops from the 1st Armored Division to let her get in the line to exchange 10,000 dinar notes at a neighborhood exchange. LYNSEY ADDARIO/CORBIS 2003

organized crime. While the religious parties have succeeded in reducing the number of thefts, there are other uncontrolled crimes, such as the stealing of electric cables and the melting of these cables in open smelting areas, a process that emits black thick smoke and further contaminates the environment.

Given the lack of security, legitimate economic activity has been thwarted, prices have gone up, and gangs have been easily transformed into crime syndicates. Further complicating economic recovery is the absence of a national or even regional telecommunications system: only three out of the nine districts in Baghdad have a working telephone system.

It is not difficult to identify all of these problems, but is it really possible to fully convey the agony of living under occupation?

BAGHDAD JOURNAL #3

One of our visits in Baghdad was to Firdos Square, the famous site where the statue of Saddam Hussein was toppled, a scene that was shown over and over again on U.S. television. Now a new, rather indecipherable three-headed statue by a young Iraqi artist was in its place. But curiously, on the column just beneath the statue, someone had written in bright red paint and in perfect English, "All done. Go home."

Sitting around the circle in the brutal heat were money changers with thick wads of bills with Saddam Hussein on them, which, ironically, is still the currency. Behind the money changers were mounds of barbed wire and U.S. soldiers sitting atop ferocious-looking tanks, weapons readied—a common scene on the streets of Baghdad.

Two elderly money changers in long flowing robes and white caps were sitting at their outdoor stand, and we started chatting. They asked where we were from. "Oh, America," one answered, crossing his arms against his chest, "I love America." "How about the soldiers?" we asked, pointing behind them. The man who "loved America" said how happy they were to be free of Saddam Hussein, but the other man pointed to the column with the graffiti. "So you think the soldiers should go home to America?" I asked. Both men broke out in big grins. "Yes, Saddam gone. That's good. Soldiers should go, too. Many Iraqis don't like them here."

They told us that if conditions in Iraq did not improve soon, ordinary Iraqis, not fundamentalists, would fight to get rid of the Americans. "We have a nine-thousand-year-old culture, you have a two-hundred-year-old culture," one of the men said, "I think we can figure out our own future."

Iraqis are puzzled why the United States, a country that can make bombs so smart they target a particular building from 30,000 miles in the air, can't give them electricity or create a functioning economy. Some are so puzzled that they have concluded that the United States is purposely trying to destroy every aspect of the economy so that they can come in and rebuild it in their own image. Others attribute the mess to incompetence, arrogance, or stupidity.

No matter the reason, in this land of 120-degree heat and no rain, the U.S. is sinking deeper and deeper into a quagmire. The Iraqis are a patient, generous people. For lack of an alternative, most are still willing to give the U.S. more time, but the clock is ticking, and patience is wearing thin.

Continued . . .

Iraqi women who worked with the Central Bank in Baghdad work at a neighborhood exchange. LYNSEY ADDARIO/CORBIS 2003

American soldiers with the 1st Armored Division. LYNSEY ADDARIO/CORBIS 2003

A PROGRESSIVE MUSLIM CRITIQUE
OF THE U.S. OCCUPATION OF IRAQ

The ongoing U.S. occupation of Iraq presents a special challenge for Muslims who self-identify as socially and politically progressive. The challenge is to speak out, rise up, and act against the unilateral American display of unbridled military power, as well as against acts of violence by some Iraqis toward that same American might or perceived Iraqi sympathizers. This double critique arises out of the Qur'anic view that to save the life of one human being—any human being—is to have saved the life of all humanity, and to take the life of a single human being, any human being, is as if to destroy all of humanity [Qur'an 5:32].

At the heart of a progressive Muslim identity is a simple assumption, the notion that all human life on this planet—Muslim and non-Muslim, female and male, civilian and military, poor or rich, "North" or "South," gay or straight—carries exactly the same intrinsic worth. This essential value of human life is due to the presence of Divine spirit in all of humanity, the same spirit that, according to the Qur'an, God breathed into each and every human being[1] [Qur'an 15:29 and 38:72]. By starting from this premise of the worth and dignity of each and every human life, progressive Muslims move to affirming the sanctity of each human life and the right of each community to a notion of global justice that allows them to realize their vision of prosperity, dignity, and righteousness, as long as that vision does not come at the expense of any other community. We have to be clear about this point: our task is not to "humanize" Iraqis—one can only humanize something that is not already fully human. The Iraqis, exactly like us, already *possess* their full God-given humanity. If we have failed to see and interact with Iraqis on a human level, if we have not listened to their cries, seen their tears, mourned their deaths, it is because they have been presented to us as inhuman, subhuman, or nonhuman.

Progressive Muslims oppose the occupation of Iraq on many fronts. First and foremost, the horrific tactics followed by the Bush administration, including the bombing of heavily populated urban sites, have led to a large number of civilian casualties. Following in the footsteps of Gandhi, Martin Luther King Jr., and the Dalai Lama, we reject this unleashing of violence against the poorest peoples of the earth. The perverse pleasure that the Pentagon and State Department derived from their death fantasy, described as Operation "Shock and Awe," does indeed shock the sensitivity of those who see Iraqis as fellow human beings with hopes and dreams and loves and joys of their own that are every bit as precious as our own. The Bush regime repeatedly attempted to persuade/delude us that this operation would be accurate and precise, that these bombs are very "smart." So-called "smart bombs" used in a misguided policy of deliberate cruelty result in nothing short of indiscriminate massacre.

The loss of human life on the Iraqi side affects Muslims powerfully, leading directly to an increase in vehement anti-Americanism all over this world. The American presence

in Iraq, coupled with U.S. support of an Israeli regime bent on brutal oppression of Palestinians and an increasingly Hindu nationalist regime in India which participates in massacres of Muslims in Gujarat and Kashmir: all these lead to a volatile and dangerous rise in hatred of America and Americans all over the world. While many Americans may wish to see ourselves as upholders of freedom and democracy, many people all over the world—and increasingly large numbers of Muslims—see the U.S. as a supporter of many forms of exploitation, domination, and oppression.

Muslims see themselves as part of a grand spiritual community (the *umma*) that stretches from Indonesia to Morocco, from South Africa to the U.S. That the word *umma* is itself derived from the word *"umm,"* meaning "mother," gives an indication of the closeness and spiritual affinity among Muslims of various backgrounds: the bonds of faith are as strong as those shared by the children born to and nurtured by the same mother. It is for this reason that the ongoing wave of Muslim casualties all over the world has been so devastating for American Muslims to bear. The wars in Afghanistan and Iraq have each resulted in civilian casualties far greater than that of September 11, yet the loss of these lives has hardly been engaged by the American media or government with the same humanity that we have treated the loss of American life, both military and civilian. The most accurate estimate of the civilian casualties in Afghanistan comes from Marc Herold, who states that "between 3,125 and 3,620 Afghan civilians were killed between October 7 [2001] and July 31 [2002]."[2] There have also been large-scale casualties in Iraq. The most recent estimate by the Associated Press puts the number of Iraqi civilians who died in the first month of the 2003 war at 3,240.[3] Other independent evaluations of the Iraq casualty count put the number even higher, between 6,139 and 7,849.[4] When pressed to explain such a high number of civilian deaths in a war that was represented as being conducted through "precision targets" and "smart bombs," General Tommy Franks responded: "We don't do body counts." For American Muslims, this callous disregard for Muslim civilians—coupled with the pomp and circumstance that surrounds the rightly joyous occasion of rescuing American prisoners such as Private Jessica Lynch[5]—can only be explained as arising out of the different worth attached to American as opposed to Muslim lives. It is this much resented double standard that Muslims in both this country and beyond see as an unspoken and unjust aspect of American foreign policy.

And yet as progressive Muslims, we cannot and will not limit our engagement simply to the evils of the American government. We have a moral duty to also speak up against the culture of violence that now pervades segments of Iraqi societies, a violence that is unleashed against UN workers, fellow Iraqis, and yes, American soldiers. No just ends can ever be attained through violent and unjust means. The ends are the very fruits of the trees of our means, and the poisoned tree of violence can never lead to delicious fruits of dignity. In addressing American violence before Iraqi violence, I am specifically following in the footsteps of Martin Luther King Jr., who stated: "I knew that I could never again raise my voice against the violence of the oppressed in the ghettos without having first spoken clearly to the greatest purveyor of violence in the world today, my own government." Our task is to do more than condemn: we must work with Iraqis in finding a way to voice their righteous rebellion of resistance—indeed, their *jihad*—against the American occupation in a nonviolent way. This is a great challenge, but I believe that we have no choice but to follow every skillful nonviolent means necessary. (Yes, Buddhist ethics of nonviolence can be combined in Malcolm X-ian urgency in a progressive Muslim agenda.)

It is this simultaneous critique of U.S. military might (disguised as "the coalition") and Iraqi violent outbursts which leaves progressive Muslims in an isolated space in the middle. And yet it is from this space in the middle that we reach out to all of humanity. In doing so we recall the Qur'anic injunction that states that notions of social justice (*'adl*) and spiritual excellence (*ihsan*) are indeed connected. May we bring some healing into this much-fractured world. May that healing begin with you and me, at this very moment.

Amin . . .

1. Omid Safi, "The Times They Are A-Changin'—A Muslim Quest for Justice, Gender Equality, and Pluralism," in *Progressive Muslims: On Justice, Gender, and Pluralism* (Oxford: Oneworld Publications, 2003).

2. Marc Herold is a professor of economics at University of New Hampshire. His data can be accessed at: http://pubpages.unh.edu/~mwherold/AfghanDailyCount.pdf. Also, see http://www.guardian.co.uk/afghanistan/comment/story/0,11447,770999,00.html.

3. http://story.news.yahoo.com/news?tmpl=story&u=/ap/20030610/ap_on_re_mi_ea/iraq_counting_the_dead_7.

4. http://iraqbodycount.net/bodycount.htm [as of September 20, 2003].

5. For initial coverage of this episode, see http://news.bbc.co.uk/2/hi/middle_east/2908477.stm. By now, some of the mythmaking that surrounded this rescue is being reevaluated: www.timesonline.co.uk/article/0,5944-648517,00.html.

PREVIOUS SPREAD: An Iraqi woman walks between rows of bodies, laid out in a building, which were discovered in a mass grave south of Baghdad. LYNSEY ADDARIO/CORBIS 2003

SEEKING HONESTY IN U.S. POLICY

During the Gulf War in 1991, when I was in charge of the American Embassy in Baghdad, I placed a copy of Lewis Carroll's *Alice in Wonderland* on my office coffee table. I thought it conveyed far better than words ever could the weird world that was Iraq at that time, a world in which nothing was what it seemed: The several hundred Western hostages Saddam Hussein took during Desert Shield were not really hostages but "guests." Kuwait was not invaded, but "liberated."

It is clearly time to dust the book off and again display it prominently, only this time because our own government has dragged the country down a rabbit hole, all the while trying to convince the American people that life in newly liberated Iraq is not as distorted as it seems.

It is returning to normal, we are assured, even as we are asked to ante up an additional $75 billion and pressure builds to send more troops and extend the tours of duty of those who are there. Deputy Defense Secretary Paul Wolfowitz tells Congress that all we need is to project a little confidence. The Mad Hatter could not have said it better.

President Bush's speech on Sunday, September 7, was just the latest example of the administration's concerted efforts to misrepresent reality—and rewrite history—to mask its mistakes. The president said Iraq is now the center of our battle against terrorism. But we did not go to Iraq to fight Al-Qaeda, which remains perhaps our deadliest foe, and we will not defeat it there.

By trying to justify the current fight in Iraq as a fight against terrorism, the administration has done two frightening things. It has tried to divert attention from Osama bin Laden, the man responsible for the wave of terrorist attacks against American interests from New York and Washington to Yemen, and who reappeared in rugged terrain in a video broadcast last week. And the policy advanced by the speech is a major step toward creating a dangerous, self-fulfilling prophecy and reflects a fundamental misunderstanding of the facts on the ground.

This is an insurgency we're fighting in Iraq. Our 130,000 soldiers in Iraq now confront an angry but not yet defeated Sunni Muslim population who, although a minority in Iraq, had been in power for a century. We are now also beginning to face terrorists there, but it is our own doing. Our attack on Iraq—and our bungling of the peace—led to the guerrilla insurgency that is drawing jihadists from around the Muslim world. The "shock and awe" campaign so vividly shown on our television screens has galvanized historic Arab envy, jealousy, and resentment of the United States into white-hot hatred of America.

Where once there were thousands, now there are potentially millions of terrorists and sympathizers who will be drawn into this campaign.

We've seen other examples of the kind of insurgency we're now facing. One was in Afghanistan against the Soviets in the 1980s, and we all should know the end of that story by now. Bin Laden was one of the outside jihadists drawn into that battle; he emerged as the head of a group of hardened soldiers he called "Al-Qaeda."

It is perhaps not surprising that the administration is trying to redefine why we went to Iraq, because we have accomplished so little of what we set out to do—and severely underestimated the commitment it would take to deal with the aftermath of war.

The president told us in his seminal speech in Cincinnati in October 2002 that Iraq "possesses and produces chemical and biological weapons . . . is seeking nuclear weapons . . . has given shelter and support to terrorism, and practices terror against its own people."

He dismissed the concerns raised by critics of his approach as follows: "Some worry that a change of leadership in Iraq could create instability and make the situation worse. The situation could hardly get worse, for world security and for the people of Iraq. The lives of Iraqi citizens would improve dramatically if Saddam Hussein were no longer in power."

Now we know that even if we find chemical or biological weapons, the threat that they posed to our national security was, to be charitable, exaggerated.

It all but disappeared from the president's speech last week, and Defense Secretary Donald Rumsfeld, one of the leading proponents of the threat, now tells us that he didn't even ask the chief weapons-of-mass-destruction sleuth in Iraq, David Kay, for a status report during his recent trip to Baghdad, relegating such weapons to the same dark corner as bin Laden, whose name rarely passes the lips of our leaders these days.

Indeed, in the most telling revision of the justification for going to war, the State Department's undersecretary for arms control, John Bolton, recently said that whether Saddam's government actually possessed weapons of mass destruction "isn't really the issue. The issue, I think, has been the capability that Iraq sought to have . . . WMD programs."

In other words, we're now supposed to believe that we went to war not because Saddam's arsenal of weapons of mass destruction threatened us, but because he had scientists on his payroll.

And the cakewalk postwar scenario that had been painted by some in the administration is anything but. More Americans have died since the president announced the end of major combat operations than during the war itself. The cost runs $1 billion per week in military support alone, and some experts say our deployment is already affecting future military preparedness.

Iraqis live in chaotic conditions as crime flourishes in the unpatrolled streets, and family squabbles are settled vigilante style; basic services such as electricity remain unavailable to large segments of the urban population.

The truth is, the administration has never leveled with the American people on the war with Iraq.

It is true that many people outside the administration, including me and many leading Democrats, thought Saddam had residual stocks of weapons of mass destruction; disarmament was a legitimate international objective supported unanimously by the United Nations Security Council. But we did not need to rush to war before exploring other, less risky options.

Invasion, conquest, and occupation was always the highest-risk, lowest-reward choice. The intrusive UN inspections were disrupting Saddam's programs and weakening him in the eyes of his key supporters, including in the Iraqi military. That would explain why the United States, according to reports, was able to thoroughly infiltrate the army before the onset of hostilities and obtain commitments from Iraqi generals to send their troops home rather than have them fight.

The administration short-circuited the discussion of whether war was necessary because some of its most powerful members felt it was the best option—ostensibly because they had deluded themselves into believing that they could easily impose flowering democracies on the region.

A more cynical reading of the agenda of certain Bush advisers could conclude that the Balkanization of Iraq was always an acceptable outcome, because Israel would then find itself surrounded by small Arab countries worried about each other instead of forming a solid block against Israel. After all, Iraq was an artificial country that had always had a troublesome history.

One way the administration stopped the debate was to oversell its intelligence. I know, because I was in the middle of the efforts to determine whether Iraq had attempted to purchase uranium "yellowcake"—a form of lightly processed ore—from Africa.

At the request of the administration I traveled to the West African nation of Niger in February 2002 to check out the allegation. I reported that such a sale was highly unlikely, but my conclusions—as well as the same conclusions from our ambassador on the scene and from a four-star Marine Corps general—were ignored by the White House.

Instead, the president relied upon an unsubstantiated reference in a British white paper to underpin his argument in the State of the Union address that Saddam was reconstituting his nuclear weapons programs. How many times did we hear the president, vice president, and others speak of the looming threat of an Iraqi mushroom cloud?

Until several months ago, when it came out that the country was Niger, I assumed that the president had been referring to another African country. After I learned, belatedly to be sure, I came forward to insist that the administration correct the misstatements of fact. But the damage had already been done.

The overblown rhetoric about nuclear weapons inspired fear and drowned out the many warnings that invasion would create its own formidable dangers.

Middle East experts warned over and over again that Iraq's many religious and ethnic factions could start battling each other in a bloody struggle for power. Former British foreign secretary Douglas Hurd fretted that we would unleash a terrorist-recruiting bonanza, and former U.S. national security adviser Brent Scowcroft warned of a security meltdown in the region.

The U.S. army's top general at the time, Eric Shinseki, meanwhile, questioned the "cakewalk" scenario. He told Congress that we would need several hundred thousand soldiers in Iraq to put an end to the violence against our troops and against each other. His testimony was quickly repudiated by both Rumsfeld and Wolfowitz.

As we now know, he was close to the mark. Our 130,000 soldiers are failing to stem the violence. Even as Rumsfeld says jauntily that all is going well, Secretary of State Colin Powell is running to the United Nations to try to get more foreign boots on the ground. One of the administration's staunchest supporters, British Foreign

Secretary Jack Straw, says ominously that we risk strategic failure if we don't send reinforcements.

And the infighting that Middle East experts feared could still erupt. The majority Shiite Muslim population, brutalized during Saddam's rule, is content with a tactical truce with our forces so long as they are free to consolidate their control and the United States continues to kill Sunni Muslims so that they don't have to. That truce is threatened not only by Shiite political ambition but also by ongoing skirmishes with the Sunnis.

The recent car bomb at the An-Najaf mosque that killed one of Shiite Islam's most influential clerics and head of the largest Shiite party in Iraq almost resulted in the outbreak of civil war between the two groups. Widespread belief that Sunni elements were behind the assassination and that the United States failed in its responsibilities for security has brought Shiite armed militias back onto the streets, actively seeking to avenge the death of their leader. Such a war within a war would make our occupation infinitely more dangerous.

Some now argue that the president's speech Sunday [September 7, 2003] represents a change of course. Even if the administration won't admit it made any mistakes, the mere call for international involvement should be enough to persuade the world to accept the burden of assisting us as we continue to control both the military and the economic reconstruction.

That may well be true, but we cannot count on the international community to do our bidding blindly. While the administration scurries back to the United Nations for help, our historic friends and allies still smart from the gratuitous insults hurled at them nine months ago. This is the same United Nations which Richard Perle, a not-so-invisible hand behind the war, recently called an "abject failure."

As Zbigniew Brzezinski, who was President Carter's national security adviser, has pointed out, at a time when our military might is at its zenith, our political and moral authority is at its lowest ebb. Essential trust has been broken, and it will take time to repair. At a minimum, we need to jettison the hubris that has driven this policy, the pretensions of moral rectitude that mask a jodhpurs-and-pith-helmet imperialism that cannot succeed.

In the meantime, we must demonstrate that we understand that more than military might is required to tame the anger in the region. This includes both the internationalization of the reconstruction effort and the redoubling of efforts to ease tensions on the Israeli-Palestinian front.

That is the thorn that must be pulled from the side of the region. The road to peace in the Middle East still goes through Jerusalem.

But before we can hope to win back international trust or start down a truly new path in Iraq, the administration has to start playing it straight, with the American people and with the world. Recent administration statements, including the president's speech, suggest that it still prefers to live in a fantasy world.

OVERLEAF: An Iraqi man pleads with Lieutenant Colonel Haight of the 82nd Airborne Division after being caught with a gun during a raid on a wedding party after Haight's unit heard gunshots. LYNSEY ADDARIO/CORBIS 2003

BAGHDAD JOURNAL #4

We return to the palace for our meeting with Margaret Bhadi. We've been told by Medea Benjamin that we shouldn't leave the palace without seeing the chapel, so we ask a young Iraqi woman sitting in the entry of Bremer's office where it is.

"I'll take you," Rajaa volunteers. She's an interpreter for the CPA. As we follow her down a very long corridor, we pass men in uniforms who move between offices or sit at tables in the anteroom chambers. The first set of doors she tries is locked; she tries all of them, unsuccessfully, but unperturbed, she continues to the next giant hallway. There is a notice of religious services—Christian, Jewish, and Mormon—posted outside the chapel.

She finds an open door and we enter. The chapel is huge and clad in marble, with lushly painted murals of missiles and rockets, almost comically phallic, on the walls and ceiling.

We are staggered by the absurdity of it but try not to laugh in her presence.

"We believed in Saddam, and he was taking our money and building this," Rajaa says, the wounds of betrayal obvious in her voice.

She sees our amazement and says, "This is nothing, follow me."

As we walk further down the hall, Rajaa talks about her life in Baghdad during the bombing. For two months she couldn't leave her home because she was too afraid. Now she doesn't care if she lives or dies.

A woman translator sits at the main entrance of the Palace of the Brigade, headquarters of the 1st Armored Division; she does not tell anyone in her neighborhood that she works for coalition forces. LYNSEY ADDARIO/CORBIS 2003

We exit one building and enter another. Huge statues of Saddam still stand atop the palace, four identical images, frightening and intact. This wing of the palace feels empty and vast; it is unoccupied. There are more huge rooms, also decorated with gold and marble and looming images of rockets and missiles, erect and tumescent, streaking across the painted sky. There is more, much more of the same—it's tacky and cold.

Rajaa continues to tell her stories; she can't seem to tell us fast enough, and she seems unafraid of who might be listening. She can't find enough words to describe the bombing, and she starts to cry. Everyone left Baghdad, she says. She wanted her mother to leave, to walk out of the city, but she was too old. She talks about the drugs and the alcohol, how drug use has grown alongside poverty. Guns are available everywhere for less than ten dollars U.S. Criminals freed when Saddam emptied Baghdad's prisons in October 2002 roam the streets. Many ex-policemen who had been fired in a fit of "de-Baathification" after the invasion have formed armed mafias, taking over neighborhoods, stealing, and extorting protection money. Rajaa tells about the kidnapping of two girls—one thirteen, the other fifteen—in her neighborhood. They were returned after ten days, but they'd been raped, so their families threw them out and left them on the street to die. She talks about the dirt and the absence of services—no electricity, garbage heaped in the roads—and how little she cares for her life now. This is what gives her the courage to risk working with the CPA: What difference does it make if her life is in danger because she works for the Americans, when she doesn't care if she lives or dies?

And it *is* dangerous to work for the Americans. Iraqis who do so are branded as traitors, threatened, and sometimes killed, and Moujahdeens have issued *fatwas* against those who work for the occupiers. Rajaa has to hide that she is employed by the CPA, so she takes a taxi from home each day, which eats into her earnings of $10 a day. She has the taxi drop her off far from the CPA so no one will know that she works there. I ask her about the salaries for men vs. women: she says they are the same. An attorney makes $15 and a laborer makes $5, but gender doesn't determine the salary.

"You take the oil and our jobs," she says as she is called back to her work. "You are like Saddam, who made people suffer so that they would follow him, obey him, because they had little choice."

Rajaa returns to her tasks, and Reverend Patricia Ackerman insists on finding the chaplain, which is difficult because he is well hidden. She returns from her conversation with him appalled. He's not very qualified, and he brags childishly about the huge amount of money he is making—six figures, according to him.

I leave to find the intelligence officer. He is pompous and full of himself. He wants to impress me with his knowledge, so words flow at a brisk pace. "Moderates want freedom: they want to taste democracy," he says. I ask him about Iran because he is Iranian, and he responds, "We won't attack Iran because we are changing their government. We are creating a radio show this week to support the students and begin to create the support needed." These programs are happening from his office, he is proud to announce. He continues: "Fear is the foundation of any government, and they will continue the chaos to create the atmosphere to keep their power."

Continued . . .

VEILED AND WORRIED IN BAGHDAD

A single word is on the tight, pencil-lined lips of women here. You'll hear it spoken over lunch at a women's leadership conference in a restaurant off busy Al Nidal Street, in a shade-darkened beauty shop in upscale Mansour, in the ramshackle ghettos of Sadr City. The word is "*himaya*," or "security." With an intensity reminiscent of how they feared Saddam Hussein, women now fear the abduction, rape, and murder that have become rampant here since his regime fell. Life for Iraqi women has been reduced to one need that must be met before anything else can happen.

"Under Saddam we could drive, we could walk down the street until two in the morning," a young designer told me as she bounced her four-year-old daughter on her lap. "Who would have thought the Americans could have made it worse for women? This is liberation?"

In their palace surrounded by armed soldiers, officials from the occupying forces talk about democracy. But in the same cool marble rooms, when one mentions the fears of the majority of Iraq's population, one can hear a representative of the Ministry of the Interior, which oversees the police, say, "We don't do women." What they don't seem to realize is that you can't "do" democracy if you don't "do" women.

In Afghanistan women threw off their *burqas* when American forces arrived. In Baghdad the veils have multiplied, and most women are hiding at home instead of working, studying, or playing a role in reconstructing Iraq. Under Saddam Hussein, crimes against women—or at least ones his son Uday, Iraq's vicious Caligula, did not commit—were relatively rare (though solid statistics for such crimes don't exist). Last October the regime opened the doors to the prisons. Kidnappers, rapists, and murderers were allowed to blend back into society, but they were kept in check by the police state. When the Americans arrived and the police force disappeared, however, these old predators reemerged alongside new ones. And in a country that essentially relies on rumor as its national news, word of sadistic abduction quickly began to spread.

A young Iraqi woman I met represents the reality of these rumors. Sitting in her darkened living room surrounded by female relatives, she leans forward to show the sutures running the length of her scalp. She and her fiancé were carjacked by a gang of thieves in July, and when one tried to rape her, she threw herself out of the speeding car. She says that was the last time she left the house. She hasn't heard a word from her fiancé since he went to the police station to file a report, not about the attempted rape, but about his missing Toyota RAV-4.

"What's important isn't a woman's life here, but a nice car," she said with a blade-sharp laugh.

Two sisters, thirteen and eighteen, weren't as lucky. A neighbor—a kidnapper and murderer who had been released in the general amnesty—led a gang of heavily armed friends to their home one night a few weeks ago. The girls were beaten and raped. When the police finally arrived, the attackers fled with the thirteen-year-old. She was taken to an abandoned house and left there, blindfolded, for a couple of weeks before she was dropped at her door upon threat of death if anyone learned of what had happened. Now she hides out with her sister, young brother, and mother in an abandoned office building in a seedy neighborhood.

"What do you expect?" said the eighteen-year-old. "They let out the criminals. They got rid of the law. Here we are."

Even these brutalized sisters are luckier than many women in Iraq. They have no adult male relatives, and thus are not at risk for the honor killings that claim the lives of many Muslim women here. Tribal custom demands that a designated male kill a female relative who has been raped, and the law allows only a maximum of three years in prison for such a killing, which Iraqis call "washing the scandal."

"We never investigate these cases anyway—someone has to come and confess the killing, which they almost never do," said an investigator, who looked into the case and then dismissed it because the sisters "knew one of the men, so it must not be kidnapping."

This violence has made postwar Iraq a prison of fear for women. "This issue of security is the immediate issue for women now—this horrible time that was triggered the very first day of the invasion," said Yanar Mohammed, the founder of the Organization of Women's Freedom in Iraq.

Ms. Mohammed organized a demonstration against the violence last month. She also sent a letter to the occupation administrator, Paul Bremer, demanding his attention. Weeks later, with no reply from Mr. Bremer, she shook her head in the shadowy light of her office, darkened by one of frequent blackouts here. "We want to be able to talk about other issues, like the separa-

Sunni Iraqi girls pray during Friday afternoon prayer at the Haja Dalal Al-Kubaisi Mosque in Baghdad. LYNSEY ADDARIO/CORBIS 2003

tion of mosque and state and the development of a civil law based on equality between men and women, but when women can't even leave their homes to discuss such things, our work is quite hard," she said.

Baghdadi women were used to a cosmopolitan city in which doctorates, debating, and dancing into the wee hours were ordinary parts of life. That Baghdad now seems as ancient as this country's Mesopotamian history. College students are staying home; lawyers are avoiding their offices. A formerly first-world capital has become a city where the women have largely vanished.

To support their basic liberties will no doubt require the deeply complicated task of disentangling the threads of tribal, Islamic, and civil law that have made misogyny systemic in each. This is a matter of culture, not just policy.

But to understand the culture of women in Iraq, coalition officials must venture beyond their razor-wired checkpoints and step down from their convoys of Land Cruisers so they can talk to the nation they occupy. On the streets and in the markets, they'll receive warm invitations to share enormous lunches in welcoming homes, as is the Iraqi custom. And there they'll hear this notion repeated frankly and frequently: without *himaya* for women, there will be no place for democracy to grow in Iraq.

American troops stand guard. LYNSEY ADDARIO/CORBIS 2003

ANNE E. BRODSKY AND TAHMEENA FARYAL

WOMEN: CANARIES IN THE COAL MINE OF INTERNATIONAL FOREIGN POLICY

The treatment of women by a particular society often renders them canaries in the coal mine, foretelling the prospects for a range of human rights issues from child welfare to freedom of association and dissent. In the current geopolitical climate in which the U.S. and other Western players are exploiting military might while claiming the role of societal liberators, the conditions of women's rights within Afghanistan and Iraq are a reflection not only of the indigenous cultures of the regions, but also of the intervention priorities and goals of the U.S. and its allies.

The speciousness of the assertion that women's rights are at the core of the recent American invasions' goals is revealed when one looks at the conditions on the ground post–U.S. intervention. In Iraq, since the ouster of Saddam Hussein we have heard relatively little about women, and what news is getting out has not been positive. In stark contrast to their conditions under Baath rule, Iraqi women are now wearing veils, staying at home, and avoiding school and work to protect themselves against the estimated twenty daily kidnappings and rapes. Meanwhile, girls' school attendance has dropped by more than 50 percent, honor killings are on the rise, and only three of the twenty-five members of the U.S.- and British-appointed Governing Council are women.[1] Tragically, one member of that underrepresented segment of Iraqi women, Akila al-Hashemi, was assassinated on September 20, 2003.

To get a better sense of what hangs in the balance in Iraq months after U.S. "liberation," one need look no further than Afghanistan. The experiences of Afghan women two years post-Taliban speak volumes about the long-term prospects for the women of Iraq. The women of Afghanistan, as the first "beneficiaries" of an aggressive American anti-terror foreign policy, are the canary's canary.

SUSPICIOUS PRETEXT

After September 11, George W. Bush announced his intention to bomb Afghanistan in retaliation for the Taliban's role in sheltering Osama bin Laden and Al-Qaeda. Both the President and the First Lady co-opted the oppression of Afghan women as a legitimating factor in the overthrow of the Taliban, suspiciously ignoring the fact that Afghan women had already suffered under five years of Taliban rule while the U.S. negotiated for oil pipelines and poppy eradication. Those same women had also suffered under the previous four years of atrocities committed by Jehadi fundamentalists, whose regime was the result of a decision by the U.S., Pakistan, and other Western countries to arm, nurture, and support brutal warlords in an attempt to use Afghans as pawns in the Cold War. These Jehadi warlords, including many that the U.S. coalition returned to power post-Taliban as part of the current Northern Alliance–controlled transitional government, were so brutal towards women (and the entire population) that the Taliban were at first welcomed by the people as liberating heroes. Bush wielded the claim to care about the plight of Afghan women like a convenient sympathy card, one that brought "compassionate conservative" clout to his plan to bomb the same Afghan women he was claiming to liberate. Thus violence and retribution were transformed into chivalrous liberation.

When the Taliban were driven from Kabul, the fawning U.S. press reported euphoria in the streets—people dancing, men shaving their beards and changing into Western clothes, women taking off their *burqas*. A heartwarming picture to be sure, but a closer look at the footage reveals that the jubilant "people" in the streets were mostly men and boys; there were few women to be seen, with *burqas* or without. And as the Northern Alliance marched back into Kabul, bringing back their legacy of oppression and atrocity focused first and foremost on women, Afghan euphoria quickly evaporated as women came to realize that their so-called liberation was nothing more than a PR campaign. The other sad truth facing the Afghan people was the civilian death toll from U.S. bombing, estimated by Marc Herold to be higher than the number who died in the September 11 terrorist attacks in the U.S.[2]

After reports of these glorious promises and joyous victories, however, people in the West assumed that progress had been made and would naturally continue. Afghan women also hoped that some good might come after yet more war, violence, and civilian deaths, but it didn't take long before their hopes were shattered as promises of freedom and opportunity were shown to be implausible in the fundamentalist-controlled reality that is post-Taliban Afghanistan. Meanwhile, in the West it became harder to learn of this reality; the press attention waned, moving on to the military buildup with Iraq, a country with a remarkably similar history of U.S. support through decades of lethal dictatorship.

Now, several years after the Taliban defeat, the realities of life for Afghan women are a world apart from the political and media gloss. As an Afghan man living in Jalalabad told us in June 2003, "The images the West has of Afghanistan now are like looking at the flowers from the horse."

LOYA JIRGA

There was much news of the Loya Jirga, or traditional grand assembly, which was held in June 2002 to elect the transitional government and president to run the country until general elections in June 2004. As set forth at the Bonn meeting the previous winter, the Loya Jirga was to consist of democratically selected representatives from constituencies throughout the country and regional refugee community, with 160 of 1,500 seats reserved for women. Perhaps the most important stipulation was that warlords, criminals, and those guilty of human rights abuses were to be barred from attending.

Ultimately, 200 Afghan women participated in the Loya Jirga, and one woman (now reported to have been propped up by the Northern Alliance warlords who were present in large numbers, having circumvented both the ban on their attendance and the requirement for democratic selection) ran for president. The "reality gap" between what the Loya Jirga promised and what it eventually delivered is best explained by Belquis Ahmadi, Afghanistan program coordinator for the International Human Rights Law Group and a delegate to the Loya Jirga herself:

Afghan women dress in *burqas* so they may leave the house. LYNSEY ADDARIO/CORBIS

Afghan women emerged from the Loya Jirga facing not only the discrimination and harassment that are a part of Afghan life, but a real danger to their physical security. Those who pose these threats to Afghan women are no longer international pariahs (the Taliban) but participants in the heralded new government of Afghanistan. When I first entered the Loya Jirga, I was inspired by the outspokenness of the Afghan men and women in attendance. Many women found the courage to deliver speeches before the mostly male crowd, campaign for candidates and even make efforts to confront the warlords who were there. One Afghan woman even pursued a largely symbolic run for the presidency. But such apparent signs of progress were eclipsed by a growing sense of futility in the face of threats, bribes, and intimidation by warlords and their supporters.[3]

In what could be a preview of similar tragedies in Iraq, Afghan women's further participation in the government since the Loya Jirga has been quite limited, with only two of twenty-six ministerial positions given to women by President Karzai, and very few women holding jobs in the government at all outside of the Ministry for Women's Affairs. Even that newly created ministry, focusing exclusively on women, is a mixed blessing; on the one hand, it demonstrates the importance of women's issues for the country, but on the other hand, according to Habiba Sorabi, the Women's Minister, it leads inexorably to their marginalization. Other ministries act as though they do not need to bother themselves with any issues of gender since it is believed that the underfunded and disparaged Women's Ministry can somehow do it all.[4]

ELUSIVE SECURITY

In two reports on the situation in Afghanistan, Human Rights Watch has not minced words:[5]

> The situation today—widespread insecurity and human rights abuse—was not inevitable, nor was it the result of natural or unstoppable social or political forces in Afghanistan. It is, in large part, the result of decisions, acts, and omissions of the United States (U.S.) government, the governments of other coalition members, and parts of the transitional Afghan government itself. The warlords themselves, of course, are ultimately to blame. . . . A number of serious consequences flow from the security problems and impunity documented in this report. . . . Targeting of women and girls by police and soldiers on the streets not only impairs their liberty of movement, but also has the effect of restricting their access to education, health care, and jobs, and keeps many from participating in Afghanistan's political and civic life and reconstruction.[6]

As reported both by Human Rights Watch and to us during interviews conducted in Afghanistan in the summer of 2003, harassment, threats of kidnapping, rape, forced marriage, and other violence continue to severely limit the lives of women and girls. *Burqas* are still ubiquitous on the streets, not due to the freely chosen expression of religious convictions, but rather due to fear and threat. Fear causes families to limit women's and girl's access to life and resources outside of the home to the extent that even those families who believe in greater freedoms for women are forced to behave in ways that promote and condone the same restrictions imposed by the

Taliban. Meanwhile, Afghan women, fearing to venture from their homes, opt to restrict their own activities. And this is by no means an isolated outcome; Iraq is currently in the throes of the same lamentable chaos. As Lauren Sandler wrote recently in the *New York Times*:

> Under Saddam Hussein, crimes against women—or at least ones his son Uday, Iraq's vicious Caligula, did not commit—were relatively rare. . . . Last October, the regime opened the doors to the prisons. Kidnappers, rapists, and murderers were allowed to blend back into society, but they were kept in check by the police state. When the Americans arrived and the police force disappeared, however, these old predators reemerged alongside new ones. And in a country that essentially relies on rumor as its national news, word of sadistic abduction quickly began to spread. . . . This violence has made postwar Iraq a prison of fear for women. "This issue of security is the immediate issue for women now—this horrible time that was triggered the very first day of the invasion," said Yanar Mohammed, the founder of the Organization of Women's Freedom in Iraq.[7]

While this rampant instability is damaging to any woman's life, whether in Iraq or in Afghanistan, it is devastating for those who are breadwinners for families decimated by years of war and loss. In the case of Afghanistan, the security force—4,800 International Security Assistance Force (ISAF) peacekeepers limited to Kabul only—is simply too small and localized to make a real difference. Its ratio of 1 peacekeeper to every 5,555 Afghans, versus the 1-to-65 ratio in Bosnia after its war, is the result of repeated U.S. opposition to an expansion requested by President Karzai, humanitarian groups, and the Afghan people.[8]

If nothing changes, it is impossible to fathom that the same women and families who are too afraid to allow their female relatives to go to a market will be convinced to allow them to leave the house to vote in the 2004 elections. This is just one way in which the current lack of security makes the prospect of free and fair elections in the supposedly democratic and liberated Afghanistan—to say nothing of Iraq—a myth. Further, the threats, harassment, arrests, and death sentences facing Afghan journalists who speak out against the current government (and especially against elements of the Northern Alliance) make public dissent a life-or-death decision, effectively silencing all but the most stalwart or underground of voices for democracy, security, peace, and freedom.[9]

This is yet another sad omen for the people of Iraq. The political voice of the people, expressed in the form of free electoral debate and participation, doesn't stand much of a chance in a climate of fear and violence.

SCHOOLS UNDER SIEGE

When schools and universities were reopened for Afghans of both genders in March 2002, it marked the end of a five-year ban on girls' and women's education. While many, especially in the urban centers of Afghanistan, have joyously returned to schools, only 32 percent of the 3.6 million students currently attending schools are girls.[10] Further, the 4,000 open schools, which operate double and triple sessions each day, are inadequate, leaving another (conservatively) estimated one million school-age children, the vast majority of whom are girls, out of school.[11]

With a literacy rate generously estimated at 16 percent for women over the age of fifteen,[12] there is no doubt that education should be a first priority for building an Afghanistan—and Iraq—in which women can participate. It is not just a lack of physical schools which keeps girls from education: in the first six months after girls' schools reopened, nearly one dozen schools in five provinces were firebombed or otherwise attacked. Further, countless families and teachers throughout Afghanistan have been harassed and threatened for seeking and supporting girls' education.

In addition to the aforementioned general security concerns that confine women to their homes and the specific threats against the education of girls, many girls we talked to during the summer of 2003—they were attending literacy classes run by the Revolutionary Association of the Women of Afghanistan (RAWA) instead of government schools—offered the following reasons for not being back in Afghan schools:

* Lack of support from their families for education.
* Being too old to attend first grade, even though after five years without school this is their proper academic placement.
* Being too embarrassed to attend class with much younger girls.
* Having been married young (either by force or by family pressure) and thus being officially banned from attending school with unmarried girls.

The end result, currently visible in Iraq as well as Afghanistan, is an overall decrease in the proportion of girls in school over the past eighteen months.[13]

CIVIL RIGHTS IN JEOPARDY

While the entire country waits for the first draft of the new Afghan constitution, months late in its release for comment, the 1964 Constitution is responsible for protecting the rule of law and civil society. Yet neither this nor Afghanistan's 1980 signature to the United Nations' Convention on the Elimination of All Forms of Discrimination Against Women (CEDAW) and the current government recommitment in March 2003 has protected women.

Among other civil rights abuses, women and their children continue to be imprisoned (as they were under the Taliban) for such crimes as attempting to marry a man of their choice, refusing an arranged marriage, leaving abusive husbands, or remarrying after divorce (they are even sometimes accused by the ex-husband of still being married).[14] Meanwhile, in Herat, a western province controlled by warlord Ismail Khan, unmarried girls who are seen with unrelated men are being picked up by the police and forced to undergo physical "chastity checks" at local hospitals.[15]

Remarkably, in the face of all of the broken promises and failures of "liberation," there are Afghans, particularly Afghan women, who have shown amazing resilience and resolve to struggle until a truly free, peaceful, democratic Afghanistan rises from the ashes. The women and men who wage this nonviolent battle today are many of the same who struggled tirelessly against Taliban and Jehadi oppressions, as well as against the Soviet invaders. One example of this resilience is RAWA, which still functions as an underground organization dedicated to provide medical, educational, reconstruction, political, and income-generating aid to Afghans. Even as the world once again forgets about Afghanistan and money is becoming scarce, RAWA continues to provide services that the government and international community promised but which rarely reach ordinary people. RAWA members—outspoken critics of fundamentalist crimes and advocates of secular democracy and freedom, human, and women's rights— remain at high risk in a country still controlled by armed warlords. Intimidation of shopkeepers who sell RAWA publications, an attack on RAWA's openly run Malalai hospital in Pakistan, and continued threats that arrive through email and phone calls all demonstrate that Afghanistan, to say nothing of Iraq, is still not safe enough for an independent, democratic, humanitarian, and political women's organization.

Another example of Afghan women's resistance is Shakeela, a Hazara educator in Kabul who manages an independent underground school for girls and who once marched fearlessly to Taliban headquarters to demand the release of her falsely imprisoned brother and other men from her community. Even under the Taliban, Shakeela advocated democracy, freedom, and women's rights, and she condemned the atrocities of fundamentalists and warlords, including those from her own ethnic group. While her activism and bravery won her the support of the community, which elected her as their representative (not their female representative, but their community representative) to the 2002 Loya Jirga, her outspoken condemnation of fundamentalism has made her grave enemies among the warlords and their followers.

Three sisters stand in front of their house in a village ruled by Komala Islami, an Islamic extremist group, in northern Iraq.
LYNSEY ADDARIO/CORBIS 2003

Despite their threats and a lack of financial support (the billions of dollars in international aid money that never make it to the neediest), she directs an Education Center that teaches math, science, English, and computer and tailoring skills to Afghan girls, boys, and women. The school, run with the help of an indigenous

Afghan women's group, stands as a testament to her fortitude as well as to that of so many Afghan women and men who struggle in similar ways around the country.

While the strength and resilience of the common people of Afghanistan should not be overlooked, it is no excuse for standing back and allowing terrible circumstances, many of which are the making of the U.S. and its allies, to continue. It is tragic to think of how much farther this strength and resilience could have moved the rebuilding of Afghanistan if people were working from an even playing field rather than struggling to dig themselves out of a hole created by the reempowerment of fundamentalist warlords.

REALITY CHECK

Given the realities of life in Afghanistan and Iraq, it is no wonder that the U.S. administration and mainstream press, recalling the comments of the Afghan man from Jalalabad, don't get off the proverbial "liberation" PR horse and look more closely at the flowers. Afghan women traditionally have been and continue to be the unfortunate canaries in this foreign policy coal mine. Witnessing the true conditions of Afghan women calls into question the possibilities for any better outcome in Iraq. Unfortunately, the dangers for Afghan and Iraqi women, as well as all the citizens of both countries who demand freedom, democracy, and human rights, are not just found in the present but in the future as well. When the United States and its allies' claims of peace and democracy are shown to be façades, their actions provide fuel for oppressive groups and ideologies that breed repression, violence, hatred, and terrorism, with the end result perhaps being a similar backlash to that which nurtured the likes of Osama bin Laden and replaced the criminal Jehadis of the Northern Alliance with the Taliban in 1996. Further, when Afghan and Iraqi women are not empowered as active leaders in the physical, social, and legislative rebuilding of their countries, they stand little chance of creating institutions, structures, and mechanisms grounded in the indigenous cultural understandings necessary to advance women's lives in meaningful and lasting ways.

The lessons of Afghanistan do not apply solely to Iraq and other countries that lie in the path of an aggressive U.S. foreign policy, but also to the deteriorating state of democracy and civil liberties in the U.S. itself. And just as the women of Iraq and Afghanistan do not have the luxury of inaction, neither do informed people throughout the world. There is plenty that the average person in the West can do to support the struggle of Afghan and Iraqi women for true democracy and human rights, including:

* Seek alternative sources of information. The World Wide Web is replete with links to independent Western and regional media links, including RAWA,[16] Alternet, Counterpunch, *The Nation*. European left-leaning publications like *The Guardian* report what the *New York Times* doesn't dare. Even the BBC, Reuters, and AFP offer news that you'll never find in the *Washington Post* or the Associated Press.
* Share this information by educating others, writing letters to the editor, and demanding that mainstream press also cover this ongoing crisis.
* Lobby the administration and Congress to demand that the number and location of international peacekeepers in Afghanistan be expanded and that the security of women becomes a top priority.

* Protect democracy and civil rights abroad and in the U.S. by getting involved in the 2004 presidential election. Volunteer for a candidate, register voters, educate voters, but most importantly, VOTE.
* Support the efforts of indigenous women's organizations like RAWA by contributing financially to their humanitarian and political activities.

In this truly global village, where decisions made in Washington and London have life-and-death consequences for people in Kabul and Baghdad—and decisions made in the mountains of Tora Bora have life-and-death consequences in New York City and Bali—all of us, as citizens whose governments are acting in our name, need to act now. As the late Congresswoman Barbara Jordan said in 1977: "The stakes . . . are too high for government to be a spectator sport."[17]

NOTES

1. Susan Milligan, "In Postwar Iraq, Women Lead a Life of Fear," *International Herald Tribune* online, 22 August 2003. Available at http://www.iht.com/articles/107336.htm.

2. Afghanistan's Civilian Deaths Mount," BBC News, 3 January 2003. Available at http://news.bbc.co.uk/I/hi/world/south_asia/1740538.stm.

3. Belquis Ahmadi, "Reality Gap in Afghanistan: Despite Rosy Reports, Women's Rights Remain Wishful Thinking," *Washington Post*, 8 July 2003, A17.

4. Minister Habiba Sorabi, conversation with the authors, Kabul, June 2003.

5. "'Killing You Is a Very Easy Thing for Us': Human Rights Abuses in Southeast Afghanistan," Human Rights Watch, July 2003; "'All Our Hopes Are Crushed': Violence and Repression in Western Afghanistan," Human Rights Watch, October 2002. Available at http://www.hrw.org.

6. Human Rights Watch, July 2003.

7. Lauren Sandler, "Veiled and Worried in Baghdad," *New York Times*, 16 September 2003.

8. "CARE Says Ideal Time to Expand ISAF Mandate in Afghanistan," CARE USA, August 2003. Available at http//:www.careusa.org/newsroom/pressreleases/2003/aug/08112003_afghanistan.asp.

9. "'Killing You Is a Very Easy Thing for Us.'"

10. Ibid.

11. "Taking Stock Update: Afghan Women and Girls Sixteen Months On," Womankind Worldwide, April 2003.

12. Ibid.

13. Isabel Hilton, "Now We Pay the Warlords to Tyrannise the Afghan People: The Taliban Fell But—Thanks to Coalition Policy—Things Did Not Get Better," *The Guardian*, 31 July 2003.

14. Farnaz Fassihi, "Little Has Changed for Wives of Afghan Officials, Rural Women," Newhouse News Service, October 2002; Robyn Dixon, "Rights: Despite Western Pressure for Greater Attention, Many Laws Have Not Changed Since the Taliban Left, and Jails Are Refilling," *Baltimore Sun*, 27 July 2002; Amy Waldman, "Fifteen Women Await Justice in Kabul Prison," *New York Times*, 16 March 2003.

15. "'All Our Hopes Are Crushed.'"

16. The Revolutionary Association of the Women of Afghanistan's website: www.rawa.org.

17. As quoted in Rosalie Maggio, ed., *The Beacon Book of Quotations by Women* (Boston: Beacon Press), p. 141.

BAGHDAD JOURNAL #5

On the bus to the palace we meet an American lieutenant who was working with the United States Agency for International Development (USAID). His job involved uncovering mass graves. He had been taking Iraqi women to the graves, and he told us he felt inadequate to deal with their extreme grief and asked if we might know of any Iraqi women who could help.

the governing counsel. She described what it was like to start from scratch. Women hold strong positions in all levels of Iraqi life—they are always the number two and three in a ministry or in other governing positions—so qualified was not the problem. The problem was the lack of civic organizations and thus no civic leaders. "Many of the strong women were still

An Iraqi woman weeps before American troops at a mass grave site as hundreds of bodies are pulled out of the earth.
LYNSEY ADDARIO/CORBIS 2003

We were more than an hour late arriving for our meeting with Margaret Bhadi—things move very slowly in the heat—and she had very little time left for us. The CPA is made up of members of the coalition of the willing: she came from England to advise on gender issues, and her task was to find women to appoint to

locked in their houses or staying home with their children," she said. The task was made more complicated by the problems with communication tools: without a phone you have to drive to the person's house, or find them at church—which is where she started, in the churches, joining the circle of women after a service to learn who had influence. Over the past month she had found about eighty women to invite to a conference later in the week. The conference had originally been the dream of an Iraqi woman in England, but Paul Bremer heard of her plans and stopped that conference in order to hold his own meeting, which he could control. Margaret complained that the speed with which the conference was being planned hampered her ability to do the job correctly. We could read between the lines and detect the tension between the CPA and the UN: the United Nations Development Fund for Women (UNIFEM) was planning a similar gathering in August with three hundred women. (Two days before the UNIFEM meeting, it was canceled because of the bombing of the UN in Baghdad.)

We asked Margaret the question we'd been asked that morning: Are there women who can help each other deal with the grief they experience at the mass graves? "There's this woman I met, Yanar Mohammed," she told us. She characterized Yanar as an activist and controversial figure. Yanar Mohammed founded the Organization of Women's Freedom in Iraq, an advocacy group addressing women's issues in general, and the problem of honor killings specifically. We asked Margaret if Yanar was among the eighty women participating— no, she is too uncontrollable.

Yanar Mohammed has dedicated herself to fighting injustice and saving women who are in danger of being killed in the name of honor, and her work has made her a target of fundamentalists of all sorts. Religious fundamentalism, having been held somewhat in check by Saddam's secular regime, is rising with a fervor that threatens the already shaky status of Iraqi women, particularly as the long-repressed Shia Muslim majority asserts itself with calls for Islamic rule.

Honor killings are increasing, as are rape and prostitution. Iraq, in many ways, is still a tribal society, and a woman who has sex outside of her marriage—regardless of whether with a lover or due to a rape— is seen as having dishonored the tribe. The only way to restore honor is for the woman to be killed by her male relatives. This practice was legalized by Saddam towards the end of his regime in an effort to shore up support amongst the tribes.

We heard one story about a prominent Iman who preached that no girls should be educated past the sixth grade. Supposedly a man raised his hand and asked, "If my wife is pregnant, should she see a man or a woman doctor?"

"A woman," the Iman pronounced.

"How will there be women doctors if girls don't go to school past the sixth grade?" asked the man.

The Iman had no good answer for that, and the man was later beaten for embarrassing the Iman.

Yanar continues her work in the face of such attitudes. I worry constantly about her safety. "A woman's freedom is the standard of a society's freedom," Yanar said at the end of one of our meetings.

Continued . . .

Iraqi men and women gather at a mass grave site.
LYNSEY ADDARIO/CORBIS 2003

Zakiya Abd weeps as she discusses her daughter's disappearance. LYNSEY ADDARIO/CORBIS 2003

THE PLIGHT OF WOMEN IN IRAQ: BETWEEN U.S. INVASION AND POLITICAL ISLAMIC OPPRESSION

Yanar Mohammed, founder of the Organization of Women's Freedom in Iraq and editor in chief of the newspaper Al Mousawat *(Equality), is a radical defender of women's rights in Iraq. She was interviewed by Medea Benjamin in Baghdad in July 2003.*

For the last thirty-five years, women have been oppressed by the Baathist regime. The previous achievements we in the women's movement attained were aborted, one after another. By the end of the Baathist regime, all the amendments that had been made to our civil law to improve the situation of women were reversed. In the 1990s Saddam Hussein introduced an amendment to the civil law that supported honor killings: the males in families were allowed to kill any female relative they believed brought dishonor to the family. During the 1990s, approximately five thousand women were killed in the northern part of Iraq—and some of those killings were organized by the ruling party.

We have major issues to confront. Women are not considered to be an equal part of humanity, so we are banding together. We are setting up this women's organization, and we will speak out against all the atrocities that are being committed against us as a gender. We will also address the political agendas that aim to keep women in an inferior status in this society.

Our organization works on many levels, but we start with the women who have nobody to speak for them. Though we only began to organize at the end of the war, we have many members. We have women who were fired from their jobs for a variety of reasons. We have women who have no one else to defend them, who were left by their husbands, who have many children to support. We have women who are at risk for honor killings or are suffering from domestic abuse. For some of these cases, we provide a safe haven within our headquarters, but unfortunately we don't have much space, so we can only accommodate a few.

But we've noticed dramatic changes in the women we have been able to shelter. For example, Fatima, who is staying with us, suffered domestic abuse. When she first left her home and came here, she was very shaken. She wore the veil and very concealing clothing; it was as if she were hiding under them. And nobody ever heard her voice. Now the veil is off, she is an outspoken activist, and she believes in the unlimited rights of women. She participated in a demonstration the other day, shouting with everyone else.

This is just one case, and it's just the beginning. I can see millions of women making such progress. Fatima, who had to leave school at an early age, now plans to go back to school; she will find a job, and we will help her establish a good life for herself.

Providing this type of support is the primary mandate of our organization. In addition, many of us who founded the organization have a socialist political vision that sees women in decision-making positions. We do not believe that gaining equal rights is possible if women are not also decision makers. Because of the consecutive wars fought in Iraq, 60 percent of our current population is women. With all of the soldiers that were killed, there are many women with no men to support them; social insurance for them is one big issue that we will be fighting for. We would also like to provide women with language and computer lessons so that they will be more employable. This is the first stage, establishing the organization and offering these services.

The second stage will be to set up a shelter in Baghdad where we can offer an alternative for women who are under immediate threat of honor killings. This is a big and ambitious project, and a dangerous one for us activists, but we are very serious about it, especially since we have previous experience in the north of Iraq, where many of us were members of a group called the Independent Women's Organization. This group set up a shelter for women, and all in all they saved almost four hundred women from honor killings. We housed seventy of these women for quite some time until we were confident that their relatives would not kill them. For the few cases where we could not provide the women with adequate security, we smuggled them out through Turkey and applied to the United Nations to have them taken to Europe, America, and other safe places.

So those are some of our success stories. We have high hopes to be able to do the same here in Baghdad—I'm getting reports from all over the city about honor killings, about domestic abuse. It's getting worse and worse.

Our main struggle here is against political Islam. We think that every person should have freedom of religion or atheism, but for a group of people to oppress and dictate to women that they must wear the veil [hijab], to go into the schools and give the orders that all girls should be veiled—this is not right. These people even harass women on the streets if they don't wear the full veil—"full" as in having a piece of black cloth covering your entire body. This is not a humane way for women in the third millennium to be living. These political Islamists should be stopped.

Our vision of the future is one where there will be institutions that protect and advance the rights of women. There must be an institution that reaches into every neighborhood, every house, a sort of human rights watch that looks after the life of every woman. And this institution should be local. This institution, as well as the constitution, must be based on full equality between men and women.

Our biggest battle now is the constitution. Our organization's founding statement puts the constitution in the forefront of our agenda, along with counseling against the compulsory hijab, canceling sexual apartheid in schools, and eliminating all articles in the law which are discriminatory against women—especially article 409 in the Civil Law 111, which supports honor killings and lets the murderers go free.

When people say that women always fight for women's rights, I say that is not true. You need egalitarian people; you need people who fully believe in freedom and in humanity. Those are the defenders of women. They could be men, they could be women. We have found that some of the honor killings were executed at the hands of women who were following the dominant male belief that women should be kept inferior and that they should follow the rules of patriarchy, which keep women submissive in a society.

When the Americans say that they have a number of women at the forefront working for the future of Iraq, I say that it's not enough. If their policies are not women-friendly, then the two women that I see on the governing council will not advance the cause of women anywhere. We need both women-friendly policies and real representation on these councils.

Regarding the occupation, we were against this notion of the "liberation" of Iraq, which we thought of as a big lie. While it is true that we wanted to get rid of Saddam, destroying our cities and killing our people is not the way to liberate us. This inhuman way of changing the political situation here rests in the belief that killing thousands of people is a fair-enough price for political change. Would George W. Bush accept that even five American people be killed in order to change a bad political regime in the United States? I don't think so. For him, however, the lives of tens of thousands of Iraqis was an acceptable price. This was the first reason that we did not support the current occupation.

An Iraqi woman stands off to the side as United States troops from the 1st Armored Division patrol.
LYNSEY ADDARIO/CORBIS 2003

The second reason was that we knew there would be a large political vacuum as a result. The Baathists ruled internally for thirty-five years. We feared that after their removal, chaos would ensue and atrocities would occur—and that is exactly what we are seeing these days. Hundreds of women have been raped. In general, people are living with insecurity. They do not have hope for a good future. This feeling of hopelessness is getting stronger and stronger with each passing day with no electricity, no income, no water, no services. We find it unacceptable that we have had to live without electricity for months and months now. We are convinced that this idea of liberation is a big lie.

Iraqi women. LYNSEY ADDARIO/CORBIS 2003

The occupation setting is really very scary for women. There are many people carrying out revenge killings against the previous Baath regime and its supporters. They are also committing rape, or even group rape, on the daughters of members of the former Baath regime as another tool of political revenge. We heard about a rape that happened in the city of Mosul, where a group sought to kill a Baath official. When he fled, they raped all nine of his daughters and left them; when the other members of their family came and found them raped, honor killings were enforced. Those nine girls were killed on the spot.

We have no protection. We are trapped between the unleashed dark forces of political Islam and tribal culture—both are anti-woman. These two terrible forces were unleashed by the occupying powers, and they have been given credibility to participate in the future agenda of political rule in Iraq. The tribes have been given seats and validation as if they have some legitimate political agenda. They call for the return of an ancient lifestyle where patriarchal structures are dominant and women have no worth. Saddam gave them power in the last year of his rule, providing them with financial support in order to gain their military support, and the tribes grew stronger as a consequence. But now, to our surprise, the occupying troops are also defending them, meeting with them, giving them importance. I see Bremer dancing their tribal dances with them, but I don't hear him talking much about women's rights.

And when the Coalition Provisional Authority created various women's groups, they spoke only to professional women, women who have reached a position in society where they no longer think about honor killings or the single women with no access to employmemt or social insurance because they are out of the poverty cycle—they're outside the circle where women are still oppressed. These are the women with whom Bremer's officials are meeting.

We see a very frightful future, with Iraq becoming a bourgeois society where 5 percent of people in Iraq will be very rich and the other 95 percent will be living in poverty. I walk the streets, and I see groups of young people going in and out of buildings, stealing. Why would they do that in a country that's so rich? It's because they have no social insurance, no work, no opportunity to attend school. They go to bed hungry.

My biggest fear is that the Iraqi people will be dragged through more misery than they can take. The thirteen years of sanctions they've already endured have drained them.

The Organization of Women's Freedom in Iraq calls for the immediate departure of the occupying forces and their immediate replacement by United Nations peacekeepers, who are better trained to deal with postwar situations, especially from a humanitarian point of view. The distribution of food, talking to people at the neighborhood level, dealing with individual families—the UN is more qualified to perform these services than military troops. The military can point guns at people, can kill, can drop bombs here and there, but defending a woman who is in danger of rape or providing food rations to a neighborhood: these are things that the peacekeeping forces of the UN and their organizations can do.

If they come.

Al-Muajaha

www.almuajaha.com

The Iraqi Witness
Vol. 1 Issue 3   18 June 2003

An Independent Weekly Newspaper

PAGE 2!

Baghdad's Hospitals Suffer!

PAGE 2!

A Friend of Saddam!

PAGE 3!

Hot Night With The US Army!

PAGE 4!

Saddam's Stuffed Horse!

PAGE 5!

Saddam Will Return!

RAPE!
New Violence in the New Iraq
9 Year Old Child A Victim

An Al-Muajaha a Special Report

Staff Writers Salaam Al-Jubouri, Salam Al-Onaibi, Hiba Alsoudani, Laith Hadithi, Yasser Hani, Saad Issam, Hamsa Mohammed, and Waleed Rahi'a all contributed to this report. (The names of victims have been changed for this article)

On 27 May at 4pm, a short man of average build put a gun to Warda Ali's head, dragged her off the street and into an abandoned government building, threw her face down on the ground and brutally raped her. This may unfortunately be a common crime in Iraq now, but what is different is that Warda is only 9 years old.

The failures to restore security or communications in the new Iraq have fueled rampant rumors about girls being kidnapped from their homes or from school or off the street. Sometimes the rumors say that the criminals are those released by Saddam in the amnesty last October. Sometimes the rumors involve foreigners, such as Kuwaitis, who allegedly kidnap Iraqi girls as slaves or to work in brothels inside or outside Iraq. Trying to track down these rumors becomes an endless chase from person to person, each referring you to another friend of a friend who these crimes supposedly happened to. Women rarely leave their homes unaccompanied now, and many parents are frightened to let their daughters out of the house - even to attend school.

Rumors run wild in Baghdad, and as long as Iraq has no government or functioning police force, there is no one keeping statistics on the increase in crimes, including rape. Hospitals deny that they are treating any rape cases, and, despite increased patrols of girls schools and neighborhoods, the police complain that they are unable to deal with the problem. While hard information about the general situation in Baghdad is impossible to discover, individual cases can be verified. Female patients at Al-Rashad Psychiatric Hospital were raped by [Continued on Page 5]

Practicing Freedom
Iraqis Protest Hilla Mayor

By Salam Talib Al-Onaibi

In previous issues of Al-Muajaha we followed the story of the people of Za'farania and their message to US President Bush about civilian deaths in their neighborhood due to the explosion of a munitions dump located there, and we also covered the story of students forcing the resignation of Dr. Alim Yacoub from his position as Dean of cal College because of his past association with the Ba'ath regime. In this issue we are exploring the most serious case of "practicing freedom" as we travel along this new path of democracy in Iraq: the struggle of the people of Hilla to force the resignation of their new "mayor."

With the fall of the previous government, many individuals have "appointed" themselves into positions of power. In Baghdad, Mohammed Mehson Zubeidi, who is associated with Ahmed Chalabi's Iraqi National Congress, declared himself as the new mayor and attempted to exert the powers of such a position until the US military

Must anseri y a Univ ersity's Medi of Iraq - the situation was no different.

In Babylon, the mayor today is Witwit. Though he comes from a respected, religious family in the area, which has a long history of fighting Saddam's regime, Iskander himself was a general in the former Iraqi military. He received so many medals during his career, that he was called a "friend of Saddam." He was also awarded a medal from the Ba'ath Party signifying that he had spent 25 years as a member of that party. This information is confirmed by a hand-written affidavit in Al-Muajaha's possession that was submitted by General Iskander during a court case

arrested him and sent him to Doha Base for a brief vacation. People such as this are taking advantage of the current power vacuum throughout Iraq, and when US troops entered Babylon, or Hilla- the "second city"

> "These people don't represent the city because they are just a few thousand."

in Hilla in 2002.

Strangely, "Mayor" Iskander's office manager, Saleem Abdel Mutaleb Beigan, told the press that, "He [Iskander] took his place as mayor when Mohammed Mehson Zubeidi sent one of his assistants, Jowdat Kadham Al-Obaidi, to put a mayor in Babylon 4 days after the fall of Baghdad." One of Iskander's first actions was appointing mayors for towns throughout the area, such as placing Abdel Hussein Alawi as mayor of Mahouweel, a mid-sized town outside Hilla. This process was called a "vote" by Iskander, despite the fact that no vote too actually took place, and all the new mayors were summarily chosen by Iskander from officers in the former Iraqi army who did not do well under Saddam's reign.

According to [Continued on Page 2]

A Burning Question
Who's Helping Baghdad's

By Salaam Al-Jubouri

Baghdad hospitals are suffering from severe shortages in many aspects. They are supposed to be places to recover from disease and injury, but have they become useless? Al-Muajaha visited various hospitals to understand how difficult the situation is today, and get the real story.

After the collapse of medical services during the war, and the massive lootings immediately afterwards, Al-Kindi hospital now has two American tanks and some soldiers protecting the grounds. The gate is surrounded with razor wire. The hospital serves a poor neighborhood, and is crowded with patients. People now enter the hospital through the emergency section, and injured patients are in full view of everyone entering.

Picture the scene: two ambulances pulled in very fast to the front of Al-Kindi and four patients were carried out on stretchers. The ambulance drivers informed Al-Muajaha that the men had been in an explosion. Six men were seriously burnt from munitions stored in a house. They had been driven more than 600 kilometres from Al-Rutba, a town near the Jordanian border with Iraq. The local hospital in this isolated area is no longer functional, after being bombed during the war.

The patients lay in the hospital for a while. No one tried to treat them at first, until a nurse started cover them in cream. They were horribly burnt. The strong stench of charred flesh was in the air, and you could hardly recognise two of them as people.

Dr. Ali Acka'ab, a resident doctor at Al Kindi told us, "We have no place for these men. All the Burn Units are full, so we have to move them to another hospital."

Al-Muajaha was informed that three men were moved to Al-Karama hospital for treatment, however, on visiting this hospital Al-Muajaha was told the men would also not be able to stay there and would be transferred to a third hospital.

Dr. Belal Al-Rowei, a resident doctor at Al-Karama said, "The Burn Unit in Al-Karama is occupied, we only have space for twelve people. We will transfer these men... to Al-Karkh hospital"

As darkness fell Al-Muajaha drove back to find the ambulances with the burn patients trying to find a place for treatment, Al-Muajaha witnessed one ambulance that was stopped by the American army and the driver was being questioned. A few days later Al-Muajaha continued this enquiry into the fate of these men.

No US troops guard the entrance to Al-Karkh hospital. Security consists [Continued on Page 2]

Baghdad's Merciless Streets
The Problems of Street Children in Iraq

By Amar Hasan Arebge and Nuha Atiya

Hundreds of children are wandering daily in the streets of Baghdad, the city named as the Home of Peace, looking for food, shelter and someone to care for them. They possess a hunger for love and the necessities of life that they couldn't find in the era of Dicatorism, and which is still not found in the new, Freedom era. This article is the second of a continuing series focusing on the problem of Iraq's forgotten street children.

Many of the street children in Baghdad have homes and families they live with. They work in the streets begging or selling small things, such as chewing gum or candy, in order to support their families. Others have neither families nor homes, and they sleep in the streets as well as work in them. Many older children come to Baghdad from other areas in Iraq in the belief that they will find jobs and money. Life for all these children is hard and merciless.

"Ali," a 7 year old street child, was arrested by Iraqi police a week after the war ended, and taken to Al-Rahma Orphanage (the House of Mercy) - despite the fact that he is not an orphan and lives with his family in Baghdad. Ali's father is an alcoholic and does not work. He also beats Ali's mother and sister regularly. Ali is an exceptionally loving child, full of smiles and always ready to give a hug to everyone around him, but he has few choices in his life.

"Either I have to stay with my mom and sister and protect them when my father comes drunk," Ali told us, "or I have to go in the street, in the traffic, to sell cookies and try to get money."

Amira, a beautiful 15 year Kurdish girl, has been working in the streets since she was 10. Like Ali, she has a family and home to life in, but she has to work to support her family. "If you saw me sometime, and I am smiling," said Amira, "it's not from bottom of my heart. Inside of me I am very sad because I don't like to go out from my house. But no one works, just me."

Amira's eyes tear up when see sees girls her age that are going to school. She said, "I am in pain because I can't go to school. School is a treasure, and man's future."

Amira refuses to work as a prostitute, but others are not so lucky. Lina is only 14 years old, and already pregnant. [Continued on Page 4]

A child sleeps in one of Baghdad's many alleys-photo by Mohammed Al-Junadi

The following three Op-Ed articles were printed in the summer of 2003 in *Al-Muajaha: The Iraqi Witness*, an independent newspaper in Baghdad.

WHO IS RESPONSIBLE?

FREEDOM IS NOT FREEDOM FROM RESPONSIBILITY
Dhiyah Daoud Salman

To whoever will listen to our voices, to whoever can stop our suffering—the tragedy that all Iraqis live in, and more than ever the tragedy of the schools—we will never ask for anything but an end to this suffering.

This is the real message: We teaching staff and students are in distress in so many ways. Who should we look to for solutions? In which direction should we throw our questions?

We were told to return to our schools and to work as we had been working before the war. But when we returned to give what we have to this new station of freedom and all that the word means, throwing away everything of the previous regime, we found:

a) The environmental conditions in the schools are terrible. We have broken windows, crushed doors, and stolen fans, so there is no relief in these hot days.

b) Our curriculum is unresolved. With all the political changes, teachers are not sure, in any official way, what to remove from their lessons or what to add. Without direction, how can they direct their students?

c) No one is broadcasting information in the neighborhoods about the situation in the schools, and so there are many children not attending because their parents are unware; in addition, many parents refuse to let their children go to school because it is generally unsafe everywhere.

There are many points, more than we as teachers could ever list, but our questions begin with: Who is responsible for dealing with these issues? Who will say that this terrible situation is not the fault of the members of this young generation who have only started to cross their way to a new freedom? How will their journey be through all of these difficulties?

Iraq's educators have not received any salaries as of today, and we have families, and they have to live. When we try to press our case with what little administration exists, the answer is: tomorrow, or the next day—or choose any day you wish. Waiting for a salary, how can we perform duties at our best?

We have to ask: Who is responsible? We are without services. With these short words we plead with anyone who is concerned to end this appalling state of affairs.

To teach our students the meaning of freedom in the right way, to teach them all the meanings contained in this word, "freedom," we teachers must look to the future and not stumble toward the past.

Dhiyah Daoud Salman has been a teacher for sixteen years and headmaster of Al-Khawarnaq Primary School in Baghdad for the last three years. He also works as a waiter in order to support his family.

A SENSE OF SECURITY?
My Experience with the Police in the New Iraq
Salaam Talib Al-Onaibi

Last week I was leaving the Palestine Hotel, in the heart of Baghdad, around 9 P.M.—early evening in my old life, but very late in my new one.

The Palestine, a castle surrounded by U.S. troops and barbed wire, is one of the few unquestionably safe places in the city. I hailed a taxi. We hadn't gone far, however, when two men who seemingly needed help signaled for us to stop.

The taxi driver and I behaved like typical Iraqis and welcomed the men with open arms. But after a few moments one of them put a gun in the driver's back, while the other put a knife to my neck. They asked us to empty our pockets, and we did. They stole everything—even the car. Before they drove off, they shot at us, but thank God, no one was hurt.

I had heard that the U.S. military was putting Iraqi police officers back on the street; on TV I saw footage of police on patrol. I didn't think this would solve the city's crime problem, but I thought it was at least a start—I thought there would be someone to protect us.

I could tell you how much money the robbers stole, but that wouldn't help you understand just what this incident really cost me and how much it hurt me: now I feel as if I'm not living in a city, but rather in a jungle of buildings and man-beasts.

I like to stay out late—before the war my friends called me "Night Bat." I would go out after work, and it wasn't until after midnight that my eyes would drift to the clock and I would realize it was time for sleep. During the war, when we all had to go home early—before the worst of the bombing began—I waited impatiently for the day that I could take my old life back.

After the regime fell I could move around the streets again, but the whole city had changed. Buildings were burned out, the streets were full of crushed or stripped-down cars, and everything, even the trees, was covered with dust. Most of all, something was missing inside of me—a sense of security. Every time I saw someone in the street I had to wonder to myself: Is this person a criminal, or someone in need of help?

After I was robbed, I had to know what the police were really doing, who was really responsible for law and order, and whether the U.S. was really trying to restore security, so I started my investigation the next evening at the Palestine Hotel. There are a lot of U.S. forces at the hotel, as well as many Iraqi police; it's just in front of the place—Al-Sadoun Street and Paradise Square—where the TV crews come to film police patrols. Unfortunately, I couldn't find any uniformed policemen there, or anyone else, to make a statement to about what had happened to me the night before.

The hotel staff told me to go to the nearby Al-Alwiyah Club because it had supposedly become a center for U.S. reorganization of the police and Iraqi military forces. I had never been to Al-Alwiyah before—in Saddam's time the Club was only for the privileged.

There were many desks set up inside the Club so that the names of former government workers and policemen could be recorded, but there was no work for them yet. Mohammed Al-Aubaidy, an old police major who waited in the Club hoping to find employment, told me, "This is the third time I've come here, and every time they give me an appointment to come another time. As you see, this is just a useless crowd."

Next I went to the Policemen's College, near Al-Sha'ab Stadium. I entered the building but didn't find anything but walls and empty windows. Everything had been looted. In one of the buildings there was a crowd of people trying to find someone to help them. Four policemen were taking statements from the people, but they weren't able to do anything else to help; they haven't been paid this month, and they aren't sure when their salaries will start again.

The person in charge of registering cases, twenty-four-year-old Officer Omar Lutfy Al-Alosy, told me, "We've got orders to wear civilian dress and stay unarmed. All that we have is a file to write down the name of the complainant and what was stolen."

According to Officer Al-Alosy, they don't have the authority to help anyone, and his superior, General Amer Ali Naif, had ordered some of the police off the streets a few days earlier.

"Of course I don't have the power [to stop criminals], and I can't stop them at all," remarked Officer Al-Alosy.

In the old Baath Party headquarters in Old Basra, an Iraqi police clerk fills out a report.
LYNSEY ADDARIO/CORBIS 2003

I then met General Naif, a legal advisor to the appeals court in Baghdad during Saddam's time. He corroborated what Officer Al-Alosy had said: "That's right, we received such orders, from General Zuhair Al-Naimi, the police leader, but I think the police force will start working again soon. About the weapons [private militias, such as Ahmed Chalabi's "Free Iraq Fighting Forces," have permission to carry weapons, but the police do not], I think it's hilarious."

I tried to speak with General Zuhair, but his guards wouldn't let me in, so at this point I gave up trying to report my troubles. On May 3 General Zuhair resigned as police chief because he wouldn't run the department in an "American way"; in addition he refused to "enact our laws," according to Captain Jimmy Brownlee, a U.S. Army spokesperson.

Later I heard that some policemen had been arrested in front of the Ministry of Health. A receptionist at the Ministry confirmed that the Americans had arrested two policemen after asking one of them to remove his uniform.

I asked U.S. Major Watkins, in charge of security at the Republican Palace, about the arrested policemen. He told me that the officers arrested may have been abusing their power or simply pretending to be policemen, but people should assume that anyone dressed as a police officer is, in fact, legitimate.

I went to the police station in Huriya. The station was hit with cluster bombs during the war and then looted afterwards. While I was there a U.S. military officer came to the station and put up a sign in English that read, "Police." According to the Iraqi policemen there, the U.S. asked them, "Who gave you permission to be here?"

Perhaps that question should be asked in reverse—by the policemen of the Americans.

——

Salaam Talib Al-Onaibi is a twenty-eight-year-old computer engineer in Baghdad.

WHO IS RESPONSIBLE?
Hamsa Mohammed

In our daily lives, are we seeing and reading the truth? We have to dive beneath the surface appearances that are presented to us.

When the American and British armies entered Iraq, they called themselves liberators. They said they came to liberate Iraqis from an oppressive, murderous government, and to prevent the spread of weapons of mass destruction. Did these "liberators" cross all the continents to arrive in Iraq simply for the safety of the Iraqi people? Who will cover the costs of these noble volunteers?

And while we are on the subject: May I ask where, exactly, Saddam and his world-threatening weapons are today?

I want facts. After thirteen years of an embargo that prevented anything from entering Iraq without United Nations authorization, no one has found any weapons of mass destruction. After eight years of weapons inspections using the most modern techniques (from 1991 to 1998), no one has found any weapons of mass destruction. In these last months of renewed international inspections and renewed Anglo-American war-making, no one has found any weapons of mass destruction. Can we conclude that the fact is that there are no weapons of mass destruction? Or maybe Saddam is storing them in the White House beneath Bush's bed?

Saddam Hussein was not Iraq. It doesn't make sense to punish twenty-four million people—to make them suffer hunger, illness, and death—because of one person and his imaginary weapons. It is illegal and inhumane to murder an entire nation based on suspicions. Who is responsible for all the deaths caused by the sanctions?

If suspicions were enough to punish Iraq, then when is the very real evidence of Israel's weapons of mass destruction going to be enough to punish Israel? Justice should be evenly applied. Anything else is the judgment of the strong on the weak. It is the law of the jungle.

The end of both Saddam and the sanctions is a dream that most Iraqis have been eagerly awaiting. Iraq is rich with its fortunes, and rich with a civilization that dates back thousands of years. We can rebuild our country by ourselves. But now we have a new Saddam—the Americans. And now we have a new sanctions regime—the Americans have put their hands on every piece of paper that leads to every single drop of Iraq's oil. We still cannot control our own future.

They say they are here to bring freedom back to Iraqis, but the first hands we see are the hands of Paul Bremer and Jay Garner, our new rulers, and Philip Carroll, appointed as the man responsible for Iraqi oil. I'm just wondering: Is "Philip Carroll" an Iraqi name?

Who is responsible for these appointments? And who is responsible for the distribution of all the contracts to American companies for "rebuilding" Iraq? Are Iraqis responsible? Or Americans? Or Americans wearing Iraqi clothes (such as Ahmed Chalabi)?

The American soldiers say their task is to keep us safe and provide security for civilians, but the looting and other crimes continue to this day. And what about the massacres in Mosul and Falluja and elsewhere? Dozens have been killed. What about the Al-Zafarania accident, where at least nine innocent people lost their lives? What about the "controlled explosions" of weapons the Americans are conducting all over town, which frighten people every day? Are these explosions really controlled? Go to the Adhamia and judge for yourselves—three houses were destroyed because of such explosions, and many people were wounded.

Who is responsible? Who will take responsibility for these disasters?

What Iraq needs now is a government representative of Iraqis—not Americans—which will organize and maintain security, and take responsibility for all that Iraq suffers from.

––––––

Hamsa Mohammed is a twenty-two-year-old Iraqi college student at Baghdad University where she is captain of the women's volleyball team. She hopes to be a writer.

BAGHDAD JOURNAL #6

I have a meeting at the United Nations Development Program (UNDP). The UNDP is about a mile from the Andaluz Apartments, where I am staying. This is the first time that I've been out on my own—and we've been told over and over again not to go out alone, but no one is available to come with me, and I have an appointment to keep. I've decided to walk because I've heard that cabs aren't always safe for women traveling alone.

I walk along the Tigris in the heat and the dust, my heart pounding in my ears. About halfway there, a tank blocks the street. For blocks I walk straight towards a huge cannon, seemingly aimed at me.

Hundreds of Iraqis are lined up behind the tank, waiting in front of a metal gate guarded by GIs. They are communications workers who haven't been paid for weeks. They are still waiting when I return an hour later.

I walk past boarded-up, bombed-out buildings. One building is in the process of reconstruction; an Iraqi man and his sons are working away, and it looks as if they've almost completed the job. Why is it that they can make so much progress, I wonder, when so much of the rest of Baghdad remains a war zone? Why hasn't the CPA, with all the power of the United States behind it, done more to improve conditions here? An occupier is responsible for the conditions in the place it occupies: it is responsible for security, for essential services, for people's health and safety. This place is not safe.

A man, obviously drunk, stumbles towards me, grabs me, and tries to steal my purse. For some reason, I stay calm; he seems harmless. Other men come down the street to rescue me. They reprimand him and tell him to leave me alone. Afterwards, they apologize for his behavior.

In February, seeing someone intoxicated here was a rarity. On this walk I see about fifteen men who are obviously drunk. Street kids are everywhere, and I pass a huddle of them sniffing glue.

The streets are empty of women.

As I continue to walk, I hear repeated and frequent catcalls from the passing taxis. This is also new. The men seem drunk or high on something—perhaps just on their sudden freedom.

The UNDP buildings have been totally bombed-out and looted, the back buildings have been rebuilt, and new furnishing and equipment have been installed—another example of a reconstruction not involving the CPA. My contact at the UNDP, Omar, tells me it was all done with Iraqi labor.

"Who is actually confronting their fear and who is running from it?" he asks as we sit together. "Iraqis are afraid of civil war—it is how Saddam kept us under his control, the threat that without him we would kill each other." Omar is very serious and concerned; this is very difficult for him and the solution is not clear. "The mistake has already been made," he says. He is upset about the talk that a constitution is being written by some student in his twenties in a university in New York. "It is rather absurd and another expression of disrespect. The constitution needs to flow from our culture and our religion. I don't believe in the civil war fear anymore; together we can do better than what we are living with now. Iraqis need to rebuild their lives and their country."

Omar talks about all the friends and relatives he knows who are in custody at the airport and the anger that is felt in the neighborhoods. He calls over his colleagues, and each has a story about someone they know being taken away in the night with no word on their whereabouts or their condition. Even with their official positions at UNDP, they have no access or information.

After my meeting at the UNDP I walk to the Palestine Hotel, which is close to the Andaluz Apartments. I want to find Terry, who works for a nongovernmental agency funded by the United States Agency for International Development (USAID). We had met the night before at the hotel; Terry had stories about

Baghdad neighborhoods with no water and sewage spilled in the streets, and I wanted to know more.

I am drenched with sweat from fear and heat. This is an area where we hear gunfire every night, and I know that it's not safe even now.

GIs guard the entrances to the two big hotels where foreigners stay; they frisk me and ask me for ID as they stand by their Humvees in the blazing heat, and street kids cluster around. One of the soldiers tells me how he washed the hair of a cute little girl yesterday, and I am both touched and concerned—I think of the kids, so dirty and uncared for, and the soldiers, standing here all day with no shade, so vulnerable despite their body armor and gear, verifying the IDs of the occasional pedestrian and checking the GMCs that barrel through the checkpoints to the hotels.

As I approach the lobby of the

Private First Class Christopher Pusateri of the 82nd Airborne Division passes his sunglasses around to a group of Iraqi kids while patrolling in Baghdad. LYNSEY ADDARIO/CORBIS 2003

Palestine, vendors hawk newspapers. One is in Arabic and English: "Baghdad Now, A Bi-weekly First Armored Division Publication." Inside are articles about the new Iraqi police force, about the need for good sanitary practices ("A Partnership to Remove Trash"), and most interesting to me, "The Coalition Mission." "The United States and its Coalition partners are dedicated to returning Iraq to the Iraqi people as soon as possible," the article states. "However, they stand by their pledge to ensure a safe and stable country before withdrawing its troops."

The article goes on to talk about "Operation Neighborhood"—"one of the many programs underway to help the Iraqi people rebuild their communities and country. Rebuilding neighborhoods is one of the first steps toward rebuilding Iraq." It promises that newly formed neighborhood councils, the CPA, the U.S. military, and its coalition partners "are working to eliminate those who would stand in the way of a new Iraq—Ba'athists, Fadayeen, and criminals. There will be more soldiers and police officers on the streets preventing crime and apprehending criminals. Iraqis can also help create a safe and stable community by turning in large-caliber weapons. . . . In a modern, free society the majority of Iraq citizens have no need to carry weapons."

I am thinking about sending this article to the NRA.

Continued . . .

Baghdad Now: A Bi-weekly 1st Armored Division Publication, Issue One, 1 July 2003.

The Coalition Mission

The United States and its Coalition partners are dedicated to returning Iraq to the Iraqi people as soon as possible.

However, they stand by their pledge to ensure a safe and stable country before withdrawing its troops.

Several programs are underway to help the Iraqi people rebuild their country. Soldiers and staff of the Office of the Coalition Provisional Authority are working together in Iraq's communities to rebuild its infrastructure, provide a safe and secure environment and promote self-government.

Military engineers have been going into neighborhoods in Baghdad and other cities to help citizens rebuild their communities. Operation Neighborhood is a program that teams engineers with members of the community in its rebuilding projects.

Recently, soldiers from the 1st Armored Division went to the Abu Ghurayb neighborhood rebuild their community marketplace June 5.

Engineers from the 94th Engineer Battalion repaired the local primary school and cleared tons of rubbish from the streets. They helped reestablish the local economy by building and setting 30 market stalls. They also improved the area's recreation facilities by smoothing the local soccer field.

Operation Neighborhood is one of many programs underway to help the Iraqi people rebuild their communities and country. Rebuilding neighborhoods is one of the first steps toward rebuilding Iraq.

In addition to making needed repairs, Operation Neighborhood provides jobs to residents.

On a larger scale, engineers are working to rebuild the city's waters, electric, sewage and roadways.

Throughout the city of Baghdad, residents are joining together to form local neighborhood advisory councils. These councils will form the foundation of a new government for the Iraqi people – one that represents their needs and responds to their communities.

The United States and its Coalition partners are dedicated to returning Iraq to the Iraqi people as soon as possible.

City residents are forming their neighborhood councils in each of the city's 90 district neighborhoods.

The neighborhood councils will elect district councils over the next several weeks. The election of the district councils is the second step leading to the formation of the Baghdad City Council on June 30th.

The neighborhood councils give the people of Baghdad a voice in their own government and a forum for citizens to address their concerns.

Neighborhood councils will have many resources at their disposal to solve problems. It can also seek assistance from the district or city-wide council.

Councils work directly with military commanders and representatives of the Office of the Coalition Provisional Authority to solve

Baghdad

problems in their neighborhoods.

Backing up those councils will be a trained and professional police force.

OCPA, the U.S. military, its coalition partners and members of the community are working to eliminate those who would stand in the way a new Iraq – Ba'athists, Fadayeen, and criminals.

There will be more soldiers and police officers on the streets preventing crime and apprehending criminals.

Soldiers will seek out and apprehend members of the former regime, terrorists and members of the Iraqi military who have not surrendered or continue to fight against Coalition Forces.

Iraqis can also help create a safe and stable community by turning in large-caliber weapons.

The intent of the heavy weapons turn-in program is not to disarm the Iraqi people but one of many programs designed to promote a safe and secure communities

All members of the community are encouraged to participate in this effort. Those who do not possess large-caliber weapons are encouraged to get those who do to turn over their weapons, show weapons cashes to authorities and to report illegal weapons sellers to authorities.

In a modern, free society the majority of Iraq citizens have no need to carry weapons. By working with the newly formed government and police force, taking part in community rebuilding efforts and helping fight crime on their communist, the Iraqi people can hasten the day when Coalition Forces leave their country.

"Coalition Mission," *Baghdad Now: A Bi-weekly 1st Armored Division Publication*, Issue One, 1 July 2003.

At a propane distribution, thousands of Iraqi civilians clamor for aid, as American soldiers from the First Cavalry Division take down an Iraqi civilian. LYNSEY ADDARIO/CORBIS 2003

STRETCHED THIN, LIED TO, AND MISTREATED

ON THE GROUND WITH U.S. TROOPS IN IRAQ

An M-16 rifle hangs by a cramped military cot. On the wall above is a message in thick black ink: "Ali Baba, you owe me a strawberry milk!"

It's a private joke but could just as easily summarize the worldview of American soldiers here in Baghdad, the fetid basement of Donald Rumsfeld's house of victory. Trapped in the polluted heat, poorly supplied, and cut off from regular news, the GIs are fighting a guerrilla war that they neither wanted, expected, nor trained for. On the urban battlefields of central Iraq, "shock and awe" and all the other "new way of war" buzzwords are drowned out by the din of diesel-powered generators, Islamic prayer calls, and the occasional pop of small-arms fire.

Here, the high-tech weaponry that so emboldens Pentagon bureaucrats is largely useless, and the grinding work of counterinsurgency is done the old-fashioned way—by hand. Not surprisingly, most of the American GIs stuck with the job are weary, frustrated, and ready to go home.

It is noon and the mercury is hanging steady at 115 degrees Fahrenheit. The filmmaker Garrett Scott and I are "embedded" with Alpha Company of the Third Battalion of the 124th Infantry, a Florida National Guard unit about half of whom did time in the regular Army, often with elite groups like the Rangers. Like most frontline troops in Iraq, the majority are white, but there is a sizable minority of African-American and Latino soldiers among them. Unlike most combat units, about 65 percent are college students—they've traded six years with the Guard for tuition at Florida State. Typically, that means occasional weekends in the Everglades or directing traffic during hurricanes. Instead, these guys got sent to Iraq, and as yet they have no sure departure date.

Mobilized in December, they crossed over from Kuwait on day one of the invasion and are now bivouacked in the looted remains of a Republican Guard officers' club, a modernist slab of polished marble and tinted glass that the GIs have fortified with plywood, sandbags, and razor wire.

Behind "the club" is a three-story dormitory, a warren of small one-bedroom apartments, each holding a nine-man squad of soldiers and all their gear. Around two hundred guys are packed in here. Their sweaty fatigues drape the banisters of the exterior stairway, while inside the cramped, dark rooms the floors are covered with cots, heaps of flak vests, guns, and, where possible, big tin, water-based air-conditioners called swamp coolers. Surrounding the base is a chaotic working-class neighborhood of two- and three-story cement homes and apartment buildings. Not far away is the muddy Tigris River.

This company limits patrols to three or four hours a day. For the many hours in between, the guys pull guard duty, hang out in their cavelike rooms, or work out in a makeshift weight room.

"We're getting just a little bit stir-crazy," explains lanky Sergeant Sellers. His demeanor is typical of the nine-man squad we have been assigned to, friendly but serious, with a wry and angry sense of humor. On the side of his helmet Sellers has, in violation of regs, attached the unmistakable pin and ring of a hand grenade. Next to it is written, "Pull Here."

Leaning back on a cot, he's drawing a large, intricate pattern on a female mannequin leg. The wall above him displays a photocollage of pictures retrieved from a looted Iraqi women's college. Smiling young ladies wearing the *hijab* sip sodas and stroll past buses. They seem to be on some sort of field trip. Nearby are photos clipped from *Maxim* of coy young American girls offering up their pert round bottoms. Dominating it all is a large hand-drawn dragon and a photo of Jessica Lynch with a bubble caption reading: "Hi, I am a war hero. And I think that weapons maintenance is totally unimportant."

The boys don't like Lynch and find the story of her rescue ridiculous. They'd been down the same road a day earlier and are unsympathetic. "We just feel that it's unfair and kind of distorted the way the whole Jessica, quote, 'rescue' thing got hyped," explains Staff Sergeant Kreed Howell. He is in charge of the squad, and at thirty-one a bit older than most of his men. Muscular and clean-cut, Howell is a relaxed and natural leader, with the gracious bearing of a proper Southern upbringing.

"In other words, you'd have to be really fucking dumb to get lost on the road," says another, less diplomatic soldier.

Specialist John Crawford sits in a tiny, windowless supply closet that is loaded with packs and gear. He is two credits short of a BA in anthropology and wants to go to graduate school. Howell, a Republican, amicably describes Crawford as the squad's house liberal.

There's just enough extra room in the closet for Crawford, a chair, and a little shelf on which sits a laptop. Hanging by this makeshift desk is a handwritten sign from "the management" requesting that soldiers masturbating in the supply closet "remove their donations in a receptacle." Instead of watching pornography DVDs, Crawford is here to finish a short story. "Trying to start writing again," he says.

Crawford is a fan of Tim O'Brien, particularly *The Things They Carried*. We chat, then he shows me his short story. It's about a vet who is back home in north Florida trying to deal with the memory of having accidentally blown away a child while serving in Iraq.

Later, in the cramped main room, Sellers and Sergeant Brunelle, another one of the squad's more gregarious and dominant personalities, are matter-of-factly showing us digital photos of dead Iraqis.

"These guys shot at some of our guys, so we lit 'em up. Put two .50-cal rounds in their vehicle. One went through this dude's hip and into the other guy's head," explains Brunelle. The third man in the car lived. "His buddy was crying like a baby. Just sitting there bawling with his friend's brains and skull fragments all over his face. One of our guys came up to him and is like: 'Hey! No crying in baseball!'"

"I know that probably sounds sick," says Sellers, "but humor is the only way you can deal with this shit."

And just below the humor is volcanic rage. These guys are proud to be soldiers and don't want to come across as whiners, but they are furious about what they've been through. They hate having their lives disrupted and put at risk. They hate the military for its stupidity, its feckless lieutenants and blowhard brass living comfortably in Saddam's palaces. They hate Iraqis—or, as they say, *"hajis"*—for trying to kill them. They hate the country for its dust, heat, and sewage-clogged streets. They hate having killed people. Some even hate the politics of the war. And because most of them are, ultimately, just regular well-intentioned guys, one senses the distinct fear that someday a few may hate themselves for what they have been forced to do here.

Added to such injury is insult: The military treats these soldiers like unwanted stepchildren. This unit's rifles are retooled hand-me-downs from Vietnam. They have inadequate radio gear, so they buy their own unencrypted Motorola walkie-talkies. The same goes for flashlights, knives, and some components for night-vision sights. The low-performance Iraqi air-conditioners and fans, as well as the one satellite phone and payment cards shared by the whole company for calling home, were also purchased out of pocket from civilian suppliers.

Specialist Eric Martin, 24, of Ricetown, Wisconsin, with the 3rd Infantry Division, 2nd Brigade, listens to music as Private First Class David Brock plays video games. LYNSEY ADDARIO/CORBIS 2003

Bottled water rations are kept to two liters a day. After that the guys drink from "water buffaloes"—big, hot, chlorination tanks that turn the amoeba-infested dreck from the local taps into something like swimming-pool water. Mix this with powdered Gatorade and you can wash down afamously bad MRE (Meal, Ready-to-Eat).

To top it all off they must endure the pathologically uptight culture of the Army hierarchy. The Third of the 124th is now attached to the newly arrived First Armored Division, and when it is time to raid suspected resistance cells it's the Guardsmen who have to kick in the doors and clear the apartments.

"The First AD wants us to catch bullets for them but won't give us enough water, doesn't let us wear do-rags, and makes us roll down our shirtsleeves so we look proper! Can you believe that shit?" Sergeant Sellers is pissed off.

The soldiers' improvisation extends to food as well. After a month or so of occupying "the club," the company commander, Captain Sanchez, allowed two Iraqi entrepreneurs to open shop on his side of the wire—one runs a slow Internet cafe, the other a kebab stand where the "Joes" pay U.S. dollars for grilled lamb on flatbread.

"The *haji* stand is one of the only things we have to look forward to, but the First AD keeps getting scared and shutting it down." Sellers is on a roll, but he's not alone.

Even the lighthearted Howell, who insists that the squad has it better than most troops, chimes in. "The one thing I will say is that we have been here entirely too long. If I am not home by Christmas my business will fail." Back "on earth" (in Panama City, Florida), Howell is a building contractor with a wife, two small children, equipment, debts, and employees.

Perhaps the most shocking bit of military incompetence is the unit's lack of formal training in what's called "close-quarter combat." The urbanized mayhem of

Mogadishu may loom large in the discourse of the military's academic journals like *Parameters* and the *Naval War College Review,* but many U.S. infantrymen are trained only in large-scale, open-country maneuvers—how to defend Germany from a wave of Russian tanks.

So, since "the end of the war" these guys have had to retrain themselves in the dark arts of urban combat. "The houses here are small, too," says Brunelle. "Once you're inside you can barely get your rifle up. You got women screaming, people, furniture everywhere. It's insane."

By now this company has conducted scores of raids, taken fire on the street, taken casualties, taken rocket-propelled grenade attacks to "the club," and are defiantly proud of the fact that they have essentially been abandoned, survived, retrained themselves, and can keep a lid on their little piece of Baghdad. But it's not always the Joes who have the upper hand. Increasingly, Haji seems to set the agenda.

A thick black plume of smoke rises from Karrada Street, a popular electronics district where U.S. patrols often buy air-conditioners and DVDs. An American Humvee, making just such a stop, has been blown to pieces by a remote-activated "improvised explosive device," or IED, buried in the median between two lanes of traffic. By chance two colleagues and I are the first press on the scene. The street is empty of traffic and quiet except for the local shopkeepers, who occasionally call out to us in Arabic and English: "Be careful."

Finally we get close enough to see clearly. About twenty feet away is a military transport truck and a Humvee, and beyond that are the flaming remains of a third Humvee. A handful of American soldiers are crouched behind the truck, totally still. There's no firing, no yelling, no talking, no radio traffic. No one is screaming, but two GIs are down. As yet there are no reinforcements or helicopters overhead. All one can hear is the burning of the Humvee.

Then it begins: The ammunition in the burning Humvee starts to explode, and the troops in the street start firing. Armored personnel carriers arrive and disgorge dozens of soldiers from the 82nd Airborne to join the fight. The target is a three-story office building just across from the engulfed Humvee. Occasionally we hear a few rounds of return fire pass by like hot razors slashing straight lines through the air. The really close rounds just sound like loud cracks.

"That's Kalashnikov. I know the voice," says Ahmed, our friend and translator. There is a distinct note of national pride in his voice—his countrymen are fighting back—never mind the fact that we are now mixed in with the most forward U.S. troops and getting shot at.

The firefight goes on for about two hours, moving slowly and methodically. It is in many ways an encapsulation of the whole war—confusing and labor-intensive. The GIs have more firepower than they can use, and they don't even know exactly where or who the enemy is. Civilians are hiding in every corner, the ground floor of the target building is full of merchants and shoppers, and undisciplined fire could mean scores of dead civilians.

There are two GIs on the ground, one with his legs gone and probably set to die. When a medevac helicopter arrives just overhead, it, too, like much other technology, is foiled. The street is crisscrossed with electrical wires and there is no way the chopper can land to extract the wounded. The soldiers around us look grave and tired.

Eventually some Bradley fighting vehicles start pounding the building with mean 250-millimeter cannon shells. Whoever might have been shooting from upstairs is either dead or gone.

The street is now littered with overturned air-conditioners, fans, and refrigerators. A cooler of sodas sits forlorn on the sidewalk. Farther away two civilians lie dead, caught in the crossfire. A soldier peeks out from the hatch of a Bradley and calls over to a journalist, "Hey, can you grab me one of those Cokes?"

After the shootout we promised ourselves we'd stay out of Humvees and away from U.S. soldiers. But that was yesterday. Now Crawford is helping us put on body armor, and soon we'll be on patrol. As we move out with the nine soldiers the mood is somewhere between tense and bored. Crawford mockingly introduces himself to no one in particular: "John Crawford, I work in population reduction."

"Watch the garbage—if you see wires coming out of a pile it's an IED," warns Howell. The patrol is uneventful. We walk fast through back streets and rubbish-strewn lots, pouring sweat in the late afternoon heat. Local residents watch the small squad with a mixture of civility, indifference, and open hostility. An Iraqi man shouts, "When? When? When? Go!" The soldiers ignore him.

"Sometimes we sham," explains one of the guys. "We'll just go out and kick it behind some wall. Watch what's going on but skip the walking. And sometimes at night we get sneaky-deaky. Creep up on Haji, so he knows we're all around."

"I am just walking to be walking," says the laconic Fredrick Pearson, aka "Diddy," the only African-American in Howell's squad. Back home he works in the State Supreme Court bureaucracy and plans to go to law school. "I just keep an eye on the rooftops, look around, and walk."

The patrols aren't always peaceful. One soldier mentions that he recently "kicked the shit out of a twelve-year-old kid" who menaced him with a toy gun.

Later we roll with the squad on another patrol, this time at night and in two Humvees. Now there's more evident hostility from the young Iraqi men loitering in the dark. Most of these infantry soldiers don't like being stuck in vehicles. At a blacked-out corner where a particularly large group of youths is clustered, the Humvees stop and Howell bails out into the crowd. There is no interpreter along tonight.

"Hey, guys! What's up? How y'all doing? OK? Everything OK? All right?" asks Howell in his jaunty, laid-back, north Florida accent. The sullen young men fade away into the dark, except for two, who shake the sergeant's hand. Howell's attempt to take the high road, winning hearts and minds, doesn't seem to be for show. He really believes in this war. But in the torrid gloom of the Baghdad night, his efforts seem tragically doomed.

Watching Howell I think about the civilian technocrats working with Paul Bremer at the Coalition Provisional Authority; the electricity is out half the time, and these folks hold meetings on how best to privatize state industries and end food rations. Meanwhile, the city seethes. The Pentagon, likewise, seems to have no clear plan; its troops are stretched thin, lied to, and mistreated. The whole charade feels increasingly patched together, poorly improvised. Ultimately, there's very little that Howell and his squad can do about any of this. After all, it's not their war. They just work here.

PREVIOUS SPREAD: U.S. troops patrol the streets while convoying through Baghdad. LYNSEY ADDARIO/CORBIS 2003

RESISTING EMPIRE:
LESSONS FOR IRAQ FROM PALESTINE

As I sit here, not far from the Muqata'a, Yasir Arafat's besieged and mostly destroyed office, I wonder how the Iraqi people are ever going to rid themselves of their occupation. Nothing Palestinians have done in the last decade of so-called "peacemaking" has managed to extricate them from their occupation. Indeed, looking back there was little chance the peace process would lead to peace; like Palestinians, Iraqis don't have the luxury of a wasted decade before they take matters into their own hands.

Listening to the shouts of schoolchildren pledging loyalty to their erstwhile leader, I can't help wonder what lessons this occupation has for Iraqis struggling against Israel's chief benefactor. Palestinians have tried seemingly everything: armed guerilla struggle, popular insurrection, terrorism, negotiations, mass nonviolent civil protests. Yet Israel, like the "house" in a Vegas casino, always wins in the end—this despite the fact that its ever intensifying occupation is reaching a level of brutality and dehumanization that is shocking in its banality as much as its scope.

Palestinians continue to put their faith in symbolic leaders like Arafat, yet these leaders almost always are corrupted and in the end will fail their people when integrity, honesty, brains, and courage are needed most. It's not surprising that the political leadership of the increasingly irrelevant Palestinian Authority (PA) are almost entirely middle-aged or older men with histories of corruption and accommodation with power—Israel has eliminated or exiled anyone with better credentials. At the same time, however, one of the main reasons that Arafat is still personally so important for Palestinians is that however inept and venal his rule, he ultimately has refused completely to sell out Palestinian national independence. As one Palestinian friend put it, "He's a dictator, but a nationalist one," and this dynamic, especially for a nation under such threat to its existence, is what has helped him remain a central figure, even as Palestinians increasingly consider him irrelevant on a day-to-day basis of struggle and survival.

The Iraqis chosen by the U.S. to lead their country to supposed independence appear little better than their counterparts in the PA, and in fact, the plan to privatize and sell off to foreign interests literally the entire Iraqi economy save for the oil industry (where we can assume the U.S. has already secured sweetheart deals with its protégés in the Oil Ministry) reveals the extent of the corruption shared between the occupier and the occupied elite. The pattern for such a sell-off of the national economy—if not national independence per se—follows the same path as most other processes of "independence" where the "mother" country retained preferential positions in crucial economic sectors. In Palestine the 1994 Paris Protocols went so far as to prevent "either side" from developing any new industry that could compete with an existing industry of the other. Needless to say, with Israel having one of the most advanced economies on earth and Palestine reeling from three decades of occupation,

Palestinian leaders wound up signing away the rights to develop almost any new industry save boutique flowers and other specialized agricultural production—much of which is held up and allowed to rot at checkpoints whenever Israel wants to send a message. Let's not forget that both these economic plans were sold under the aura of a "New Middle East" built on the foundations of democracy and free markets; Iraqis can look to Palestine if they want to know where that fantasy leads.

As I talk with the young generation of emerging Palestinian grass roots leaders— well-educated twenty- and thirty-somethings from a variety of class and social back- grounds—I realize that if there is hope for Iraqis and Palestinians alike, it is going to come from truly radical young people who are committed both to comprehensive social transformation and to resistance, but in a manner that moves beyond the kind of crude nationalism, ethnic exclusivism, or violence that has proved so morally and politically counterproductive. Only such a positive culture of resistance can hope to defeat the full weight of colonialism and occupation in the global age. Yet in Palestine too many of this generation are already being co-opted and depoliticized by a sur- prising source: the international nongovernmental organization (NGO) community whose "civil society" and related "capacity building" programs have, ironically, cre- ated a Palestinian intellectual and activist/NGO class whose disconnection from the needs and realities of the grassroots—as well as the intensification of occupation— increases in direct proportion to its funding.

As the well-intentioned world NGO community rushes in to save Iraq from America, it would do well to take stock of the reasons behind the failures of the NGO/civil society system in Palestine. One the one hand, it is clear that positively rad- ical social movements and forces such as are desperately needed in Palestine or Iraq absolutely need international support. Yet it is precisely because of who the main providers of that support have been in Palestine—and are as of now in Iraq—that such problems have occurred: that is, the main groups delivering a message of human freedom, democracy, and development have wound up being associated with policies that have been disastrous for people on the ground. In Palestine it's been an NGO community that hasn't been able to tackle the root causes of occupation or focus suc- cessfully on society-wide grassroots activities and whose relatively large sums of money poured into a relatively small intellectual class have tended to weaken rather than strengthen that class's bond with the rest of society. In Iraq, of course, the UN has become the tragic example of this problem, as it offered itself as the provider of humanitarian relief and even a political counterpoint to the U.S. occupation regime when in fact it was implicated in ten years of devastating sanctions and then rubber- stamped the invasion itself; these policies have made it difficult to be seen as neutral or even sympathetic to the needs of ordinary Iraqis.

The violence that shattered the UN presence has also played a crucial role in Palestine, where a major reason for the depoliticization of the NGO class has been the violence of the Israeli occupation. In fact, both Palestine and Iraq are the product of extreme violence associated with uncompromising colonialism. In his essay in this book, Mike Davis details the legacy of British rule in Iraq; the violence of 1920 pro- foundly impacted the dynamics of politics to this day. Like Israel's occupation of Palestine, Britain's occupation of Iraq could only be implemented by extreme violence and autocratic rule, including the repeated use of poison gas and large-scale aerial bombings of civilian targets which have made Saddam Hussein infamous, and which, according to a recent biography of Hussein, "administered a shock to the country's social system from which it has never recovered. It was the British conquest of Iraq which set the stage for what is happening today."

Violence has had a similarly profound impact on Palestinian society (and Israeli society as well, with lessons that all Americans should heed if they don't want to wind up living in a society as hypermilitarized and uncivil as Israel's). For Iraqis the biggest lesson is the disempowering effect of overwhelming violence: the victims of the violence are unable to transcend it in order to develop large-scale societal means of resistance that don't mirror the same violence and associated pathologies.

Sergeant Valdez with the 1st Armored Division fires shots into the air to try to control the crowd.
LYNSEY ADDARIO/CORBIS 2003

For example, in conversations with numerous Palestinian leaders, including leaders of Hamas, most accept that the violence used by militant Palestinian groups against Israeli civilians is not achieving any concrete political goals, is counterproductive, and is playing right into Ariel Sharon's hands. However, many also feel either that they have had to engage in such violence so that Israelis would at least feel some of the Palestinian's pain and suffering, or that there was no realistic alternative available to surrender or personally/politically suicidal violence. In other words, the cycle of violence has so stifled Palestinian creative political energies that only a small but crucial segment of society can resist responding with their own extreme violence. This is destroying any chance for independence, not to mention a viable social fabric within which to continue resistance.

In this context the most important issue for Iraqis to learn from Palestine is the need to confront dehumanization: the occupation of Palestine continues to succeed because successive Israeli governments have engaged in dehumanizing Palestinians to such a degree that just living one's daily life has become a supreme but largely unacknowledged act of nonviolent resistance. This societal *summud* (steadfastness)—the result of the combination of brutality and indoctrination within Israeli society, where, for example, newly conscripted Israeli soldiers are told that Arabs are animals and every Palestinian wants to kill every Jew possible—has produced a level of psychosis within Israeli culture, which in turn has tended to create a vicious cycle where Palestinians internalize the hatred of Israelis and reply in kind. This damages the positive aspect and process of *summud* that is at the core of Palestinian identity and survival.

Everything possible must be done to prevent a similar process from occurring in Iraq: simplification and demonizing of the U.S. and the West are already at the heart of the discourse of Al-Qaeda. The U.S. is already exploiting this dynamic: in fact, their goal seems to be to sow enough chaos and violence so that Iraqi society breaks down and is left with little ability to develop any creative and politically effective means of resistance.

Given the similarly violent conditions in Palestine and Iraq, what strategies can be adopted in Iraq based on the lessons of Palestine? A lot of work remains to be done to answer this question, but here are a few of the things Palestine teaches us:

1. The occupation of Palestine has succeeded in good measure because Israel has been able to play off and accentuate class and ethnic differences within Palestinian society through political and economic control. The destruction of Palestinian civil society has made it much easier for violence to become the main form of resistance. Every effort must be made to help Iraqis build a grassroots democratic society and to ensure that the U.S. doesn't succeed in dividing the country along ethnic lines.

2. The International Solidarity Movement (ISM) remains perhaps the most important model for Iraq, and for it to work Iraqis must take the lead. What is needed in Iraq, specifically, is an ISM-type force that clearly distinguishes itself from the U.S. and the UN/mainstream NGO community so that its message cannot be implicated in the larger dynamics of the occupation. At the same time, strategically, it should develop through a two-stage process: first, by forming the nucleus of an international force that protects Iraqis from the vagaries of U.S. occupation by monitoring what the U.S. is doing and that does what the U.S. fails to do (as Occupation Watch is already doing). Then, after local legitimacy is built through these kinds of activities, a kind of ISM "Peace Corps" of volunteer doctors, lawyers, agriculturalists, and similar crucial professions must be developed which can forge links with progressive local forces. This would allow not just resistance to the occupation, but the building of an alternative social fabric on the ground with strong links to the global peace and justice movement.

3. Americans must become educated. One of the main reasons Palestine gets so little sympathy from Americans is that our view of the history of the Israeli-Palestinian conflict is so distorted and inaccurate. Having recently looked at the textbooks used for teaching California students about Iraq, it is clear to me that our government and its corporate media allies—the materials are all produced by large media companies—are similarly trying to prevent any understanding of the realities

of British colonial rule in Iraq or American foreign policy towards Iraq. Most Americans remain ignorant of our unflinching support for "the dictator Saddam Hussein" (which included putting his Baath party in power twice, in 1963 and 1968, and helping to find and kill thousands of Iraqi communists in the process), just as we have been inoculated against the real history of our involvement with coups and corrupt dictatorial regimes in every other country in the region.

An effort must be made to look at the history of the region systematically and holistically, to help Americans understand the links between our support for Israel and for Saudi Arabia, the power of the "arms-petrodollar cycle," and the coalition of big oil and defense companies which has benefited for decades to the tune of upwards of 13 percent of the profits of the Fortune 500. With the invasion and occupation of Iraq, this coalition has managed to succeed in the greatest theft in history of American tax dollars and another country's resources.

4. Needless to say, the military-industrial complex behind the current occupation is intimately related to the processes of globalization. It's not for nothing that the World Bank, that paragon of neoliberal market mythology, argued almost a decade ago that in order to create the "new social contract" necessary to bring the Middle East into the global age, civil societies will have to "lower their protective walls" while governments lower wages and subsidies in the name of efficiency and productivity, all of which was likely to necessitate a "shakedown period to clear out the accumulated structural problems" of the region.

George W. Bush and Co. clearly felt a shakedown was not sufficient; instead, "shock and awe" were necessary to free Iraq from the shackles of a history that, as the Arab economist Samir Amin long ago pointed out, has been tied into the world capitalist system longer than other region of the Third World aside from Latin America—specifically, as a marginalized and peripheral region whose main resource, oil, has become the main obstacle to autonomous and democratic development.

5. Our artists, academics, and activists must grapple with the increasingly clear fact that the occupations of Iraq and Palestine represent (like Stalinism, the Holocaust, slavery, and the genocide of indigenous Americans, etc.) the absolute failure of what the Moroccan Islamist activist and Sufi leader Abdesalam Yassine calls "armed capitalist modernity." (Yassine's phrase echoes the description posited by the socialist philosopher George Sorel a century ago of the inherent similarity between "the capitalist type and the warrior type.")

We need to create an entirely new philosophy, ethics, and aesthetics—that is, a truly new social contract—to enable humanity to imagine and work towards a better future. But in order to do that we need to be asking the right questions and demanding honest answers of ourselves as much as of those in power. From this perspective, Palestine sends a message to the Iraqi people: Be smart, don't waste one or two generations with fantasies, corrupt leaders, and illusions of peace. Do the hard work now and build social movements to bring justice and democracy from the grassroots.

More broadly, as Sheikh Yassine points out, we need to "address modernity with questions it has no interest in, and which its citizens haven't the time to ask . . ." The dialogue of the deaf leading up to the Iraqi invasion clearly demonstrates that "two-way communication is beyond reach with a modernity that is comfortably installed in a way of life hardly troubled" by the misery it produces. So Sheikh Yassine calls for "concluding a pact of mutual aid among humankind that crosses the boundaries of state structures and goes above the heads of official institutions. [For Islam] this is our ideal of beneficence strictly bound to our ideal of spiritual perfection. This plan for a worldwide humanitarian coalition responds to the utopian dream and the actuality of the flagrant imbalance that rages between north and south."

Similarly, Tariq Ramadan, the leading Muslim intellectual-activist in Europe, together with Nadia Yassine forcefully argues that Muslims and Europeans must move beyond facile denunciations of the United States. Ramadan explains: "To face this reality, we have to speak of the common risks we are facing—not just the Muslim world, but everywhere. It's important to find a way to come to universal values and to say this period is a challenge to all of us together."

We would do well to pay close attention to the words of the Yassines, Ramadan, and other clearly radical—"radical" in its most positive sense—religious figures in the Muslim world. They reveal an Islam fully engaged with the same problems as progressives in the North/West, ready to join coalitions based on similar conceptions of social justice and rights (including gender equality, as demonstrated in this case by the role of Yassine's daughter Nadia as the leader of the largest political movement in Morocco).

Since the famed antiglobalization protests in Seattle in late 1999, it has unfortunately been nearly impossible to get the leadership of the anticorporate globalization movements to even minimally engage Muslims as partners in the struggle for a truly new world order. Whether in Iraq, Pakistan, or Palestine, there are innumerable religious Muslim voices that are progressive and nonviolent, but which are largely ignored by our media and government, as well as, in large measure, NGOs and activists alike. In reality, the more "like us" the Islamist voices I have encountered are—that is, the more they support real democracy, women's rights, tolerance, and real free markets—the more vehemently they reject almost every aspect of the American-dominated globalized order. Why is it, then, that both the American Left and the antiglobalization movement persist in dismissing or outright ignoring these voices and the contributions they might make?

Today's American *Realpolitik* has taken us far from the core ideals that our country was founded on, the kinds of ideals that have inspired Muslims in the universities of Tehran as much as they inspired Catholics in the Gdansk shipyards a generation ago. If we want Muslims to become more like us, perhaps we should become more like the society we claim to be.

If the peace movement and democratic Iraqi forces are to develop a more sophisticated message and strategy and offer a positive alternative discourse to occupation, corruption, and violence, intercommunal solidarity through dialogue and committed nonviolence will be the key mechanisms. This is a daunting challenge, but if relationships can be forged between Iraqis, the larger Arab and Muslim worlds, and activists in the West, the global peace and justice movement may yet gain the upper hand in the struggle against global empire, in Palestine as well as Iraq.

Local Iraqis line up behind piles of gerry cans they hope to fill at a gas station. LYNSEY ADDARIO/CORBIS 2003

BAGHDAD JOURNAL #7

The greeting in Baghdad is *"Assalamu alaykum,"* "Peace upon you." One's hand touches one's heart, then reaches out as if making an offering. If you are an American, the greeting will be followed by a generous "Welcome."

I am standing on a dirt street in a poor suburb of Baghdad, a neighborhood of dusty stone walls that shelter boxlike concrete houses. The people who live here have had no running water for seven days; so we've been told by the USAID workers, who are helpless to get them what they need. We've joined the director responsible for the neighborhood to investigate reports that the elderly and babies are dying of dehydration and water-borne illnesses.

The streets are full of children. Sewage runs in rivulets down the ruts of the road and gathers in its craters. The smell is thick, and I try to keep my breathing shallow so as not to inhale it too deeply.

Women have come out of their houses; the younger women are dressed in bright colors and head scarves, the elders in the more traditional black *abeya*. The few men in evidence are older, in their fifties and sixties, and wear the clothes of the conservative religious.

Our guide moves into the crowd. Immediately she is approached by a woman in an *abeya* who has tribal markings on her lower lip and chin. She begins to speak in rapid, forceful Arabic. Our driver, Farouk, translates for me, struggling to keep up with the torrent of words: There is no water, no electricity, sewage in the streets, our children are suffering, can you not see what a disaster this will become? People are dying.

I move closer to the woman to ask a question. She turns to me. Her face lights up with a warm, open smile. "Welcome," she says in English, reaching out her hand. *"Salaam alechem."*

"Why can't the Americans give us our electricity and water?" she pleads with me in Arabic.

I am reminded of the repeated questions I heard in February: "Why does Mr. Bush want to bomb us?"

I still have no answers to these questions.

Iraqis gather around a water tank provided by the Iran Red Crescent Organization. LYNSEY ADDARIO/CORBIS 2003

EVERY MORNING THE WAR GETS UP FROM SLEEP

Ah! This is Baghdad: I move through it every day, to and fro,
While I squat in this cold exile. I look for it
In the demonstrators who move along Rashid Street carrying banners,
In the strikes of textile workers,
To whom we throw bags of bread and political tracts.
At dawn, carrying paint, we spray the walls with our slogans:
"Down with Dictatorship!"
In the coffeehouses extending along the river on Abu Nawwas,
In the fishermen by the bridge,
In the monument of Jawad Selim which is riddled with bullets,
In Majid's coffeehouse, where the geniuses and informers sip tea,
Where a poet expelled from college gazes at a window
Behind which three Palestinian girls gaze down the street forever.

Ah! Every morning the war gets up from sleep.
So I place it in a poem, make the poem into a boat, which I throw into the Tigris.

This is war, then.

BACK TO BABYLON

Accept and forget difference or desire that separates and leaves us longing or repelled. Why briefly return to play in broken places, to mock the ground, to collect infant shards, coins, fossils, or the familiar empty canisters and casings that glint from poisoned roots in the blackened dust? We make bad ghosts, and are last to know or believe we too will fade, just as our acrid smoke and those strange flakes of skin and strands of hair will, into largely undocumented extinction. Lie down, lie down; sleep is the best thing for being awake. Do as we've always been told and done, no backward glances or second thoughts, leaving sad markers buried in the sand. Sleep now, dream of children with their heads still on, of grandmothers unburdening clotheslines at twilight, of full kettles slow-ticking over twig embers. Ignore boneless, nameless victims that venture out on bitter gravel to claim remains while we rest.

Pay at the window for re-heated, prejudiced incantations. Take them home and enjoy with wide-screen, half-digested, replayed previews of solemn national celebration. Then sleep, by all means; we'll need all the energy we can muster for compiling this generation's abridged anthology of official war stories, highlights of heedless slaughter, to burnish our long and proud imperial tradition. At some point, by virtue of accidentally seeing and listening, we may find ourselves participating in our own rendering. Few of our prey will be left alive enough to water the sun with their modest, time-rubbed repetitions, to rephrase their particular, unifying laws. Our version of events has already made its money back in foreign distribution and pre-sales; all victory deadlines must be met.

It can get so quiet, with or without the dead watching our constant deployments. From our tilted promontory we may see one last woman scuffle away across cracked parchment of dry wash beneath us, muttering to herself—or is she singing at us?—as she rounds the sheared granite face and disappears into a grove of spindly, trembling tamarisk shadows lining the main road. We'll soon hear little other than our breathing, as shale cools and bats rise to feed, taking over from sated swallows. Night anywhere is home, darkness a cue for turning inward, quiet an invitation to review our expensive successes before morning extraction from the twin rivers of our common cradle.

February 2003.

RADIO CORRESPONDENT

I.
At 8 years old
I stood on the equator
beside ant hills that were taller than me
in a game park in post-colonial Kenya
with Mount Kilimanjaro—its clouds
    and snow
shimmering in the distance
as I tried to coax harmony from a goat-
    skinned drum

Masai tribes people had danced in this
    same place
the previous evening
their bare feet
stomping dust
into low clouds
that reddened the sunset
by putting little bits of earth into the sky
and calling the sky and the night
closer to the ground
collapsing the distance
between earth and the stars
between the drum and the sun
between prayer and celebration
between Hollis and the snows of
    Kilimanjaro
and my 8-year-old soul

I never wanted to leave that place
As night fell a symphony of wildlife
flooded my ears
I crawled on top of a small boulder
and strained to touch the sky
I wanted to slip the moon beneath my
    tongue
let constellations trickle down my throat
and sing me closer to the universe

but maybe that would be too much
to swallow

II.
One day your heart will abandon you
Your tongue will not work
And your ears will create their own sounds
The betrayals will no longer be outside
    of you

The world is coming apart
And I'm shitting blood in the Palestine
    Hotel
As other Americans liberate Iraq
With bombs and murder
Photoplay
I want to run to my balcony
And work
But I haven't had
A solid bowel movement
Since I got here
And my system is unravelling
A porcelain throne of blood
Is beneath me

III.
So much chatter
In the sky
Empty streets
No more horns
Bleating warning and permissions
So much dead traffic and language
Allah has retreated into the Euphrates
as Jesus shepherds cluster bombs

There are no new ways
to describe destruction
all that is new

is your fear   blindness and   prayers
invested in the rubble
commingled with the smoke
and licks of flames
the hearts on the ground
and hearts swirling above them
in machines
separated by much more
than airspace
the lean wild dogs
don't run the banks of the Tigris
in the daylight
they stay hidden in the rubble of
bombed-out buildings
hiding like cicadas in the half-built
   promises
unfinished construction
shelter and pause before the gravity
   strikes
at night they run the banks of the river
crooning
aboriginal
inscrutable
as they sing the air raid sirens awake
tax dollars and jet engines make you run
to your balcony
break out your Sony
and attempt thin
and one-dimensional recordings
of the city
Baghdad is unstrung
in a corset of sound
murder and chaos are concussive
they don't just shout in your face
they grab you by the collarbone and

blow into it
the tune is so familiar
you want to leave your skin and your
   body behind
you weak motherfucker
what made you think you could do this
put down your superficial electronics
and be present
the air bends more than it shakes
it will push itself into everyday sounds
car doors closing
dishes breaking
engines backfiring
it will find ways to remain close to you
camouflaged and close
familiar
for all your days

and the shit
hasn't even
really begun

Baghdad 3/21/03

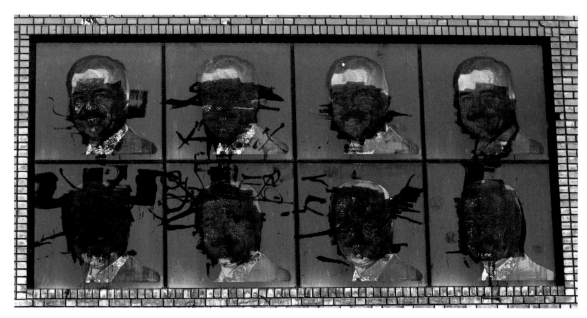

Defaced mural of Saddam Hussein. LYNSEY ADDARIO/CORBIS 2003

CONTRIBUTORS

Lynsey Addario is a photojournalist based in Istanbul, Turkey, where she photographs for the *New York Times*, the *New York Times Magazine*, *Time*, and *Newsweek*, among others, through her New York–based photo agency, Corbis. In January 2003 Lynsey moved her base to Istanbul, in order to situate herself closer to feature and news stories in the Middle East. In February 2003 she traveled to Iraq, where she spent almost seven months covering the war for the *New York Times Magazine*, *Time*, and the *New York Times* newspaper.

Fadhil al-Azzawi was born in Kirkuk, north Iraq, in 1940. He has a BA in English literature from Baghdad University and a PhD in journalism from Leipzig University. He has edited literary magazines and newspapers in Iraq and abroad and has been publishing his work since the 1960s—seven volumes of poetry, eight novels, a collection of short stories, two works of criticism, and numerous translations into Arabic from English and German. His poetry has been translated into many languages, and he is soon to have a major selection of his works published in English by Boa Editions, Ltd. He left Iraq in 1977 and has settled in Germany. He is a consulting editor of *Banipal*.

Medea Benjamin is a powerful and charismatic force in human rights activism. She has struggled for social justice in Asia, Africa, and the Americas for more than twenty years. Benjamin is the founding director of the human rights organization Global Exchange; she also helped form the coalition United for Peace and Justice and is the co-founder of Code Pink: Women for Peace.

Tiosha Bojorquez Chapela was born in Mexico City in 1973. After spending some years in various provinces of Babylon, he returned to Mexico, where he is working as a translator and scriptwriter while finishing one degree in Linguistics from the National School of Anthropology and History (ENA), and another degree in the department of English Literature at the National Autonomous University of Mexico (UNAM).

Kristina Borjesson, an Emmy- and Murrow Award–winning investigative reporter, has worked for CBS and CNN, and she is the author of *Into the Buzzsaw: Leading Journalists Expose the Myth of a Free Press*.

Anne E. Brodsky is Associate Professor of Psychology and Women's Studies at the University of Maryland Baltimore County (UMBC) and author of *With All Our Strength: The Revolutionary Association of the Women of Afghanistan* (Routledge, 2003).

Mike Davis is a MacArthur Fellow and the author of several books, including *Dead Cities*, *City of Quartz*, and *Ecology of Fear*. He lives in San Diego.

Jodie Evans has been a political, environmental, and social activist for more than thirty years, and she is the co-founder of Code Pink: Women for Peace. She visited Iraq in February and July of 2003.

Tahmeena Faryal is a Pakistan-based member of the Revolutionary Association of the Women of Afghanistan (RAWA) and serves on their Foreign Affairs Committee.

Lisa Fredsti is a writer and researcher based in Venice, California. She is currently working on a pop biography of the late Chinese premier Zhou Enlai.

Sandra Fu is a Los Angeles–based freelance writer and a senior editor for Morphizm.com.

Amy Goodman is host of the award-winning nationally syndicated daily grassroots news hour, *Democracy Now!*, broadcasting on public radio/TV stations nationally, and streaming at www.democracynow.org.

Amir Hussain is a member of the Department of Religious Studies at California State University, Northridge (CSUN). His area of research is on the study of Islam, specifically contemporary Muslim societies in North America.

Eman Ahmed Khammas is a journalist. She has written numerous reports on the conditions of occupation in Iraq and is currently the director of Occupation Watch. Khammas lives in Baghdad, is a Sunni Muslim who is married with two children, and speaks ardently for nonviolent means to political change.

Naomi Klein is the author of *No Logo: Taking Aim at the Brand Bullies* and *Fences and Windows: Dispatches from the Front Lines of the Globalization Debate*. She writes an internationally syndicated column for *The Nation* and *The Guardian*.

Mark LeVine's research, activism, and music engage the histories and political and cultural economies of the modern Middle East, Islam, and globalization. He has worked with artists such as Mick Jagger, Ozomatli, Hassan Hakmoun, Dr. John, and Chuck D, and is the author of *Overthrowing Geography: Jaffa, Tel Aviv, and the Struggle for Palestine, 1880–1948* (University of California Press, 2005) and the tentatively titled *Why They Don't Hate Us: From Culture Wars to Culture Jamming in the Age of Globalization,* forthcoming from Oneworld Press.

Yanar Mohammed is the founder of Defense of Iraqi Women's Rights (DIWR), a Toronto-based women's group founded in 1998. After the fall of the Baath Regime, Mohammed went to Baghdad and was a founding member of the Organization of Women's Freedom in Iraq (founded June 22, 2003). She is also the editor in chief of *Al-Mousawat* (Equality) newspaper , a radical defender of women's rights in Iraq.

Viggo Mortensen is a co-editor of this book and founder of Perceval Press. He dedicates the poem "Back to Babylon" to the people of Iraq and the United States of America.

Christian Parenti is the author, most recently, of *The Soft Cage: Surveillance in America From Slavery to the War on Terror* (Basic, 2003), and is a fellow at City University of New York's Center for Place, Culture, and Politics.

Pilar Perez is an activist, art curator, and co-founder of Perceval Press. She has edited numerous books that combine art, social issues, and politics.

Jerry Quickley's hard-hitting poems and essays are widely anthologized—from New York to Munich, from Bordeaux to Baghdad, he perfects the art of creative revolution. In Iraq as a radio correspondent and documentary filmmaker during the early days of the war, he recently returned to occupied Iraq to complete his documentary project and continue to broadcast independent, unembedded radio reports.

Omid Safi is an assistant professor of Islamic Studies at Colgate University in Hamilton, New York. He specializes in Islamic mysticism, contemporary Islamic thought, and medieval Islamic history. He is a member of the steering committee for the Study of Islam at the American Academy of Religion, the largest international organization devoted to the academic study of religion. He is the author of *Progressive Muslims: On Justice, Gender, and Pluralism* (Oneworld Press, 2003).

Lauren Sandler, a journalist, is investigating issues of women and culture in Iraq for the Carr Foundation.

Joseph Wilson was deputy chief of mission at the U.S. Embassy in Baghdad from 1988 to 1991. In July, he called into question the Bush administration's assertions about Iraq seeking uranium from Africa by revealing that he had been asked by the U.S. government to look into such claims—and had reported in early 2002 that they were unfounded. He is an adjunct scholar at the Middle East Institute in Washington, D.C.

Nadia Yassine was born in 1958 in Casablanca, Morocco. In 1980 she earned a bachelor's degree in political science. She is the author of *Toutes Voiles Dehors* (published in Morocco and France), translated into English as *Raising Full Sail Towards Original Islam* (not yet published). Yassine is a prominent figure of Islamic renaissance, not only in Morocco, but internationally as well. Through interviews with international newspapers, magazines, and TV channels, she has been solicited to expound the viewpoints of her movement, *Jamâtu Al Adl Wal Ihssân* (Justice and Spirituality Association), which is concerned with domestic and foreign issues involving the Muslim world.

Howard Zinn is professor emeritus of Political Science at Boston University and is the author of the best-selling *A People's History of the United States,* and many other books, including *The Zinn Reader* and *Artists in Times of War.*

ORGANIZATIONS

Alternet:
an online magazine created by
the Independent Media Institute
(www.alternet.org).

American Friends Service Committee:
a Quaker organization providing
worldwide peace and justice programs
(www.afsc.org).

Antiwar.com:
a resource site for antiwar news
articles, viewpoints, and activities
(www.antiwar.com).

Baghdad.com:
a World News Network of extensive
resource for news articles and events
(www.baghdad.com).

Baghdad Bulletin:
independent coverage of the
redevelopment of Iraq
(www.baghdadbulletin.com).

Baghdad Independent Media Center:
independent news produced by
Iraqis in Iraq
(www.almuajaha.com).

Bring Them Home:
U.S. military families and veterans
opposed to the occupation
(www.bringthemhomenow.com).

Center for Defense Information:
an independent monitoring agency
of military activity in Iraq
(www.cdi.org).

Code Pink: Women for Peace:
is a women-initiated grassroots
peace and social justice movement that
seeks positive social change through
proactive creative protest and
nonviolent direct action
(www.codepinkalert.org).

Common Dreams:
a cutting-edge website publishing
progressive visions
(www.commondreams.org).

Costs of War:
a running daily count of the
cost of war in Iraq
(www.costofwar.com).

Democracy Now!:
an online website of Amy Goodman's
Pacifica Radio show
(www.democracynow.org).

Electronic Iraq:
an Internet portal of breaking news
from Iraq
(www.electroniciraq.net).

Fairness and Accuracy in Reporting:
a national media watch documenting
media bias and censorship
(www.fair.org).

Fellowship of Reconciliation:
an interfaith organization committed
to international nonviolence
(www.forusa.org).

Global Exchange:
an international organization
promoting fair trade and peace
(www.globalexchange.org).

The Guardian:
an independent British newspaper
(www.guardian.co.uk/iraq).

**Human Rights Watch for Iraq and Iraqi
Kurdistan:** a website that monitors
human rights alerts in Iraq
(www.humanrightswatch.org).

International Occupation Watch Center:
a website that monitors U.S. and British
corporations and occupation forces
(www.occupationwatch.org).

International Red Cross Focus on Iraq:
offers neutral humanitarian aid to
victims of war
(www.icrc.org).

Iraq Action Coalition:
a media and activists' resource
center for Iraq
(www.iraqaction.org).

Iraq Body Count:
public independent database of civilian
deaths resulting from military action
(www.iraqbodycount.net).

Iraq Coalition Casualty Count:
a website that provides a breakdown
of coalition force deaths during and
after the war
(www.lunavillc.org).

Media Alliance:
a nonprofit membership
organization dedicated to advancing
all independent media
(www.mediaalliance.org).

MoveOn.org:
an online leader for waging political
campaigns through the Internet
(www.moveon.org).

National Priorities Project:
a website that provides tools for
citizens to effect U.S. budget and
policy priorities
(www.nationalpriorities.org).

Peace Action:
the largest grassroots peace group in
the United States
(www.peace-action.org).

Peaceful Tomorrows:
the families of September 11 victims
seeking peaceful solutions
(www.peacefultomorrows.org).

**Revolutionary Association of the
Women of Afghanistan:**
an organization established for women's
rights and social justice in Afghanistan
(www.rawa.org).

United for Peace and Justice:
a coalition of 650 U.S. organizations
opposing the war in Iraq
(www.unitedforpeaceandjustice.org).

Women's Action for New Direction:
an organization that empowers women
to act politically to reduce violence
and militarism
(www.wand.org).

ACKNOWLEDGMENTS

This book was largely conceived of and inspired by Jodie Evans and Pilar Perez, who, along with Mark LeVine, brought together the diverse voices and points of view presented. Lisa Fredsti must also be acknowledged for lending her incomparable research skills to this project.

Heartfelt thanks go to the various contributors from around the world whose work speaks to a shared interest in finding a way to understand the complex situation created by the occupation of Iraq by U.S.-led forces—a shared interest in the common good of all nations.

Special thanks for additional assistance go to Peter Rothberg, *The Nation;* Denis Moynihan, *Democracy Now!;* Kim Fararo, the *San Jose Mercury News;* April Jenkins, Corbis; Carol Shayne, Corbis; Scott Thill, Morphizm.com; Ramzi Kysia, *Al-Muajaha;* Patricia Foulkrod, Code Pink; Linda Gregg; and Mariana Botey.

We must also mention those who assisted us with the production of the book: Dana Fredsti for transcribing the various interviews, Sherri Schottlaender for her invaluable copyediting assistance with the essays, and Michele Perez for helping make sense of the wide-ranging material made available in this publication.

Viggo Mortensen

BACKACHE, STRESS, AND TENSION

Understanding Why You Have Back Pain
and Simple Exercises to Prevent and Treat It

HANS KRAUS, M.D.
Photos by Melanie Trice

Foreword by
Robert H. Boyle

Skyhorse Publishing

For permission to use the following materials, the author wishes to thank:

Charles C. Thomas—for material and illustrations from my books, *Principles and Practice of Therapeutic Exercises*, copyright © 1949, 1963, and *Hypokinetic Disease*, copyright © 1961.

The Lancet—for statistics from "Coronary Heart-disease and Physical Activity of Work," by Morris, J. N., Heady, J. A., Raffle, P. A., Roberts, C. G., and Parks, J. W., in *Lancet* 2:1053, November 21, 1953, and 2:1111, November 28, 1953.

Dr. Lloyd Appleton—for the graph on "Discharge of West Point Cadets with Psychiatric Endorsement."

New York State Journal of Medicine—for use of the diagram in my article "Preventive Aspects of Physical Fitness," in Vol. 64, No. 10, May 15, 1964.

Sports Illustrated—for the quotation from the article "The Soft American" by John F. Kennedy, December 26, 1960.

Dr. Jean Mayer—for the table from his *Nutrition in Clinical Medicine*, copyright © 1960.

Dr. Jean Mayer and Harper & Row—for the conclusion from the chapter "Exercise and Weight Control" in *Science and Medicine of Exercise and Sports*.

ALL NAMES OF PATIENTS MENTIONED IN THIS BOOK ARE FICTITIOUS.

Skyhorse Publishing books may be purchased in bulk at special discounts for sales promotion, corporate gifts, fund-raising, or educational purposes. Special editions can also be created to specifications. For details, contact the Special Sales Department, Skyhorse Publishing, 307 West 36th Street, 11th Floor, New York, NY 10018 or info@skyhorsepublishing.com.

Skyhorse® and Skyhorse Publishing® are registered trademarks of Skyhorse Publishing, Inc.®, a Delaware corporation.

www.skyhorsepublishing.com

10 9 8 7 6 5 4 3 2 1

Library of Congress Cataloging-in-Publication Data is available on file.

ISBN: 978-1-61608-341-0

Printed in China

617. 564

Contents

Foreword
to the 2012 Edition

IF YOU SUFFER FROM LOW BACK PAIN, THIS BOOK CAN BE your life saver. I know because I had back pain so crippling after a car accident that I thought I would spend the rest of my life in a wheelchair. But I became a new man after Dr. Hans Kraus started me on the therapeutic exercise program shown on pages 85–165.

How could that have happened? The answer is simple. Hans and his associates at Columbia-Presbyterian Medical Center in New York City had, as he recounts in this book, found that slightly more than 80 percent of the cases of low back pain suffered by some 3,000 people came from tense and/or weak muscles, not the spine, and that therapeutic exercises could correct the problem.

As Dr. Frederick Seitz, the president of the National Academy of Sciences, stated when this book was first published in 1965, "Every individual who has suffered backache should become familiar with the principles and corrective measures to which Dr. Kraus has devoted so much of his career."

As a senior writer for *Sports Illustrated*, I was well aware of Hans's outstanding reputation. Originally trained as an orthopedic surgeon, he became a world pioneer in the field of physical medicine and rehabilitation, and he was, in the words of the *New York Times*, "the originator of sports medicine in the U.S." Thanks to Hans, in 1955 President Dwight Eisenhower started the President's Council on Physical Fitness and Sports. His next visit to the White House came in October of 1961, to examine President John F. Kennedy's debilitating back pain. Before winning the presidency in 1960, Kennedy underwent three failed back operations, two so disastrous that he received the last rites of the Catholic Church when it was feared that he might die.

Hans found Kennedy "so weak that he couldn't do a single sit-up and . . . so tight that his leg muscles felt 'as taut as piano wire,'" according to Susan E. B. Schwartz's book, *JFK's Secret Back Doctor: The Remarkable Life of Medical Pioneer and Legendary Rock Climber Hans Kraus*. Asked to touch his toes, Kennedy could not even reach his knees. Hans prescribed an exercise program, and said that he would need to come to the White House at least three times a week to check on progress. Kennedy was hesitant: "I don't know," he said. "What if the reporters start writing again about my health problems?" Always to the point, Hans shot back, "It's your decision. But when you get worse, what will they write then?"

By the summer of 1963 JFK was greatly improved. Admiral George Burkley, the official White House physician, watched the president perform exercises that would "credit a gymnast," and for the first time he could romp and play with daughter Caroline and son John. In November he was assassinated.

In 1965 Hans asked me to assist him in editing *The Cause, Prevention and Treatment of Backache, Stress and Tension*, and I readily agreed, grateful for what he had done for me. The book offered the opportunity to spread the word to others who needlessly suffered from back pain that can bring life to a despairing stop.

Today, given that back pain remains a mystery to many doctors and that the number of afflicted has ballooned to mega-epidemic proportions, Skyhorse Publishing has performed a public service in bringing this self-help medical classic back into print.

Publication comes at a truly critical time. Low back pain now strikes eight out of ten Americans sometime in life. In the main, there are, as Hans prophetically noted, two causes: Physical inactivity brought about by the ceaseless proliferation of labor-saving devices and appliances causes millions upon millions to lead a largely sedentary existence, while they are simultaneously bombarded by the stresses and tensions inherent in a frenetic twenty-first-century society. As a result, people sit and seethe and muscles tense and stiffen, unrelieved by the daily physical exercise that came naturally to previous generations. As Hans put it, back pain is one of the diseases born of modern civilization.

While it is impossible to put a price on pain, medical treatment of back pain now approaches $80 billion a year—*repeat $80 billion a year*—attributable in good part to unsuccessful surgeries that often leave patients worse off and in utter despair when therapeutic exercise could have done the job. "Once someone has had a back operation, even once, you never know," Hans told biographer Schwartz. "Backs don't like to be operated on."

Born in 1905 in Trieste, a then major port on the Adriatic Sea for the Austro Hungarian Empire, Hans was the first of three children born to Ella and Rudi Kraus. A prosperous shipper, Rudi hired a young Irish expatriate named James Joyce to teach him and his wife English. In 1915 when Italy entered the First World War against Austria-Hungary, the military ordered Trieste evacuated, and the Kraus and Joyce families moved to Zurich in neutral Switzerland. There young Hans would go to the Joyces' apartment for English lessons. "My parents and I knew that Joyce was a writer," Hans told *The New Yorker*. "He was not then the James Joyce that the world knows now, but I was greatly impressed by him. He was a very friendly and very charming man who treated me like a grownup, and not like a child, and he taught me not only English but Italian." (Years later when a friend exclaimed to Hans in mounting excitement, "Just think, Hans, James Joyce, James Joyce, was your parents' English teacher in Trieste, and then he taught you in Zurich! James Joyce was your English teacher! He discussed ideas in *Ulysses* with you while he was writing it! James Joyce, your very own English teacher!" Hans replied, "Ja, he dint do a goot chob, dit he?")

Rudi saw to it that his children led a vigorous outdoor life, and for Hans, starting at age four, mountaineering became a lifelong enthusiasm after he clambered up his first hill and, at age eleven, ascended the 9,500-foot-high Vrenelisarti in Switzerland. He continued climbing into his seventies and won an international reputation with first ascents in the Alps, the Tetons and the Wind River Range in Wyoming, the Cascades in Washington, and the Bugaboos in British Columbia.

Invited to join the first two American expeditions to Mount Everest, prior commitments—one to treat President Kennedy—forced him to decline. He was also celebrated for his proficiency at rock climbing, and he pioneered a number of routes on the challenging cliffs of the Shawangunks ("the Gunks") near his weekend home in the Hudson Valley with his friend Fritz Weissner who, in 1939, without oxygen, came within 750 feet of the top of K2.

After the First World War, the Kraus family moved to Vienna where Hans attended a commercial gymnasium—a business high school—instead of a college-bound, liberal arts-science gymnasium because his father wanted him to join the shipping company. But that career path changed dramatically, William Oscar Johnson reported in an *SI* profile, after sixteen-year-old Hans and a teenage friend were climbing the Pluider Kogel in the Austrian Alps.

"We were putting up a first ascent on the face," Hans said, "and before the first ridge my friend fell. We had no pitons, we had no equipment. It was an unpardonable thing. I tried to hold the rope to keep him from falling. I gripped the rope as tight as I could, but, of course, I could not stop him. The rope ripped and burned through my hands as he fell. My palms and fingers were denuded of their skin. They were stripped to the fascia. In some places the tendons showed."

Scrambling 2,000 feet down, Hans found his friend's battered body and went for help with his rope-burned hands "in terrible shape, bleeding heavily and growing stiffer. The local doctor said I should be very happy to be alive, that I was incredibly lucky, but he also said that I would never be able to move my fingers again. He predicted that I would be equipped with stiffened claws because of what the rope had done to my hands. He bound them in bandages and said that was all that could be done."

At home Hans learned his first lesson in the value of exercise as he soaked his hands in hot water twice a day: "As I soaked them, I moved the fingers. Slowly at first, painfully they moved. But they did move. I kept it up. By some instinct, the idea of movement instead of immobilization worked for me. My hands were never quite perfect again, but

I could move my fingers very well." He resumed climbing and skiing, and he fenced, boxed, and did gymnastics.

After graduating from the commercial gymnasium, Hans decided to become a doctor, despite his father's objections. He worked during the day and for ten months went to night school to make up for the liberal arts and science courses he had missed. He then took the eighteen entrance examinations, not for admission to college, but for direct admission to the University of Vienna Medical School. He scored As in all eighteen, and his father gave in.

While an intern in surgery, Hans learned more about using exercise as a healing agent for muscle injury, and that ethyl chloride spray could speed healing by allowing immediate movement. *The Journal of the American Medical Association* published an account of his techniques, and surgeons at Columbia-Presbyterian Medical Center had him demonstrate them.

In 1938, after Nazi Germany seized Austria, the Kraus family settled in the New York area and Hans served on the staff of Columbia-Presbyterian. Later he became affiliated with Bellevue and Metropolitan hospitals in the city and served as an associate professor of physical medicine and rehabilitation at the New York University College of Medicine. In private practice, his skiing connections soon brought him patients. His wife, the former Madi Springer-Miller, was on the 1958 United States ski team, and in 1974 he was elected to the Ski Hall of Fame for his medical contributions to the sport. One of his many grateful patients was skier Billy Kidd, who appeared on the cover of *Life* when he became the first American to win a gold medal in the FIS World Championships. "Thanks for putting me here," Kidd wrote on a copy of the *Life* cover he inscribed to Hans.

In 1974, at the urging of YMCA physical educator Alexander Melleby, an initially reluctant Hans agreed to help establish the Y's Way to a Healthy Back program based on his exercises. By the time the program ended a decade later, following Melleby's retirement, more than 300,000 people in the United States, Canada, Australia, and Japan, had participated, and the largest follow-up study ever done anywhere on sufferers of back pain found that 80.7 percent of 11,809 people experienced improvement after just six weeks.

As one who has benefited doing Hans's exercises for almost fifty years, I can tell you that while they are simple to do, the results are profound. However, as Hans always advised readers, consult with your physician to make sure that you do not have a condition that could make the exercises inappropriate for you.

—Robert H. Boyle

BACKACHE, STRESS,
AND TENSION

chapter 1

Test Yourself

PROGRESS BRINGS BENEFITS. IT ALSO BRINGS PERILS. MAN has been on earth for more than 100,000 years, and yet in the last hundred years, a brief flash in the infinity of time, he has changed his environment in revolutionary fashion. He has moved from a life of hard physical activity to a life of inertia in which machines do the work. He has moved from the quiet of the countryside to the city with its ceaseless irritations.

Nowhere is this more true than in the United States. On the face of it we have benefited greatly by progress. We are the most prosperous nation in the world. We have a superabundance of automobiles, appliances, and other labor-saving devices. In medicine we have conquered tuberculosis, polio, diphtheria, and a host of other diseases. Yet at the same time progress also has brought perils of its own. We have so altered the physical balance of our lives that we are now beset by a new wave of degenerative diseases. We have become so physically inactive that underexercise, often in conjunction with over-irritation, has become the most serious threat to the health of Americans. Approximately one out of every two Americans is underexercised, and you may be among them. If you are, you should be seriously concerned about your health. Underexercise is a major factor in causing back pain and tension syndrome (stiff neck and headache), and even emotional instability, duodenal ulcers, diabetes, and heart disease.

These degenerative afflictions are known as the hypokinetic diseases, the sicknesses caused by insufficent exercise. These are the diseases of an advanced civilization, and only in the last ten or fifteen years have we started to cope with them. Fortunately there is a way for you, or the members of your family, to find out if you are underexercised and a potential target for disease. You can test yourself by taking the six simple tests shown below. These are known as the Kraus–Weber tests, and they are for everyone, regardless of age, height, or weight. Designed to test the key muscle groups in your body, they reveal whether or not you have the necessary strength to handle your own body weight and the flexibility to match your height.

Before you test yourself, make yourself comfortable. Take off your shoes. Try to put yourself in a relaxed frame of mind. Do not rush. Do not push. Do not strain. Simply take the tests as directed. If you have back trouble or any other health problems, check with your physician before taking these tests.

Test 1

Lie flat on your back on the floor with your hands clasped behind your neck and with your legs straight and touching. Now keep your knees straight and lift your feet so that your heels are ten inches above the floor, as shown in the image. You pass this test if you can hold that position for ten seconds. This test shows if your hip flexors have sufficient strength.

Test 2

Lie flat on the floor again with your hands clasped behind your neck. Have someone hold down your legs by grasping the ankles as shown. If you live alone, hook your ankles under a heavy chair that won't topple. All right,

now pass the test by rolling up into a sitting position. You pass if you can do one sit-up. This test reveals whether or not your hip flexors *and* stomach muscles combined are strong enough to handle your body weight.

Test 3

Once again, lie flat on the floor with your hands behind your neck, only this time have your knees flexed, heels close to buttocks. Make sure your ankles are held down. Now roll up into a sitting position again. This tests the strength of your stomach muscles.

Test 4

Turn over onto your stomach. Put a pillow under your abdomen, clasp your hands behind your neck, and lie flat on the floor. Have your helper hold the lower half of your body steady by placing one hand in the small of the back and the other on your ankles. Now lift your trunk and hold it steady for ten seconds. This test reveals whether or not your back muscles are strong.

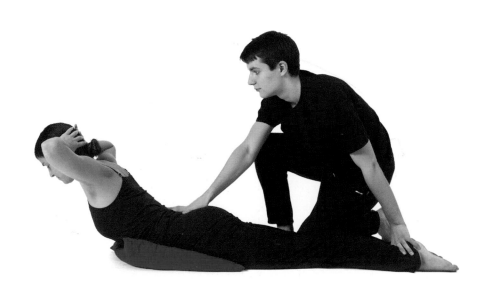

Test 5

Stay on your stomach, fold your arms under your head, and make sure that the pillow is still under your abdomen. Have your helper hold your back steady with both hands. Now lift your legs up, be sure to keep your knees straight, and hold the position for ten seconds. This tests the strength of your low back muscles.

Test 6

This is the last test. Stand up straight and make sure your feet are together. Now relax, lean over, and touch the floor with your fingertips without bending your knees. If you can pass this test, you have sufficient flexibility in your back muscles and hamstrings, the muscles in the back of your thighs. If you fail, it is because these muscles have become shortened and tense, not because your arms are too short or your legs too long.

These K-W tests are among the most important you can take to check your health. If you passed all six, you are meeting *the minimum levels of muscular fitness*. That is, you have sufficient strength and flexibility for your weight and height. But if you failed even one of the six tests you are underexercised or overtensed and you need help. In fact, if you had difficulty passing any one of these tests, you should consider yourself below par. This may seem severe or unfair, but you would not be considered healthy if you had perfect vision and hearing, a good pulse rate, but an abnormal red-cell blood count.

This book is directed not only to anyone who is underexercised but also toward anyone already suffering from back pain, stiff neck, or tension. Back pain and underexercise are intimately related. Clinical studies show that more than 80 percent of all back-pain cases are caused by underexercise. Clinical evidence also shows that if you failed one or more of the above tests, and do not yet have back pain, the odds are excellent that you will suffer from back pain in the future. And back pain is often merely the first of the hypokinetic diseases to strike the underexercised.

Back pain, or tension syndrome, is no joy. The pain can strike almost anywhere from the neck to the waist. It can be the pulsing throb of a tension headache so excruciating it is torture to try to focus your eyes; tense neck muscles can cause this. Tense neck and shoulder muscles can also cause a horrible stiff neck that makes it agony to turn from side to side. Some people, often those with desk jobs, suffer stabbing pain between the shoulder blades. But the worst of all is low back pain. A bad case of low back pain makes you think that you're crippled for life. If your muscles are weak and tense, low back pain can strike at any time. Suddenly all the tension that has been building up in your system seems to focus across the lower back, just above the buttocks. In an instant, as you go to turn or twist, or to stoop or straighten up, muscles go into a wracking spasm. You cannot move. You are locked into position. You wonder what hit you. You wonder if you dare straighten up. You try to, and you immediately feel as though someone has stuck a knife in your spine. You try to get to a chair, and the pain increases even more. Finally you manage to lie down. When the pain is really piercing, you cannot get up. You can't move your legs. Even a slight shift in bed triggers the pain. For a day or two the pain persists. Then slowly it ebbs. At last you manage to hobble out of bed. Then the pain seems to go away, and you gingerly test your back. A week, a month, maybe two months later, the pain attacks again. This time it's worse. You wonder what's wrong. Nothing seems to help.

All this is very familiar to physicians; they hear it from patients all the time. But these patients can be helped, and you can be helped. If these patients had been in reasonable condition, if they could have passed the six K-W tests, probably, they never would have needed help. If they had led more balanced lives—if they had exercised, and exercised correctly—they would have felt fine. They would have had healthy backs, sound backs, fit backs, not sick backs, not muscularly deficient backs.

Let me give you a case in point of a sick back sufferer who was warned five years ahead of time that he was bound to have trouble. I'll call him Pete Hamilton. He is a magazine staff writer, and we first met over the telephone when he called me at my country place. This was in 1955, and the K-W tests were "news" because of a report I had given to the then president, Dwight Eisenhower.

"I want to know all about the Kraus-Weber tests, what they mean, everything," said Mr. Hamilton over the phone. "If you don't mind, I'd like to fly up to see you today. I have to do the story quickly."

"All right," I said. "Come on up and we'll talk."

Pete Hamilton arrived that afternoon. He was a pleasant young man in his late twenties. He was of medium height and was just starting to run to fat. He was perhaps five or ten pounds overweight. But what really struck me about him was his intensity. He was all wound up. He exuded tension. In fact, when I met him at the airport, he was suffering from a tension headache. He said he didn't like to fly and that he had gotten the headache on the way up.

Well, everything went fine that day. I gave Mr. Hamilton all sorts of facts, and we talked and talked until ten or eleven that night. The next morning, after we had breakfast, he asked, "Would you mind putting me through the Kraus-Weber tests?"

"Not at all," I said. "I'd be delighted."

He took off his shoes and got down on the floor. I gave him the six tests. He had good strength; he had no trouble whatsoever moving his body weight. But as I had figured from watching him, he was tense. In fact, he was so tense that he failed the floor-touch test, which gauges the flexibility of the back muscles and the hamstrings. When I say he failed, I mean he really failed. Strain and grunt as he did, he couldn't get his finger tips to within six inches of the floor. I checked his hamstrings, and they felt as unyielding as piano wire.

I said, "If I ever saw a candidate for back pain, you're it. You're simply too tense. Tell me, what do you do for exercise?"

"Nothing," he said.

"Don't you exercise at all?" I asked. "Don't you ever work out in a gym? Don't you swim?"

"No, Doctor," he said. "I was as active as could be when I was a kid. But when I reached sixteen or seventeen, I started to study a lot and I just sort of let exercise slide by. Besides, I'm very busy with my work, and in addition to that I live in the city, and unless I happen to live across the street from a tennis court or a pool, I just can't be bothered to take the time. I feel okay. I know I'm tense, but that's me, I'm just naturally a tense person."

"That may be you," I said, "but that shouldn't be you. Tension is very bad for your muscles. It shortens them.

15

That's why you can't even get close to the floor with your finger tips. I strongly recommend that you start a regular exercise program to relieve the tension and make you relaxed."

"I'm sorry, Doctor," Pete said, "but I'm just too rushed to do that."

"You're wrong," I said. "But you run your life your own way and see what happens."

Pete Hamilton went off and wrote his story. I read it, and he had done an accurate job. He told everyone what was wrong with under-exercised and overstimulated living, and he told everyone why they should exercise. Of course, he didn't write in the story that he himself was "too busy" to exercise. Pete was one of those people who believe in fitness for everyone but himself.

I didn't see Pete Hamilton until five years later, and when I did he limped into the clinic, bent over at the waist, a look of agony on his face. He smiled ruefully and slowly backed into a chair to tell me what had happened.

"After I saw you, Doctor," Pete began, "I moved out to the Midwest to work as a correspondent. Then my wife and I moved to the West Coast. Two years ago we moved back to New York. We bought a house up in the country, and I began commuting. About a month after we moved in, I happened to use the car to go to the office. It was raining when I started back home, and to make the story brief, I went into a skid, a bad skid, on the parkway. There were cars coming at me from the opposite direction, and since I didn't want to slam into them head on, I yanked the wheel in the opposite direction, and I really went for a ride. The car turned around three times before stopping, but the odd thing was that I was okay. So I thought. I didn't have a scratch, although the car was smashed up against a guardrail. But the next day at home—I had the day off—I felt a slight pain in the lower back. It bothered me, but I didn't think it was bad. Then, a few minutes later, I went to pick up a piece of paper from the kitchen floor, and, wham, I fell down. It was as though someone had swung an ax into the base of my spine. I was flat on my face and I couldn't move my legs. I stayed there for a half hour until my wife found me. She called the volunteer fire department.

They came, put me in a stretcher—boy, did that hurt—and took me up-stairs to bed. My wife called our doctor, and he called an ambulance. I spent a week in the hospital in traction.

"I wore a brace when I came home, but the back just got worse. Two months later it went out again. This time I spent three weeks in bed. I just couldn't face the hospital again. At Christmas my back went out again. In the spring I was laid up for a month. Two months ago the back went out again. Now I am desperate. My doctor says I may need a spinal fusion, but before he operates, he wants you to see me. Doctor, is there *anything* you can do?"

When I finished examining him, I said, "Let's forget about surgery now. When you skidded in that car, your back muscles couldn't relax. They had no give to meet this emergency. They had been shortened by constant tension, and you tore a muscle slightly. Since you are tense, the muscles have never had a chance to relax and heal the tear. This may be all that's ailing you. Now here's what we will try. First, get rid of the brace. It will only weaken your stomach muscles, and the ex-amination shows you have all the strength you need. What you need are relaxing exercises, exercises to stretch your hamstrings and back muscles. These will help those shortened muscles to become flexible and resilient. You will get rid of the tension. Do not do any bending or lifting for the present. Come to the clinic three times a week for the next two months. The therapist will give you certain exercises to do. Learn how to do them properly, then we'll examine you again. Above all, don't worry."

Three months later Pete Hamilton was fine. He could walk erect. He could touch the floor with his finger tips. The pain was gone. The tension was gone. Soon he was on his own, doing a daily set of prescribed exercises that he had learned in our clinic. Not long ago Pete Hamilton called to ask me to treat a friend. During the conversation he said, "Doctor, I want you to know that I feel just great. I do the exercises every day, and I have no pain. I run, I swim, I chop two or three cords of wood a winter, but above all, I don't feel tense all the time. If I start to feel tense, I'll take a half hour, shut out the world, and do my exercises. After that I'm as relaxed as can be."

I'm glad that Pete is fine now. I'm only sorry that he did not avoid all the pain and anguish that he had been warned about. But you don't have to do anything as dramatic as wrecking your car to hurt your back. That sudden jab of pain which can lock your muscles tight can strike at any time. You may stoop over to pick a flower and suddenly your back muscles are in spasm. Back pain may strike when you start to get up from a chair, or when you're tying your shoelaces, or swinging a golf club or a tennis racket, or simply turning a doorknob. When it strikes, you know it. And when it strikes once, it will come back, again and again, unless you do something about it.

Severe back pain is one of the most common medical complaints today, and yet it is one of the least understood. Why? Because the underlying causes of back pain are so subtle and so insidious. Being out of shape has become one of the accepted facts of American life, and most people are in such poor shape that the abnormal is thought of as the normal.

Back pain occurs most often for two reasons. First of all, millions of Americans are underexercised. We live in a sedentary age. Progress has robbed us of our physical heritage. One hundred years ago you would have had to do hard physical tasks in the ordinary routine of living. You would have walked, run, ridden a horse, chopped wood, plowed fields, or done household chores that were muscularly demanding. But look at the easy life you lead now. Instead of walking or running, you drive a car. And the car has power steering—you don't even have to move your arms. Instead of climbing stairs, you take an elevator. When you want heat, you don't shovel coal; you simply turn up a thermostat. When you do laundry, you just dump it in a machine. And when you want to dry it, you dump it in another. You do not have to wash dishes; a machine does it for you. There are appliances all over the house. Mixers have done away with the egg beater. Vacuum cleaners have supplanted the broom. There are electric razors and even electric toothbrushes. When you ski, you take a chair lift up the hill; when you play golf, you ride a cart. In short, you lead a mechanized push-button life, and so do many other Americans. And millions are underexercised as a result.

The other contributing factor is tension. In years past you would have worked off your tension doing physical tasks. Nowadays, not only do you not do physical work, but you live in a hectic age of crowded cities, and suburbs as well. You are overstimulated and over-irritated every day. There is the rush to the office in the morning, the annoyance of traffic jams, late trains and slow buses, the constant chatter of TV commercials, the pesky appliance that won't work, the continuous ring of the telephone, the loud radio next door. When you are irritated by any one of these or similar annoyances, muscles actually tense in preparation for action. Repeated irritations will make the muscles stiff and short. The next time the phone rings or a commercial blares; notice how you stiffen and tense. Think of how many times a day countless irritations like this occur.

On top of these external irritants there are internal irritations. You may be worried and under strain because of a personal problem, which can be anything from money worries to unhappy sex relations. These internal problems can make you tense just from thinking about them. Your emotions affect your muscles. The two are bound together, not only physiologically but semantically. The word "emotion" literally means "to move." Your muscles reflect your emotional problems. When you say that a certain problem is "a pain in the neck" or "a headache," or that so-and-so is "a pain in the behind," you are speaking the truth.

The underexercised and over-irritated life we lead today is especially bad for children, who should be developing strong and resilient muscles for adulthood. Children rarely suffer from back pain, but youngsters with weak and tense muscles will be lucky if they suffer only back pain when they reach their twenties. When you grew up a generation ago, you led a far more vigorous childhood than the majority of youngsters do today. If your muscles act up, you at least have a base on which to build: the muscles you developed as a youngster. But the situation has gotten worse in recent years. For one thing, television has a doubly bad effect on youngsters. A child gets no physical benefit whatsoever from watching television. Also, a child gets tense from television. His muscles will become tense and shortened, and he will assume poor posture. Instead of getting tense watching cowboys and Indians indoors, a youngster should be outdoors getting rid of tension playing cowboys and Indians.

Back pain may begin early in life, in the twenties or thirties. It hits men and women alike. It can hit men and women at any time, but there are two periods in a woman's life when she is most likely to suffer. These are after she has a child and when she is in menopause. A woman in change of life is prone to back pain because she is under tension and because her hormonal balance is upset. A woman who has just had a child is in danger because of all the lifting she has to do. She also may be under stress. Take the case of Jane C., a very attractive suburban mother. As a young girl, Jane grew up in the city. She enjoyed good health, but she never was physically active. Jane got married when she was twenty-two. She and her husband moved to a suburban town, and they were very happy. A year after they were married Jane gave birth to a boy. A month before the baby was born, she woke up one night in bed with a dull ache in the middle of the lower part of her back. Her husband rubbed the ache for her, and she went back to sleep. But when Jane woke up in the morning, the ache was still there, and she dragged herself through the day. She didn't feel irritable; she just felt blah. She thought the ache came from being in the late stages of pregnancy, and she was right. The only trouble was that she also thought it would go away after she had the baby, and she didn't say anything to her obstetrician.

But when Jane came home from the hospital with the baby, the dull ache had become sharp pain. And it wasn't just in the lower back either; it smarted sharply down into her left buttock. She tried to put the pain out of her mind as she looked after the infant—nursing him, changing him, feeding him—but as the months went by the pain grew in severity.

One night, when the baby was about four months old, Jane couldn't sleep. Now the pain was shooting down her left leg. From the lower back to above the back of her knee, it was one pulsing throb. She found it impossible to get back to sleep, and the next morning she made an appointment with her obstetrician. He examined her and found nothing wrong.

The pain continued, and Jane called her general practitioner. It was the same story. When the baby was a year and a half old and Jane was at her wit's end, the pain suddenly stopped.

Two years later Jane became pregnant again. Two months before this baby was due the back pain returned. This time the pain began by shooting down her left leg. She had a restless, irritable pregnancy. She was glad to see that the baby, another son, was fine and healthy, but right after she returned home with him she started to resent him. She hated herself for feeling this way, but the more she had to tend the baby, the more she resented him because the pain was just too much and she blamed the baby for her discomfort. Now she couldn't even get to sleep at night. She tossed fitfully for hours, and when she did lapse into sleep, it was the sleep of the exhausted. One again she saw her obstetrician. Again he could find nothing wrong. Her G.P. finally referred her to our clinic.

We examined her carefully, had X-rays taken, and finally put her through the K-W tests described at the beginning of this chapter. After Jane took them, I looked over her medical history once more and then told her, "You have nothing to worry about as long as you follow directions. Let me tell you what the trouble is. First of all, as you know even better than I do, your lower back muscles are very, very tender. That is because they are tight. Why are they tight? Not because you're a tense person—although you are starting to get tense from worrying about your back—but because you don't have any strength in your stomach muscles. The pain started in the eighth month of your first pregnancy, and you got it because your weak stomach muscles forced you to carry the weight of the child with your back muscles. Your stomach muscles were weak because you never had made them strong when you were a child. Now, the pain got worse after you had the baby because you had to bend over and lift him, you had to carry him, and you had to change his diapers. Then, when he was a year and a half old, he could walk by himself, and so you didn't have to lift him as much and the pain subsided.

"But with the second pregnancy and the second child, the pain came back. You have simply put too much of a load on your back muscles. Now, what you have to do is to build up the strength of those stomach muscles, and you are going to do that by following a daily exercise program. At first you will need more rest and a corset for your back—until your muscles get strong enough to support it unaided."

That day Jane began exercising to strengthen her stomach muscles. She did the exercises every day, and her back pain gradually subsided. By doing exercises prescribed to correct the weakness that had made her back unbearable, Jane was able to avoid future difficulty.

Often tension has a great deal to do with back pain. In fact, tension, or lack of flexibility, is responsible for more attacks of back pain than any other single cause. Even if you are physically strong, you can be struck with a bad back, caused by tension, that will render you helpless. If you are over-irritated, overstimulated or even overeager, your tense mental state will be reflected in your muscles, and unless you exercise properly, the tension will accumulate. This can happen to a strong person over a period of years. Here is the case of an ex-college football star whom I'll call Steve B.

Steve grew up in a poor family. He had to hustle for everything he earned. He was a big, strapping boy, and he was tough. When he was seventeen, he was six foot two, weighed 220 pounds, and was an A student. Above all, he could really play football, and scouts from all over the country were after him. He not only had the muscle they were looking for, but he also had an intense desire to win. His childhood had made him extremely competitive.

Steve got many offers to play football. Some schools offered cash on the line, but Steve was looking for the school that would give him the best education. He finally accepted a scholarship at a prestigious eastern school. For three years he played varsity ball. He did extremely well, but he did even better in his studies. Upon graduation he joined a large industrial firm as a trainee. In five years he was a plant manager. But in the course of time, Steve changed without realizing it. He was so busy that he gave up running every morning and working out in the gym. When he was only in his mid-thirties, he was made a vice president. He was busier than ever. There were business lunches and social meetings. His work became his life. He grew tense without knowing it. His weight began to creep up on him. He was 240, then 250. He carried it well, but he was running to flab. He didn't exercise at all, but everyone who knew of him thought he was as strong and tough as he had been in the days when he was the terror of the football field. No one thought this more than Steve himself. He still had that strong competitive drive, but now it was devoted to business instead of football. The bathroom scale told Steve he was getting heavier, and his panting breath told him he was getting out of shape, but Steve paid no heed. The changes were slow and subtle; Steve accepted tension as a fate common to all executives who led the busy life he did. Like a lot of people, he accepted the abnormal as normal. Sure he was tense, but wasn't everybody else?

Then Steve's back "went out." It was not at all dramatic. It was simply the response to the inevitable. It was a gray January day, and snow had fallen all night long. Steve had an important appointment, and he had to drive to the office. The snow was two feet deep, and he had to shovel a pathway from his garage to the street. As he shoveled hurriedly, it seemed like hard work compared with what it had been in the past, but, always the competitor, Steve battled to get the job done. When he had finished shoveling, he felt a muscle twinge low in his back. He paid no attention to it. However, when he arrived at the office, he found it difficult to get out of the car. As he tried to straighten up behind the wheel, he felt a sudden stabbing pain in the lower back. He finally had to clamber out in a stooped position.

Steve struggled through, the day and managed to drive home. The pain was worse when he went to bed. He stayed in bed for a couple of days and then came to our clinic for help.

Examination showed that his stomach muscles and hip flexors were weak and that his hamstrings were stiff and tense. When I told him this,

he protested, "Doctor, I'm an athlete. I played football. I'm as strong as an ox."

"You *were* an athlete," I replied, "and if you're as strong as an ox, why can't you shovel a driveway without straining your back? You've changed. Your body has changed. You were strong, but that was fifteen years ago. You've been up to your neck in business. You don't exercise. You're extremely tense. Do you think that because you once played football when you were young that you're fine now? You must face facts."

He didn't say a word.

"Now look," I said, "there is no reason for you to become despondent. You're not permanently crippled. You just have to take stock of your condition. I can tell you what you should do, and it is up to you to cooperate if you want to get better."

First Steve needed treatment to relieve his pain. Two weeks later he embarked on therapeutic exercises designed to strengthen his stomach muscles and hip flexors and loosen his tight hamstrings. Within three months he returned to his former strength and flexibility, and he lost fourteen pounds besides. The tension ebbed. He felt fine. To this day he has continued exercises. Steve has given himself a new lease on life.

And now what about you? What can you do? You can do quite a lot.

First of all, you can exercise. You can and should exercise *correctly*, and doing this will help correct any deficiency you may have. But first a word of caution.

In recent years there has been a growing interest in exercise. There are exercise and fitness books by the dozen. Some of them even offer good exercises. But the question is, are these exercises for you? They may not be. Before you ever start exercising on a regular basis, you have to know what your individual needs are. The majority of people do not know what their needs are, yet they buy exercise books and go at the exercises with a vengeance. In doing this they often injure themselves. As a matter of fact, we regularly see two or three new patients a week who have injured themselves because they were faithfully doing the exercises handed down for everyone in one popular exercise book. Not all of us are alike in our muscular problems, and all of us cannot do the same set of exercises without risk of injury. You may lack strong stomach muscles. Your friend, Joe, has strong stomach muscles but no flexibility in his low back muscles and hamstrings. Your friend, Betty, lacks flexibility in her hamstrings and has weak hip flexors as well. All of you cannot go and do the same set of exercises from the same book and benefit because you may all have different problems. At least one of you is likely to get hurt. For instance, if you are tense and you start doing isometric exercises, the latest exercise fad, you are going to have even more tension, and you can hurt yourself badly. Isometric exercising calls upon you to tense a muscle without actually producing any movement of the limbs or body. Enthusiasts claim that if you do this tensing just a few minutes a day, you will get in excellent shape. This is not borne out by fact. Physical medicine has been aware of isometric exercises for a long time, and while the exercises will increase strength to a certain point, the gain in strength will then level off, and much more exercising of an entirely different kind is then needed to produce a really strong muscle. But the potential danger in isometrics is that they are likely to make your muscles stiff and tense—the last thing you want them to be.

Whether or not an exercise book recommends isometrics or some other form of exercise, you should be wary, even if you already are in excellent condition. Most of these books cannot consider your own particular needs. Instead they blithely give exercises for everyone. I would no more think of telling everyone to do the same set of exercises than your family doctor would tell all his patients, no matter whether they had a broken leg, sinus trouble, or heart disease, to take the same medicine. Let me cite a very recent case as an example.

Robert F. came to see us with severe pain in his upper back, between the shoulder blades. Mr. F. likes to be physically active, so when

he became very busy at the office and had no time for the tennis he ordinarily played to stay in shape, he started doing exercises to make up for the lack. He bought a very popular book, a best-seller, in fact, read it, and started doing the exercises every day. One exercise called for him to lie on the floor and arch his upper back quickly. He started with ten repetitions of this and worked his way up to twenty a day when the pain started. But he mistakenly thought there was something wrong with him so he worked his way up to forty a day, until the pain just refused to allow him to continue. When Mr. F. came to the clinic, his upper back muscles were in severe spasm. I told him to cease his exercises immediately. It took several days to relieve the pain, and then we gave him an exercise program that would relax and stretch the upper back muscles instead of making them tense and stiff. He did, and the tension subsided.

In brief, exercises must be prescribed individually to treat a specific condition. First, you must know what is wrong. You can find out what is wrong with your key posture muscles by taking the Kraus-Weber tests. Each one of those six tests is for a key muscle group in your body. For instance, if you are unable to touch the floor with your finger tips (Test 6), your lower back muscles and hamstrings are stiff and tense. Therefore you should do relaxation, limbering, and stretching exercises. If you are unable to roll up to a sitting position with your knees flexed (Test 3), your stomach muscles need strengthening exercises. It may be that you will need to do both strengthening and flexibility exercises at the same time. What you need to do, and what you can do through exercise, is spelled out completely in Chapter 6.

But exercise alone is not the answer. Proper exercise is an important key to good health, but it is only one of several keys. If you take the proper approach, you can stop the effect of tension before it even starts. You can do the same for your children either at home or in school. You can learn what sports are best for you and for them. Some sports and activities are sure to be tension builders. Others are not only tension relievers but help improve your heart and blood vessels. You should know the difference. You may be overweight and on a diet. Is your diet really necessary? It may not be.

In short, you must study yourself: your mind, your daily routine, your work and living habits, your emotional attitudes, and your body. By all means find out where you are physically weak or strong, but also try to learn what actually prompts tension or pain. You must try to find out about yourself. Once you do, you can approach your problems with a sense of purposeful direction.

ADVANTAGES OF THE PHYSICALLY ACTIVE AS COMPARED TO SEDENTARY

ACTIVE		SEDENTARY
LOW	WEIGHT	HIGH
LOW	BLOOD PRESSURE	HIGH
LOW	PULSE RATE	HIGH
LOW	NEURO-MUSCULAR TENSION	HIGH
HIGH	MUSCLE STRENGTH AND FLEXIBILITY	LOW
HIGH	BREATHING CAPACITY	LOW
HIGH	ADRENO-CORTICAL RESERVE	LOW
HIGH	TIREDNESS LEVEL	LOW
HIGH	EMOTIONAL STABILITY	LOW
HIGH	HEART STRENGTH	LOW
LATE	AGING	EARLY

chapter 2

Why Back Pain Comes

THE TREATMENT OF BACK PAIN HAS ALWAYS OFFERED A fertile field for the quack. America's first notorious quack, Elisha Perkins, who died in 1799, believed—and he was apparently sincere about this—that certain metals could yank pain from the body. He invented a device called a "tractor," consisting of two short metal rods, which he sold for $25. A patient was supposed to work the tractor by running it down over the pain.

Generally you can spot a quack because he usually has something to sell. It might be a magic board that tests against your back, or it might be a "healing" belt. Whatever it is, it is always a gimmick, it costs money, it is guaranteed to cure, and it is worthless.

There are several reasons why quacks have had a field day with back pain sufferers. First of all, back pain is a relatively new problem. In the past back pain was rare, and when it did occur, it was usually earned by serious disease or injury, such as ruptured discs. Help was sought through the normal approaches of medicine and surgery. It is only recently that "everybody" has started having a bad back, but unless a patient is afflicted with a mechanically unstable spine or a serious disease, the ailment is considered unimportant. In recent decades medical attention has focused on major surgery and research, and if back pain cannot be related to a major disability, it is considered to be of little significance. It is no wonder then that many physicians are uninterested in what might be called the garden variety of backache.

Increasing numbers of physicians and surgeons have begun to realize that garden-variety back pain is of a complex origin and must be regarded as one of the major ailments of a mechanized society. But instead of turning to braces and surgery, which are necessary only in relatively few cases, these physicians and surgeons have returned to one of the oldest and most valuable tools of medicine: therapeutic exercise. Compared with surgery, therapeutic exercise may seem undramatic, but in case after case its use has been extremely rewarding.

A century ago exercise was prescribed quite widely by physicians. In Sweden, Pehr Henrik Ling, a student of anatomy, developed a system of therapeutic exercises that was used by physicians in most countries. One of his pupils, Dr. George H. Taylor, brought his ideas to the United States and wrote a widely consulted book, *Exposition of the Swedish Movement Cure*. Exercise was regarded both as a way of promoting health and as a way of correcting bodily defects. But then, with the dramatic strides in medicine, particularly in surgery and in the development of drugs, which came toward the end of the nineteenth century, exercise began to lose out not only in medicine but in the schools as well. By the 1920s the medical aspect of exercise had been all but forgotten in the United States. Of course, at the time we were still a somewhat physically vigorous people—progress had not yet robbed us of daily physical activity.

I came upon the value of exercise through happenstance more than thirty years ago, when I was a young hospital intern in surgery. One of my jobs at the time was to serve on emergency duty, taking care of fractures. In addition to this, I had to review the results of hundreds and hundreds of cases involving wrist fractures. I had to find out how the patients were doing. Had their breaks healed? Did they still feel pain? What did follow-up X-rays show? As I went through case after case, a common pattern began to emerge: the patients who made the best recoveries were those who had exercised the most after the fracture. It made no difference if their fractures had originally been worse than those suffered by others. The fact was that the recovery rate of patients who exercised was better and quicker than that of patients who did little or no exercise.

After I reported this to our chief surgeon, the hospital started reviewing the results of other fracture cases. The findings were similar: exercise was decidedly helpful. As a result, the hospital decided to start a special department where all fracture patients could receive exercises. Shortly afterward, any patient who had spent any time at all in bed in the hospital was given special exercises to reestablish muscular strength and flexibility through systematic training.

In those early years—and this is long before the six K-W tests were even thought of—I learned a great deal from an athlete, coach, and exercise teacher named Heinz Kowalski, who ran a local gym. Originally he had been a circus acrobat, and he was an artist in conditioning the people, mostly athletes, who came to his gym for help. As I watched Kowalski, I began to see that some of his techniques could be used to treat the sick or the physically deficient. A specific instance comes to mind. Kowalski and I used to work out together at the gym, and one day I asked him, "How is it that you never send anyone with a sprain to the hospital? You send us fracture patients, but I don't know of one person you've sent us with a sprain."

"Oh," Kowalski said in his calm way, "you wouldn't know how to treat a sprain."

"What do you mean?" I asked. "We're physicians, surgeons. We certainly know how to treat sprains."

"I don't know about that," he said. "When you get your hands on someone with a sprained shoulder or a sprained ankle, you wrap him up in bandages and keep him immobilized for weeks. I don't do that.

In my family we had to perform every night in the circus. We couldn't be out of action. When we got sprains, we performed in spite of them. We knew what to do. The minute we got a sprain, we treated it with hot steam, alcohol applications, and movement. The pain went away and we could go on with our performance. The exercise did it good. The next day we were fine."

I was interested in what he had to say. Obviously hot steam and alcohol have their drawbacks—it is easy, as I found out the hard way, to scald yourself—and so I looked about for something else that would ease the pain and allow movement. After trial and error I found it— ethyl chloride spray. It is often more effective than ice or heat. When this fluid, which should be used only by physicians, is sprayed on the skin, it evaporates quickly and dulls the sense of pain by freezing. The pain must be lessened so the injured part can be moved. The movement is essential to the healing process; otherwise, the effect of the ethyl chloride is temporary. Nowadays many physicians find ethyl chloride most helpful in treating sprains and strains and in relieving the pain of back muscles in spasm.

Later on, Harold Anson Bruce, the great track coach, also taught me certain principles. Bruce was a living lesson in conditioning. He showed that you don't have to run to flab at the age of forty. When he was seventy, he competed in the national cross-country tryouts and placed fifteenth in a large field.

In 1940 I had the good fortune to work with Dr. Sonja Weber in the Posture Clinic of Columbia-Presbyterian Hospital in New York City. The clinic had been established to treat children who had posture problems. Some of the youngsters were afflicted with injuries or birth deformities, but most of our young patients were well and their bones and functions were considered normal; they had been sent to us simply because they had "poor posture."

We spent many hours in detailed examinations of the youngsters. We photographed them, made line drawings, and conducted all sorts of studies, trying to find out more about the muscles of these otherwise normal children who had bad posture. At first we had little success. We noticed that the children quickly learned to assume good posture when examined or observed but then slipped back into poor posture when they thought no one was looking.

After more investigation it occurred to us that poor posture was often the result of a muscular inability to move properly. To check on proper movement, we decided to measure the strength and flexibility of the back, stomach, and hip muscles used to hold the body erect. We spent several years experimenting with muscle measurements and muscle tests. We prescribed various corrective exercises. From time to time we would compare the results of these exercises with physical changes in the patients.

Finally we agreed on a battery of fifteen muscle tests, of which the six key tests later became known as the Kraus-Weber tests. Using them, we could quickly and easily determine which muscles were weak or tense. We could understand why children slouched, why their stomachs stuck out, why they had round shoulders or sway-backs. After giving the children the tests and noting which ones they failed, we would then give each child a specific set of exercises to correct his or her particular condition. Those who exercised according to our prescriptions often improved. Those who did the exercises and then stopped reverted to previous defects as their muscles deteriorated.

In 1944 Dr. Barbara Stimson asked Dr. Weber and me to participate in a special back clinic she had organized at Columbia-Presbyterian Hospital, under the auspices of Drs. William Darrach and Clay Ray Murray. Later on the work was pursued at Dr. Howard Rusk's Institute for Physical Medicine and Rehabilitation at New York University. Dr. Stimson had started the clinic to find the cause for the ever-increasing number of back pain sufferers. Back pain had become a problem in the armed services, in industry, and in everyday life. The clinic staff at Columbia-Presbyterian Hospital included orthopedic surgeons, internists, neurosurgeons, psychiatrists, and neurologists. X-ray and routine laboratory tests were made of every back-pain patient. In more than 80 percent of the cases, nothing at all abnormal was found. Dr. Weber and I were then asked to study the muscular efficiency of these patients. We decided to use the six key tests we had developed for children at the Posture Clinic. Upon administering the tests to the back patients, we at

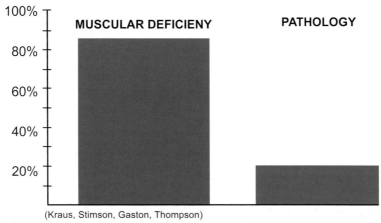

LOW BACK PAIN

Over 80% of low back pain is due to muscular deficiency

(Kraus, Stimson, Gaston, Thompson)

80% of low back pain is due to lack of adequate physical activity.
(H. Kraus, B. Stison, S. Gaston, W. Thompson).

once discovered that not only were they weak and tense but we could see exactly where the deficiencies were. Exercises were prescribed to fit each individual case.

The benefits of the exercises were soon evident. The patients who did them faithfully often found relief from back pain in a few weeks or months. Those who did not exercise continued to suffer. Their suffering was understandable, because muscles are healthy only when they are properly used.

It took us only a little more time to realize something else: we had not only discovered an effective way of relieving muscular back pain, but, more importantly perhaps, we had found, in the six Kraus-Weber tests, *a way of predicting potential back trouble.* We discovered this when we began giving the Kraus-Weber tests to "healthy" people. Even though these people were considered well and had no pain, we often found that a person who failed even one of the six Kraus-Weber tests was a prime candidate for back trouble.

Dr. Weber and I both began to speculate about the general causes of back pain. We were very aware of the fact that people from all walks of life, from the armed forces to industry, were coming up with complaints. Discussing the problem back and forth, we wondered if many people had become weak and tense because now they were leading lives that were largely sedentary. In order to determine whether or not sedentary living habits were actually at the root of back trouble, we decided to test American school children and compare them with European school children who lacked such "benefits' of progress as television sets and automobiles. In 1952 we tested more than 5,000 healthy American children between the ages of six and sixteen in a half dozen urban and suburban areas in this country. These children, mind you, had all the care and medicine that an affluent society could give them.

These youngsters did poorly on the Kraus-Weber tests. They were amazingly weak and tense. Then we went to other less mechanized countries. In Austria, Italy, and Switzerland we tested about 3,000 children in the same age group. The difference was startling. Very few were weak or tense. In brief, we found:

- that 57.9 percent of the American children failed one or more of the six tests, while only 8.7 percent of the European children failed;
- that 44.3 percent of the American children failed the flexibility test, while only 7.8 percent of the European children failed;
- that 35.7 percent of the American children failed one or more of the strength tests, while only 1.1 percent of the European children failed.

Realizing that we had important facts to reveal to both physicians and physical educators, we presented our findings at the annual meeting of the New York State Medical Society in 1954. The reception was somewhat cool, but it was warm compared with the chilly welcome we got at the annual meeting of the American Association for Health, Physical Education and Recreation. The physical educators politely applauded but simply refused to admit there was a problem.

We carried on with our work. We continued our clinical studies of back patients and accumulated evidence that back pain was only one of the ailments afflicting the underexercised. We began to see, as we pieced our data together bit by bit, that many back patients were sick in other ways. They were emotionally upset or under strain; they suffered from "tension," ulcers, and headaches. We then started to survey medical literature to discover if other "sedentary diseases" besides back pain had been found.

We discovered a wealth of material. We found that the protective value of exercise and physical activity extended to much more than muscles alone. Besides back pain, underexercise was correlated with coronary heart disease, duodenal ulcers, diabetes, obesity, "tension," and emotional instability.

Some of the findings were fascinating. Two British researchers, Doctors J. A. Heady and J. N. Morris, found that death from coronary heart disease occurs twice as often among the physically inactive as it does among the active. A striking example of this was a comparison study they made of drivers and conductors on double-decker buses in London. The drivers, who had to sit behind the wheel all day, were more than twice as susceptible to coronary heart disease than were their far more active colleagues, the conductors, who spent the working day climbing up and down the stairs of the buses. On this page is a graph of Morris and Heady's findings.

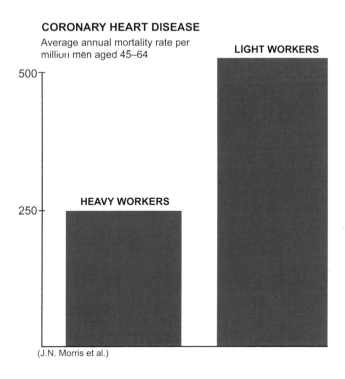

CORONARY HEART DISEASE
Average annual mortality rate per million men aged 45–64

LIGHT WORKERS

HEAVY WORKERS

500

250

(J.N. Morris et al.)

Medical researchers had also found that the physically inactive person has high neuromuscular tension, high blood pressure, high pulse rate, less vital breathing capacity, and low adrenocortical reserve. Diabetes, too, is reported to have a high incidence among the physically inactive. Dr. Jean Mayer of Harvard has done significant work on the close relationship between overweight and underexercise, showing that exercise often has more effect on your weight than does your diet. (I have more to say about this in Chapter 9). Dr. Lloyd Appleton of the U.S. Military Academy at West Point discovered that 12.9 percent of the cadets who finished in the lowest category on the Academy's physical-fitness test received psychiatric discharges. By contrast, no psychiatric difficulties were encountered in the most physically fit cadets.

At the same time that we were looking into the medical literature on the diseases caused by underexercise, we started getting reports from abroad on follow-up studies of the Kraus-Weber tests. An Austrian physician, Dr. Willi Nagler, was doing extended studies of Austrian school children we had studied previously, and his findings proved to be most

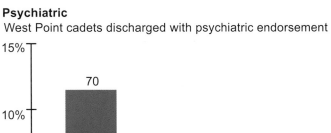

Psychiatric
West Point cadets discharged with psychiatric endorsement

Lack of physical fitness goes parallel with emotional difficulties.
(L. Appleton)

significant. As Austria recovered from the war and moved into an era of prosperity, complete with television, automobiles, and appliances, the rate of failure on the K-W tests almost doubled.

Like the American youngsters, the Austrian children were starting to pay the penalties of progress by becoming underexercised. Reports came in from all over the world and, basically, they showed that physical fitness declined with mechanization and urbanization. Failure rates on tests shot up as a country became more prosperous. As the most prosperous nation in the world, the United States was in an ignominious position. It had—and still has—the most physically unfit youngsters. In tests administered by the Asian Foundation, Pakistani youngsters also rated much higher than their American counterparts. This was also true in Japan where researchers at Kyushu University studied 6,000 children.

These facts were disputed by physical educators. They declared the tests "invalid" and the findings inconclusive, even though they could not offer logical reasons for their opposition. In time the American Association for Health, Physical Education and Recreation composed their own test based on the movements of 5,000 American children. The test included running, jumping, and throwing a softball, and an average standard was established for the average child in different age groups. The test was then given in school systems all across the country, and most of them, of course, could happily state that their children were meeting the average standards.

No one seemed concerned that these "average" standards might not be up to standards in other countries until two physical educators, W. R. Campbell and R. H. Pohndorf, gave the test to 10,000 British boys and girls. Excluding the softball throw, the British youngsters scored 24 percent higher than American youngsters.

Dr. Weber and I decided to study a group of adult Americans who were, almost by definition, physically inactive. We picked psychoanalysts, who sat in their offices all day listening to their patients. We followed case histories of twenty-six analysts with back pain from two to 10 years, and we sent out hundreds of questionnaires to members of the American Psychoanalytical Association. Here is what we found:

We got clear answers to our questionnaires from 423 psychoanalysts. Of these, 144 exercised regularly and had no complaint of back pain; 107 did not exercise and did have pain; 47 analysts had back pain that was relieved by exercise; 52 had pain despite physical activity; 29 did not exercise and had no pain; 44 had disc trouble. The results were even clearer with the twenty-six analysts we personally studied. We prescribed exercises and encouraged them to move around for five minutes between patients. Our most recent follow-up survey reveals that of the twenty-six analysts, seven had no pain whatsoever, eighteen had definite relief, and one still had pain. This analyst, we later learned, had stopped his exercise therapy.

As we delved further and further into medical research on the underexercised, I could not help but recall that, in the past, physicians often told patients who were getting overweight that they should become more active, that they should chop wood, run, and even climb mountains. But in recent years too many physicians, it seemed, were giving overweight patients a diet—crash, gradual, or otherwise—and said little, if anything, about exercise. I still remember a book that proclaims, "Exercise Is Bosh." Indeed, even the *New York Times* Sunday Magazine Section carried an article by, of all people, a physician saying the same thing. None of these writings, and there are many others, are substantiated by facts.

In any event, the idea that underexercise was responsible, in whole or in part, for many ills was regarded as extremely radical in medical circles as recently as the 1950s. This I found when my associates and I presented our findings at the 1955 annual meeting of the American Medical Association.

We used the term hypokinetic disease to describe all the ailments—from back pain to heart trouble—induced at least in part by underexercise. Hypokinetic comes from the Greek, and by hypokinetic disease we mean all the sicknesses prompted by insufficient motion. Nowadays hypokinetic disease has become a most respectable term—there have even been United States Government posters saying: "Fight Hypokinesia"—but at the time it was really Greek to most people.

True, we won a prize for the exhibit we presented on "hypokinetic disease," but most of the audience did not believe in exercise at all, and they were practically shouting at me when discussing my paper.

Among other things, my associates and I were accused of being unpatriotic. We were told, of all things, that we were maligning American athletes. Then one of the audience got up and said that we were wrong about American youngsters being weak and tense, because he happened to have a three-year-old boy he could not follow around the house. I suppose he considered this clinical evidence. His baby, he declared in ringing tones, was more active and faster than he was. I could only congratulate him on having such a healthy child; politeness forbade my commenting on the underexercised father.

There was one physician in the audience, however, who stood up and agreed with us wholeheartedly. This physician was Dr. Jessie Wright, who had been in charge of several children's clinics for many years, and she could bear out what we had found. She, too, felt that children—and adults as well—were becoming less flexible, less strong—in short, less physically fit than their forefathers had been, and that they were worse off as a result.

The controversy spilled over into the press, and an article that I wrote for the *New York State Journal of Medicine* was picked up in a magazine published by the Amateur Athletic Association, and this came to the attention of a former athletic great, John B. Kelly. At the time he was best known to the public for being the father of Grace Kelly, but he had twice won Olympic gold medals for rowing and had been an adviser on physical fitness to the late president Franklin D. Roosevelt. When it came to physical fitness, Kelly played no political favorites. He called the article to the attention of the then president, Dwight Eisenhower, whom Kelly knew to be concerned with the problem. President Eisenhower then held a special sports luncheon at the White House, and he invited me and one of my research assistants, Mrs. Ruth Hirschland, to attend.

When we delivered our report, President Eisenhower, as the press later remarked, was shocked. The President subsequently established the Council for Physical Fitness. The physical educators now became interested but, in trying to get away from the word "physical," succeeded in having the name changed to the Council for Youth Fitness, ignoring the point that underexercise threatens not only children but the entire adult population. Almost all of them regarded the idea of formal exercise as unpalatable. Instead, they suggested various sports and games as an alternative. This sounds very well, but, as I point out in Chapter 7, some sports are better than others for physical conditioning and some sports may even be harmful. Sports were not and are not the answer. The answer was and is basic exercise programs geared to the correction of muscular deficiencies and development of good hearts and lungs.

At the time I simply did not realize that many physical educators had such an ingrained dislike of exercise. I found this out in 1957, when I attended a meeting with a number of physical educators. It was a very friendly session. After a few minutes we got down to the main problem. I asked. "Why are you against exercise?"

"We can't use exercises," one physical educator said.

"Why not?" I asked.

He smiled. "Very simple," he said. "Twenty-five years ago we gave exercises to school children. And as far as I'm concerned, that's enough. We were looked down on as the boobs of the school system. We had no status at all. So we changed our emphasis. Now who are we? Well, we're not the boobs we used to be. Now we're respected members of the academic community. We're educators, physical educators if you wish. We're not 'exercise teachers' any more. We're educators, coaches, and administrators. You want to know the truth? Exercise is finished! It's passé; it's out of date. You want us to turn back the clock. Well, I'm telling you, Doctor, we don't care what your findings show, we're not going back to the old days. We've worked hard to get where we are, and we're going to stay there."

Well, at least this was an honest answer. In the same way, the Council for *Youth* Fitness became increasingly bogged down in talk. At council meetings there was no point in bringing up exercise. Instead the physical educators discussed different forms of "fitness:" mental fitness, moral fitness, youth fitness, psychological fitness, and so on.

The situation got worse. Even physicians did their best to avoid the problem. I remember that, at a yearly council meeting, I made the elementary proposal to a group of physicians that we collect all the medical literature relating to the merits or demerits of physical activity as a cause of disease. I couldn't even find one physician to second the motion, but another motion—that there was no such thing as any standard for physical fitness—was quickly made, seconded, and passed! The only dissenting vote was mine. I protested. Medicine had all sorts of standards, I said. There was a standard for blood pressure. There was a standard for blood count, pulse rate, blood sugar, and body temperature. But all this was pooh-poohed. Finally I said, with some irony, "All right, I hereby make the motion that a twelve-year-old child should be able to run ten steps without collapsing." I had no sooner said this than a pediatrician jumped up and said, in all seriousness, "Yes, but that is about as far as I would go on this motion."

When John F. Kennedy was elected president, he renewed interest in physical fitness and he went right to the heart of the problem. He announced his concern in two articles he wrote for *Sports Illustrated*. In 1960 the late president reviewed the shocking results of the Kraus-Weber tests administered to youngsters in both America and Europe, and in 1962 he wrote in *Sports Illustrated* that a survey personally ordered by him revealed "that more than 10 million of our 40 million school children are unable to pass a test which measures only the minimum level of fitness, while almost 20 million would be unable to meet the standards set by a more comprehensive test of physical strength and skills.

"These figures," President Kennedy continued, "indicate the vast dimensions of a national problem which should be of deep concern to us all. It is paradoxical that the very economic progress, the technological advance and scientific breakthroughs which have, in part, been the result of our national vigor have also contributed to the draining of that vigor. Technology and automation have eliminated many of those physical exertions which were once a normal part of the working day. New forms of transportation have made it unnecessary to walk to school or to the office or the corner store. New forms of entertainment have consumed much of the time which was once used for sports and games.

"No one can deny the enormous benefits which these developments have brought—the reduction of drudgery and tedious tasks, the opportunity for greater leisure, the increased access to intellectual stimulation and quality entertainment. But at the same time we must not allow these advances to become the instruments of the decline of our national vitality and health. We cannot permit the loss of that physical vigor which has helped nourish our growth and which is essential if we are to carry forward the complex and demanding tasks which are vital to our strength and progress."

Before his tragic death President Kennedy said that he intended to take a new look at the fitness program. He was well aware of the fact that little had been done to meet the problem.

Meanwhile other physicians took great interest in the problem, among them Dr. Paul Dudley White, the heart specialist, Dr. Wilhelm Raab, director of the Cardiovascular Research Unit at the University of Vermont College of Medicine, and Dr. Hans Selye of McGill University, who has done pioneering work in stress. Their research and experience strongly buttress the data that my associates and I have collected showing that lack of exercise combined with constant irritation produces an imbalance, a sickness in our emotional and physical functions.

As research piles up, the climate is gradually changing. Many physicians are now beginning to look upon exercise with favor, though there are still some diehards. After Dr. Kenneth Lane published a fine paper, "Role of Pediatricians in Physical Fitness of Youth," in a 1959 issue of the *Journal of the American Medical Association*, there were only ridiculing letters to the editor.

Still, acceptance comes, however slowly. In 1964 the American Medical Association published a pamphlet on physical fitness. It notes, among other things, that physical activity is good protection against back pain caused by sedentary living, a helpful way of controlling weight, and a preventive of degenerative disease. The AMA pamphlet mentions that "diseases of the heart and blood vessels, diabetes, and arthritis strike the obese more often and more seriously than they strike those of desirable weight." The pamphlet further states that exercise may help relieve tension. Two pamphlets, *Vim* and *Vigor*, issued by the President's Council for Physical Fitness, also proclaim that exer-

cise will make youngsters "radiate confidence" and allow them to win friends.

The fact is, however, that exercise cannot be made palatable on the grounds that it will help you glow with charm and grace. The blunt fact is that, exercise, properly done, will help you prevent the onslaught of disease. Back pain is only one of the diseases that afflict the under-exercised, and as I discuss back pain you should bear in mind that it is representative of many troubles that may come either to you or your children. If you or they are underexercised, you can start now to correct this condition, this sickness. It is not easy. It needs daily attention. But it is well worth it. Right now you accept as normal the overweight man of twenty-five or thirty who cannot run up two flights of stairs without huffing and puffing. You accept the fact—you even expect—that a businessman is tense and nervous and has high blood pressure, bad back, or ulcers. All too many doctors advise a forty-year-old who plays tennis to slow down and "act your age." Friends tell you that over-weight, tension, muscular weakness, and occasional painful back are "normal." Nothing could be further from the truth.

chapter 3

The Importance of the Muscles and the Spine

IN ONE WAY OR ANOTHER MOST OF US ARE STATUS conscious, but when it comes to status, muscles do not rank. They are one of the most important parts of your body, but they are the least respected. This attitude is even reflected in popular speech. You will praise the brain or heart, but you have no respect at all for muscles. You speak in complimentary terms of a person when you say, "He's brainy," "She's got a brain," "She's got heart," or "He's a hearty fellow." But what do you say about muscles? You speak of them with contempt: "He's all muscle," "He's muscle-bound," "He's a muscle man," "Muscle Beach," and "He's muscling in on us."

Few physical educators show much respect for muscles either. Instead of seeing to it that youngsters grow up with strong and flexible muscles, too many of them think only of coaching winning teams or of becoming administrators.

Medical students are not instructed in therapeutic exercise or muscle evaluation. When you go for a thorough checkup, you are given an electrocardiogram; your blood pressure and pulse rate are taken; your nervous system, eyes, and ears are examined; your blood and urine are analyzed; and your heart and lungs are examined. X-rays are taken of whatever body area is suspected of being diseased or injured. This is as it should be. But are your muscles examined for strength and flexibility? Very rarely. If tests are given, they gauge neurological deficiencies. Tests to detect whether your muscles can manage your body weight are uncommon, and so is appraisal of flexibility and muscle tension; yet, your muscles have a tremendous effect on your overall health. Muscles are not only important and vital inherently, but they exert great influence, for better or worse, on your metabolism and emotional life. Their use keeps your cardiovascular system in good shape. If you don't use your muscles sufficiently in running or other strenuous activities, your heart does not get the stimuli it needs to keep strong and healthy.

Your muscles do countless things for you. When, you walk, you use your muscles. When you work with your hands, you use your muscles. When you move your back, you use your muscles. Your muscles, moreover, are your only means of communication with the outer world; they are irreplaceable organs of expression. When you show your thoughts and feelings by facial movements, when you talk, when you write, when you dance, you use your muscles. You must use them constantly to show what you feel and think. This applies to the abstract thinker as much as the day laborer. The thinker who is afflicted with back pain, stiff neck, or tension headache simply cannot function in top shape.

Besides allowing you to move and to express your thoughts, your muscles are the only organs which permit you to exert your will. In fact, you can use your muscles to train your will. For thousands of years some religions have deemed training of the body the first step toward disciplining the mind and spirit. It is no wonder that symbolic movement and posture are an integral part of worship.

Use of your muscles affects your metabolism. If you exercise sufficiently, you will set up a natural balance against overweight. Until the last century, most people had to work hard physically for their food. Their muscles and organs used up what they ate. In addition to regulating weight and metabolism, the heavy labor done by the muscles kept the heart and blood vessels in good condition. There is no denying that the death rate was higher in the "good old days," but the reason that we live longer now than people did in the seventeenth or eighteenth centuries is due largely to preventive medicine's victories over most types of contagious diseases, antibiotics, sewage disposal, and milk control. As a matter of fact, the upsurge of longevity has come to a halt. In 1964 the U.S. Public Health Service reported that American life expectancy is on the decrease.

Yes, people now live longer than their ancestors did, but how many people really feel vibrant and alive? The answer, as I check our clinical records, is all too few.

Your muscles are only as good as you make them. When you do not use the muscles of your body properly, they suffer and so do you. Neglect or abuse the muscles that keep your body erect, and you are bound to get back pain, stiff neck, or tension headache. When muscles are weak through lack of exercise and tense because of irritation, they cannot do their share of keeping the body erect and too much strain falls on the bones and ligaments of your spine. Let us take a look at the spine and the muscles involved in its function.

Your spine runs from your head to your buttocks. It consists, in order, of seven cervical or neck vertebrae, twelve dorsal vertebrae in the middle back, five lumbar vertebrae in the so-called small of the back, and, finally, the sacrum, a bone of roughly triangular shape that connects the spinal column with the pelvis. The vertebrae, the bony parts of the spine, are not directly linked to one another but are separated by ligamentous rings with a soft inner part rather like a jelly doughnut. These rings are known as discs, and they are notorious as a source of serious back trouble. Fortunately "slipped" discs are not quite as common as you might think. As you will see in Chapter 5, many persons who think they are suffering from disc trouble actually are victims of muscle strain in the back, and this condition can be corrected through exercise instead of surgery.

Besides the discs, there are strong ligaments joining the vertebral bodies with one another and with the sacrum. On the back part of each vertebra is a bony ring. This holds the spinal cord. The center of this cord consists of nerve cells. Surrounding it are large cables of nerve fibers that ultimately join the lower and upper part of the brain. From there smaller nerve cables branch out into all parts of the body. These are the nerve cables that transmit all sensations to us. They help conduct reflexes, and they contain all the connections to the muscles. These nerves, traveling through their cable links, transmit orders from the brain and the spinal cord that make muscles move and contract.

The spinal column is formed in the shape of a gentle "S." The ligaments and discs together make the spinal column an elastic structure. But in order to function correctly—and in order to offset sudden blows or continuous strain—the spinal column needs help. This help is given by the trunk muscles. All of them—not only the back muscles, but stomach muscles and hip flexors as well as hip extensors—support the spinal column. They combine to keep it erect. They allow the column to move. They protect the column by acting as an outer guard. If your muscles are really in good condition, they can even offset damage to the spinal column itself. As a case in point I will cite the story of a friend of mine, a mountain climber. I'll call him Alex. For years he has spent all his free time in the mountains. He regularly spent his weekends climbing the cliffs of the Shawangunk Mountains near New York City. He is in superb condition.

One Monday morning Alex unexpectedly showed up at our clinic. "What are you doing here?" I asked.

"Guess what!" he said, with a big smile. "I have a bad back."

I couldn't believe it. Furthermore, he was smiling about it.

Alex sat down painfully and told me what happened. "I went climbing yesterday, as usual," he said. "But this time I found no partner and foolishly decided to climb alone. I went up the southern 'pillar' and enjoyed the rock and the sun and being alone. Just when I was ready to pull myself up to the second belay place, my right hand slipped and I fell. Down I went, bouncing off the rock a couple of times. Anyway, I came to a stop after some fifty feet straight down. I was lucky that my fall was broken by a bush and I landed on a wide ledge. I was knocked unconscious, and when I came to, I thought I was dead. But I wasn't. I felt for broken bones, but I couldn't feel any. I got up carefully. I ached all over, but the pain in the back was the worst. I'm still quite beaten up but not badly enough to go to the hospital. I just want to find out whether I have broken anything in my back."

We examined his back. Alex had a large swelling, a hematoma, covering the back from his buttocks to his shoulders. We took X-rays of the spine and couldn't believe it. There was no injury at all, and except for minor cuts and a slightly sprained ankle, the swelling on his back was his only serious injury. We drained the blood from the swelling. Three days later we did so again. A week afterward the back was black and blue, but the only pain Alex felt was in his sprained ankle. His strong and resilient back muscles had helped shield his spine from severe damage.

Besides strong and resilient back muscles, strong stomach muscles and hip flexors are essential for the avoidance of back pain. When people complain of back pain, they invariably blame the back muscles. The pain is in the low back, to be sure, but the pain may be there because the stomach muscles or the Hp flexors are weak. The muscles are weak because they are the most inactive ones in a sedentary life. Say you spend most of the day sitting down. When you sit, you still have to keep your back muscles active in order to avoid toppling over. At the same time you let your stomach muscles go slack, and your hip flexors are more or less inactive as well. This is as it should be, but if you do a lot of sitting and no exercise, these muscles are bound to become weak.

And when they become weak, they impose a severe strain on the back muscles, and the back muscles simply are not up to carrying this strain of keeping your spine erect.

Keep this up consistently, add nervous irritation to your sedentary life, and the back muscles will get tense and stiff. Finally, when they are unable to stand the strain, they will rebel by going into spasm and causing pain. Weakness and tension often combine to produce pain, but tension does not necessarily have to be the result of emotional disturbance. The normal tension of work, especially of work done in a cramped position, may be enough to produce acute muscular tension that results in pain.

We had a good illustration of this years ago. The patient was Dr. D., a psychiatrist in his middle fifties. Dr. D. was at the top of his profession, and his profession called for him to be sitting down all day. As a youngster he had been bookish and had done little exercise. When he became an analyst, he stopped doing what little exercise he had done. As a matter of fact, I figured that Dr. D. had spent close to thirty years just sitting down. For the last two years, he said, he had suffered back pain on and off. Examination revealed that his back was stiff. It was especially stiff on the left side. "That's the side to which I turn to face my patients," he said. I suggested that he change his seating arrangements. The examination also disclosed that Dr. D. had very weak stomach muscles. But one thing really struck me about Dr. D. He was completely relaxed otherwise. He was weak, but he had no trace of anxiety or mental tension. He was, in fact, so relaxed that when I had finished the examination, I said to him, "I hope you will excuse me for being personal, but you're rather unusual. You are one of the few patients I have seen who is really serene."

He smiled and said, "Yes, I guess I am. I'm very happily married, and my wife and I have raised good and useful children. I myself was brought up in a very devout home, and I was told as a boy that every human being has at least one good side and that he should be loved for that good side. I believe that, and I've always been very happy, both in my family life and in my work."

Dr. D. was an ideal patient. Since he had no emotional source of tension, he managed to deal with his working tension by frequently changing his position at work. He interrupted his day as often as possible by lying down and actively relaxing. He learned how to do this very quickly. For several months he came in and was treated by a therapist who administered exercises that limbered and stretched his back and leg muscles and strengthened his abdominal muscles. Dr. D. cannot fit sports or outdoor activities in his pattern of living. But he avoids back pain by continuing his exercises regularly at home and moving around in the office.

In order to produce strength, a muscle shortens and tightens. It becomes tense, and it performs whatever task you want it to do, whether it be lifting a pencil, moving your legs, or turning your head. After the muscle has performed the task, it normally returns to its initial length and goes into a state of relaxation. It stops being tense; other muscles take over, become tense, do their job, and in turn let go and return to a state of relaxation. It is this flowing rhythm of tensing and relaxing muscles that makes for smooth movement.

The more you use a muscle, the stronger it will become. Your stomach muscles and hip flexors, for example, are mainly developed by running and lifting. If you do little running and lifting, these muscles will not develop. They will be weak and will impose an unnatural strain upon the back muscles, as was the case with Dr. D. Luckily for him, he had no emotional tension to compound the problem. But he was a rarity. Most persons are tied in knots with tension.

Tension prohibits muscular relaxation. A muscle must relax. Relaxing is a part of its function. If a muscle fails to relax, it stays tight. It loses its stretch, its suppleness, its give. Over a period of time it becomes permanently shortened. When this happens, the muscle loses most of its ability to release tension. If you have tense and shortened muscles, you are susceptible to all sorts of "tension syndrome"—back pain, stiff neck, or headache—because your muscles never have the chance to let go or relax, and neither do you.

Your muscles can be trained, if you take the trouble to train them properly. They can become strong and relaxed through purposeful exercise, or they can become shortened and tense from lack of exercise and over-irritation. Like mischievous children, muscles are more inclined to stick to bad habits than persist in good ones. How they behave is up to you. Overtensing and shortening of your muscles are very bad habits, and once acquired, they may be hard to break. You can see this around you all the time. Look at people you know are tense. How do they move their bodies? Certainly not smoothly. Their body movements are not fluid or rhythmic but jerky and stiff. They freeze themselves into a position, whether they are sitting in. a chair, standing, or driving a car. They force their muscles into a steady alert reaction. Their muscles, already under tension, are forced to become even more tense. The muscles of the neck, shoulder girdle, and back are particularly tense, and they become the prime target areas for even more tension.

Look at your friend who is usually tense. Watch him at the wheel of a car when you're with him. It's the morning rush hour, and he is late for the office. Whenever a horn blows behind him or he misses a green light or a car cuts in front, you can almost see his shoulder muscles tense with each irritation. This happens to you, too, and the irritations keep up all day long. Each time you are irritated the muscles become tense. As the irritations keep up, the muscles keep tensing, and they never get the chance to respond normally and relax.

Irritations come from all over. There are external irritations, such as traffic jams, the ringing of the telephone, a sudden loud noise, an unexpected slap on the back, a shout from your children. These are just samples of hundreds that occur every day. Then there are internal irritations; just thinking about them can make your muscles tense. You do not like your job; a member of the family is desperately ill; your sexual relations are a problem. All these internal irritations can make your muscles extremely tense—tense to the point of inducing muscle spasm and pain. Sexual difficulties, for instance, can have a devasting effect. Take, for example, the case of Harry G.

Mr. G. was an accountant in his late thirties. Five years prior to treatment he had been married. He saw us on the recommendation of his psychiatrist. Mr. G. had back pain. He was extremely tense. He was also nearly impotent, which was why he had been seeing the psychiatrist. Three months after his honeymoon he strained his back while trying to change a flat tire. Up to then, sexual relations had not been completely satisfactory; after he hurt his back muscles, he came to dread intercourse because it produced pain. In time he actually equated intercourse with pain while simultaneously he began to brood about his apparent lack of masculinity. Muscular pain and emotional tension like this can really wreck a person. Back pain and his feeling of interiority became part of a continuous vicious cycle that almost destroyed Harry G. emotionally and physically.

While the psychiatrist worked on Mr. G.'s mind, we worked on his back. Slowly but gradually his back began to improve. Slowly but gradually the psychiatrist was able to allay his fears. It took almost a year before Mr. G. began to show signs of definite improvement. When the vicious circle was broken, his life returned to normal.

Unfortunately too few persons know how to move their muscles and their bodies, much less control their emotions. Instead of mastering their emotions, they have let emotion master them, unaware that emotions are the wellsprings of muscle tension. Since many persons lack both emotional and physical discipline, their lives become subject to moods, emotional storms, anxieties, and hostilities. These factors only make muscle tension all the worse and they are an important source of hypokinetic disease.

MECHANIZED, URBANIZED, UNBALANCED INDIVIDUAL

Over-Rested   Over-Fed   Over-Stimulated
Over-Protected   Under-Exercised   Under-Released
Under-Disciplined

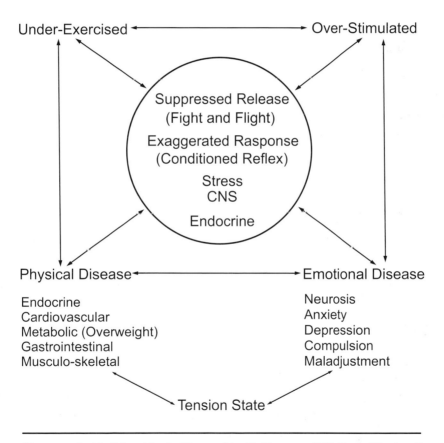

Under-Exercised   Over-Stimulated

Suppressed Release
(Fight and Flight)

Exaggerated Rasponse
(Conditioned Reflex)

Stress
CNS

Endocrine

Physical Disease   Emotional Disease

Endocrine
Cardiovascular
Metabolic (Overweight)
Gastrointestinal
Musculo-skeletal

Neurosis
Anxiety
Depression
Compulsion
Maladjustment

Tension State

(Documented in "Hypokinetic Disease" by H. Kraus and W. Raab Charles C Thomas, Publisher.)

chapter 4

Fight or Flight: Why Tension Builds

A FEW THOUSAND YEARS AGO, A SHORT TIME IN THE HIS-
tory of a species, man lived in caves. He led the life of a brute animal.
He was physically involved in the struggle for existence. So were his
wife and children. Like all animals, their bodies were endowed with an
amazingly complex and efficient preparation for action. In an instant
their bodies were ready to fight or to flee. In either case they responded
with a physical action. They either fought or they fled.

Civilized man—and civilized woman—has the same physiological
structure. When you are faced with a stressful situation, your body prepares to act. But unlike your ancestors, you neither fight nor flee. The
rules of civilized society prevent this, and usually you do nothing but
sit and seethe. This constant suppression of a natural physical response
puts an unnatural strain, on your system.

Here is a typical case. Angela J.
was a slim brunette secretary in her
late twenties. Her posture was bad,
her neck stiff. She was as tense as any
girl who ever came to our clinic.

"For the past three years," she
said, "I have had pain, both in my
neck and in the back of my shoulders.
No matter what I do, the pain just will
not go away.

"I first got a pain in the neck when
I went to work for the Blank Company"—and here Angela named a large
corporation—"three years ago. I'm a
secretary. There's an awful lot of work to

63

do; we're almost always short handed, and I would have quit, but I have friends there. A month after I started work I got a stiff neck. I had it a couple of days. I remember thinking that I had caught it working near a new air conditioner. It went away. But about a month after that I had to fill in for another girl and I got a stiff neck again. This time there was no air conditioner nearby. I tried to do different things for the pain, like putting hot packs on it, but I just couldn't seem to loosen it up.

"After I went back to my regular boss I was all right for a little while. Then I started getting pain between my shoulder blades. First it was at the end of the day, then at lunch. Now it starts in the morning.

"Last month it started to get worse. I got the pain between the shoulders before I even went to work. Yesterday was the worst day I've ever had. My boss was off on a trip, but he phoned long distance and told me he wanted to change some letters he had dictated the day before. I had

just finished typing them up, and I was furious. I took the new dictation down on the phone, and I started to retype the letters. I was halfway through the first one when the pain simply became too much to take. I got up and walked away from the typewriter and tried to relax. I couldn't. So I sat down again and started to type. But I simply could not continue. My neck felt locked, and in between my shoulder blades it felt as though my muscles were in knots. I had to stop work. I feel hopeless."

I assured Angela that she need not feel hopeless, and I asked her what she thought prompted the pain. She guessed it was her work, but then she dismissed this by saying that was "only in her head."

I agreed that the pain was started by what was in her head. I told her that her muscles reacted to the constant mental irritations and frustrations of the job by getting ready to strike out or run away. Since Angela neither ran away nor struck out, since she never fulfilled "the fight or flight response," her muscles remained tense, in a state of constant readiness. Inasmuch as this had happened day after day after day over three years, her muscle tension had finally reached the state where it became painful. At first she had felt the pain at the end of a long day. Then, as the tension started to accumulate, it took less and less irritation to produce the pain. The phone call from her boss had brought her pain to a climax.

"In short," I told Angela, "you undergo rage without hitting, and fear without fleeing. Instead of resolving the situation, you stay at your work, hunching your shoulders and seething inwardly. Instead of fighting or fleeing, you seethe. Your neck and shoulder muscles haven't relaxed in three years. Now they have gotten so tense that they rebelled by going into spasm."

I told Angela to stay away from work for a week while she began treatment. It was an involved case, requiring physical therapy to relieve her muscle spasm and medication to relieve pain and to calm her nerves. She then needed exercises to limber her neck and shoulder muscles, and she had to learn exercises that would relax her.

Two weeks passed before Angela could return to her job. Even then she still required treatment. Three weeks after returning to work her neck and back muscles began to become painful again. This time I suggested that she look around for another job where working conditions were easier, where there would be little if no tension. After all, I told her, a good secretary can always get another job, and she would still have her friends. Angela did as suggested and had no trouble at all in getting another position with fewer irritating demands. Since then she has kept up her exercise program, and she has been doing well. Her neck and shoulders remain sensitive to strain and irritation, but Angela now recognizes the warning signs of "fight or flight" and knows how to handle them.

Failure to respond with a physical action to fight or flight is the main cause of tension. It has become particularly important as more and more people lead lives without exercise. Under exercised muscles never get a chance to get rid of tension.

What happens to you physiologically when you are challenged or irritated? A number of things. Adrenalin pours into your system; your heart beats faster; you breathe quicker; your blood pressure rises, and your muscles tense. In the days when men and women led primitive lives, they completed this response either by fighting or running away.

But what do you do? You do nothing except seethe. Your muscles, your mind, your heart, and your organs all prepare to act, but you do nothing. You may want to fight, you may wish to flee, but modern civilization prevents you from carrying out your natural impulses. When the boss tells you off, you have to "grin and bear it," and you only get more tense. Then there are occasions when you cannot respond physically even should you wish to do so. You cannot throw the telephone at the pest on the other end of the line. You cannot punch the insane driver doing seventy miles an hour who just missed hitting you with his car. In such situations you neither fight nor flee. Instead, you do as you usually do; you seethe. This happens to you all the time, and this constant suppression of physical response puts a strain on the muscles that tense and want to react.

Think of all the times during the day when your body gets ready to respond to a challenge or an irritation. Then think of all the times you do absolutely nothing. All this has an appalling effect on your ready-to-respond system, especially when the pattern is repeated day in and day out, month after month, year after year. Now I am not talking about lurid or dramatic situations where you are called upon to defend your life or your honor. I am talking about the flood of daily irritations that bedevil and bother you. You don't have to be facing a mugger with a knife to have your system sound battle stations. Your system actually prepares for action when the phone rings, when someone shouts at you, when you hear a sudden noise, when you are interrupted at work, when you hear your child fall down and burst loudly into tears. Your whole being gets set to respond, to fight or to flee. Your muscles suddenly tense up. They get ready to act. So do your heart, your blood vessels, your glands, and your mind. But you do nothing. All day long the irritations mount up, making your muscles tense and putting your mind in a state of anxiety and irritation. But you race your engines without ever going anywhere. As sure as anything, this is almost guaranteed to trigger back pain, a stiff neck, or a thudding tension headache. And this may be only one of many other adverse results. The same unreleased strain, if repeated often, may cause high blood pressure, ulcers, or heart disease. Surely it will upset you emotionally and make you "nervous."

Medicine owes its knowledge of the fight or flight response to a great researcher, the late physiologist, Walter B. Cannon of Harvard. Cannon wanted to know what happened to man when he underwent fear or rage, and he began by experimenting on animals. What happened to laboratory animals when they were irritated? Cannon studied their reactions. The animals tensed their muscles. They increased their heartbeats, and blood pressure rose quickly. Adrenalin was released into the blood stream and raised the blood sugar to provide emergency rations for the muscle, and sugar spilled into the urine. In the wild this preparation for action is essential. The animal reacts physically to the irritation. It fights or it flees. Then afterward the muscles relax, blood pressure drops, the heartbeat slows, and breathing becomes normal.

A cat is a perfect example of this. When a cat is not disturbed, it is perfectly at ease. Every muscle is supple and relaxed. Yet when the cat becomes irritated or angered, you can watch it become tense before your eyes. It spits, hisses; it arches its back as it prepares to fight or to flee. When the irritation reaches a certain point, the cat either attacks or runs away. In either case it carries out a physical response. The cat does not sit and stew like you do. It responds physically, and after it does it returns to its state of ease and relaxation.

Cannon went on further with his research. He found his results confirmed in human beings. For example, he and a colleague checked the urine of twenty-five Harvard football players after a Yale game. Sugar was found in the urine of twelve excited players, five of them substitutes who sat on the bench throughout. An excited spectator examined also had sugar in his urine.

Besides Cannon's pioneering research, various other investigators have conducted experiments on muscle tension. A German physiologist, Tiegel, did research showing that repeated tensing of a muscle results in a definite loss of length. The muscle shrinks, so to speak, and when suddenly you are required to stretch it, it cannot do the job and it reacts by going into spasm or, even worse, tearing. A pair of English physicians, Peter Sainsbury and T. G. Gibson did interesting experiments on tension pain. They examined a number of people who complained of habitual tension headache or muscle pain. They used a device to measure action currents in the muscles. When a muscle contracts it produces weak electric currents; the intensity of the currents is in proportion to the degree of muscle contraction. One set of electrodes was attached to the muscle or muscles producing the pain—the "target" area—and another set was affixed to "normal" muscles that did not produce pain. Then Sainsbury and Gibson put the subjects through an interview deliberately designed to bring about tension. As the interview proceeded, Sainsbury and Gibson discovered that the normal muscles started to tense but relaxed quickly afterward. The muscles that produced pain, however, not only started to tense during the interview but tensed even more afterward, bringing about pain at the peak of contraction.

There are definite "target" areas of muscle tension in tension headache: they are the occipital muscles running up the back of the head and the frontalis muscles in the forehead. Sometimes you can feel the tight occipital muscles if you have a very bad headache. Put your fingers behind your head midway between the upper part of your ears and the back of the skull, and you may feel your muscles tighten. The target areas for painful or stiff necks are the neck muscles and the trapezius muscles, which cover your shoulder blades, and the rhomboid muscles which are beneath the trapezius. The muscles of the lower back are prime target areas. Less frequently target areas are found in the legs, thighs, arms, or any place where muscles are continually subjected to tension without release and relaxation.

Sometimes you can be bothered by one particular irritation and not realize it. This reminds me of a Mrs. M., a forty-year-old career woman who came to have a stiff neck treated. She carried her neck twisted to the right side and was quite uncomfortable. We were able to limber it up somewhat on her initial visit. Mrs. M. had a very responsible job with a publishing company. After loosening her neck, I started talking about her tension and the need to find its source to minimize it. I had no idea as to what specific irritation was triggering her stiff neck until she glanced at her wrist watch and said, "This is all very interesting, but I must be back at the office at three to dictate to my secretary." As soon as she said the word "secretary," her neck at once twisted to the right.

"Don't be in such a hurry, Mrs. M.," I said. "I have an idea of what's wrong."

Mrs. M. stayed. It turned out that she could not stand her secretary. The girl was pleasant enough but inefficient to an extreme. Mrs. M. had put up with her for two years. She had thought many times of firing her, but when she remembered her own beginnings in business and the difficult time she had had, she always relented.

When Mrs. M. returned a week later, her neck was again stiff. I suggested that she change secretaries. Mrs. M. wouldn't hear of it, but when the neck pain persisted for a month, she finally resolved to transfer the girl. The girl literally was a pain in the neck.

chapter 5

Why We Get Sick Backs

ORGANIC DISEASE CAUSES ONLY A SMALL PERCENTAGE OF back pain. X-rays sometimes show "osteoarthritic" changes of the verte-brae, but these do not often cause pain. Rheumatoid arthritis, a much more serious ailment, causes pain and stiffness, but it is relatively rare. Other pathologies, such as malignancies and tuberculosis of the spine, are still more unusual. Even "disc' trouble is not as common as one might think. The same is true of mechanically unstable spine caused by congenital malformation or injury. In short, if you suffer from back pain, the chances are that your condition is caused not by organic dis-ease, but by muscles that are weak or tense or both.

A number of medical researchers have found this to be the case. Dr. Weber and I found this out for ourselves at the special back-pain clinic organized at Columbia-Presbyterian Hospital. More than 80 percent of the patients who complained of back pain were found to be suffering from muscular deficiencies, while fewer than 20 percent had patho-logical disorders. Drs. Barbara Stimson and Sawnie Gaston arrived at a similar figure. All of us were able to arrive at this conclusion because the patients treated at the clinic were thoroughly examined by a team of physicians specializing in all sorts of fields. In addition, every pa-tient was given X-rays, and laboratory analyses were made of the blood and urine. In short, nothing was left unexamined in the quest to find the reasons for complaints of back pain.

The muscularly deficient back-pain sufferers would have been considered "healthy," except for the fact that they had pain. Then when they took the six K-W tests, they all failed one or more. They simply did not have the necessary muscle strength to manage their own body weight and/or they lacked the muscular flexibility required for their own size. When given prescribed exercises, the majority improved. A follow-up more than a decade later showed that, as long as these patients did their exercises every day, they had relief from pain and their muscles were strong and resilient.

Many of these patients had localized and exquisitely tender spots which we could feel in their muscles. These spots are called "trigger points." They were first extensively described by a German orthopedic surgeon, Max Lange, more than fifty years ago and then by another well-known specialist, Arthur Steindler, in this country. In recent years many other physicians have written about trigger points. Among them are Dr. Janet Travell and Drs. Alois Brugger and Duri Gross of Zurich University, who have written an excellent monograph on the subject.

Trigger points occur in different parts of the body, but they are especially frequent in neck, shoulders, upper and lower back, and hip muscles. They can be caused by constant or acute strain of the muscles or by muscle spasm. They are, in a sense, rather like scar tissue of muscles. Trigger points are very painful, and they can literally trigger pain by provoking muscle tension, spasm, or contracture. Trigger points usually appear in your muscles if you let minor episodes of back pain go untreated, and then, once the trigger points have formed, the episodes of pain will increase, both in intensity and frequency.

When we examine a patient with chronic back pain caused by weakness or tension, we feel the muscles gently with our fingers to see if there are trigger points. If there are none, exercise therapy can start once pain subsides, usually after about a week. We use ethyl chloride spray and other physical therapy to help relieve the pain.

If a patient has trigger points, we mark the locations on the skin. Then we inject each trigger point with procaine. This kills the pain, but more important, both the needling and the injected fluid itself break up the trigger point through the force of hydraulic pressure. Once the trigger points have been injected and eliminated by subsequent treatment, the patient can embark on an exercise program.

On occasion a physician may find another kind of tenderness when he gently rolls a patient's skin between his fingers. If the skin itself is very sensitive to the touch, it is known as "fibrositis." It responds well to pinching massage if carried out regularly for weeks, sometimes months.

Some patients are quite disappointed when they learn that their pain is caused by trigger points. They had expected "slipped" discs, caused when the ligamentous disc covers tear or give so that the soft contents ooze out and press nerve roots. These patients find it difficult to accept the fact that their trouble is "only muscles." Some even feel "left out" with such an unglamorous problem because so many movie stars and celebrities seem to be suffering from discs.

Trigger points and discs can be confused. Confusion sets in because they can exhibit similar symptoms. Like discs, trigger points can prompt radiating pain in either the upper and lower back and down the back of the legs or arms as well. But here the similarities between trigger points and discs end. Trigger points do not cause reflex loss. Damaged discs can. Trigger points do not cause sensory loss, numbness, or weakness. Discs can.

Sometimes weak and stiff muscles, emotional tensions, endocrine imbalance, muscle tenderness, or skin tenderness all combine to cause pain and make a diagnosis difficult. You can understand how such a complicated condition may lead to a diagnosis of "disc trouble," even though there may be no real involvement of a disc. Occasionally these symptoms suggest at least impending disc lesion.

It has happend that some back-pain sufferers with trigger points have been incorrectly diagnosed as having disc trouble. This can be harmful, because from that moment on a patient, seeing surgery as a distinct possibility is asked to "live with" the pain and to refrain from "excessive motion." So the patient, who is really troubled by trigger points, becomes more and more inactive and thus worse off. Occasional minor spurts of activity only serve to inflict greater pain on the patient's constantly deteriorating muscles and sensitive trigger points. The downward trend becomes difficult to reverse, and complications set in, prompted by the patient's anxieties, such as the fear of surgery, the fear of disability, the fear of losing his livelihood. When a patient has reached this desperate stage, he or she loses all sense of emotional and active well-being and becomes resigned to a life of physical inactivity instead of a life of activity and vigor. Occasionally such a patient will finally undergo surgery to remedy the "disc trouble," and of course this only does more harm since the muscles are made even weaker and tenser by long confinement to a hospital bed. And yet there are some back-pain sufferers who hate to be told that they have muscularly deficient backs instead of disc trouble, because discs are glamorous!

Even in cases of disc trouble surgery is not necessarily called for. There are times, many times as a matter of fact, when exercises to retrain inadequate muscles can offset damage to the spinal column. This was true of a patient whom I'll call Mr. Jim C. Mr. C. was in his early forties, and when he came to the clinic with pain in his back and right leg, he had already been through two operations for spinal fusion and removal of a disc. Yet the pain persisted. We had no doubt that he did have disc trouble before, and we had little doubt that he did have disc trouble again. But rather than force Mr. C. to undergo surgery yet again, we thought it would be worthwhile to try different treatment. Mr. C. readily agreed; he had little desire to spend more time in the hospital flat on his back.

First Mr. C. had to take a full month's leave of absence from his job as an executive in a large manufacturing firm. This eliminated tension at work which, incidentally, had been aggravated by Mr. C.'s poor postural habits in handling the telephone. We used the first month of treatment to deal with painful trigger points in Mr. C.'s back and hip. A gradual retraining program was also started. Rest at home, use of a surgical corset, and muscle relaxants were prescribed. Later when Mr. C. returned to work, he continued to come to the clinic for exercise sessions three times a week. He did exercises at home the other days.

It took more than six months for Mr. C.'s muscles to return to normal, and during that time he was slowly weaned from his corset. Even when he felt all right he had to return to the clinic for periodic checkups. In the beginning he suffered one or two mild setbacks when he stood too long and when he started playing golf prematurely.

Mr. C. now lives a normal life, but he has to continue to keep in good condition. His back remains his weak spot, reacting when he is under too much stress of any kind. He now knows the signs of trouble, however, and he has learned how to handle them.

Exercise may also be used for treatment of "mechanically unstable spine" caused by old fractures, wornout joints of the vertebrae, and by forward sliding of the last (fifth) lumbar vertebra on the sacrum. In these cases, however, effectiveness of exercise is limited and surgery may be needed.

There are, of course, occasions when surgery is imperative. Once a very attractive young blonde in her late twenties, Miss Jane S., came to us for treatment. Six years before she had taken a trip to Europe. On the ship on the way back, she tripped and fell down a ladder. Miss S. felt pain and stiffness in her back but did not see a physician. From then on she was never entirely free from backache. When we saw her, Miss S. seemed to be in good physical condition, but there was no doubt she was stiff and felt pain. X-rays were ordered. They disclosed an old fracture of the fourth lumbar vertebra. We recommended a spinal fusion, and it was performed successfully. A reconditioning period of exercise followed. Only occasional discomfort reminds her now of past injury.

We have seen how many factors—underexercise, tension, glandular imbalance, and severe injury—may cause back pain, but other factors—overweight, flat feet, unequal leg length, and poor seating or sleeping facilities—may play a part. All these factors create a situation which gradually may lead to backache, maybe starting at night after a long day as fatigue pain, or discomfort and stiffness in the morning or after long periods of sitting as "jelling pain." Discomfort may gradually increase in degree and spread to your thighs or arms. Finally you reach the point where you are never comfortable. Often a sudden minor blow, a sudden twisting motion, sudden stooping, or lifting may set off an acute, sudden attack of pain that may force you to go to bed or even to the hospital. Even minimal injury will be sufficient to do this if you are in poor muscular condition and have had low-grade backache for some time.

In a healthy person whose back is protected by strong, resilient muscles it takes a much more serious injury to produce an attack of back pain. But the difference between injury to a healthy person and a deconditioned one goes further: the healthy person recovers much quicker under adequate care.

A case in point was Miss N., a dancer, who saw us two years after a second operation for disc trouble. After both operations she had felt fine—until she took up dancing again. Then severe pain forced her to give up performing. After the second operation she had tried several times to return to the stage only to be forced to give it up again. She thought about having a third operation. Examination revealed that Miss N. had extremely weak trunk muscles and stiff back and leg muscles. They were riddled with trigger points. Why? Because she had bravely tried to return to her demanding work without ever having gone through systematic reconditioning. It took several months of injections and exercise sessions to get her in good shape. She resumed her work and since then has missed few performances.

There are innumerable patients with similar experiences. Complete reconditioning after injury is a must for all physically active people. If they are properly reconditioned, they are not so likely to suffer again, no matter how physically demanding their work may be. Take the case of Dr. John L., a rugged country veterinarian. He was in his forties, and all his life he had been extremely active. In his spare time Dr. L. walked, ran, rode horseback, went hunted, fished, chopped wood, and played tennis. He was most vigorous physically. Even his job made physical

demands upon him. He regularly went around the countryside shoeing horses, lifting sheep and hogs, and chasing cattle. One stormy night when Dr. L. was at home reading, the phone rang. It was a farmer who lived off in the hills ten miles away. The farmer said there was something wrong with his prize bull. Dr. L., like a family physician on call, set out at once in his car. He got to the farmer's place and, after the call was finished, said good night to the farmer and started home. It was still blowing hard outside. Two miles down the road from the farmer's house a huge ash tree had fallen across the road. Rather than drive back and trouble the farmer, Dr. L. decided he might as well chop the way free. He got an ax from the back of the car and started chopping. It took him about an hour to cut up the trunk so his car could get through. Then, feeling in good spirits, he decided to lift up one of the logs and throw it instead of rolling it to the side. When Dr. L. picked up the heavy log, he felt something twinge in his back. He dropped the log and rolled it to the side with his feet, got back in the car, and drove home.

Dr. L. had back pain for a week. He thought nothing more of it when it went away. But from then on the pain would return periodically, especially when he moved something heavy. After two years of on-and-off pain Dr. L. came into the clinic for treatment. He was perfectly healthy and had excellent muscles. The only thing was that he had a trigger point in the back muscles on his leftside. We injected it with procaine and treated him for a few days. After that he learned some exercises to keep limbered. This treatment lasted only ten days. Now his outlook is good—he may never have any trouble again.

Whenever we treat back pain, we try to find its cause. A disc injury will require bed rest, maybe surgery. Fractures may need immobilization or surgery. Aside from these and other less frequent causes, we first treat "acute back strain" mainly by stopping muscle spasm.

We use ethyl chloride spray, supported by electric muscle stimulation and gentle limbering motions given by a therapist. Others use applications of ice or hot packs. Whenever possible, gentle limbering performed at one-hour or half-hour intervals should be combined with rest to avoid unnecessary stiffening of the afflicted area. Muscle relaxants or pain-relieving medication may be given. Once the pain subsides, we start the patient on a prescribed exercise program.

There are cases—they are not common, but they occur from time to time—when exercise or surgery are of little or no use by themselves. For example, take the case of Mrs. Annette C. She was in her late forties and extremely emotional. She was close to being what she called "a complete wreck," and she looked it. Her hair was frowzy and her clothes sloppy. She was sent to us by her psychiatrist. Mrs. C. complained of severe back pain. From her medical record we knew that she was undergoing menopause. She had all the symptoms of chronic back pain, including very poor and stiff muscles. She came for treatment over a three-month period, and while her muscles improved, she did not. I knew from consulting with her psychiatrist that he was making no headway. We finally suggested that Mrs. C. visit an endocrinologist. She did, and the endocrinologist agreed that her menopause might help cause her emotional problems and recurring tension pain. He gave her medication, and Mrs. C.'s emotional tension and back pain subsided.

Similarly a Mr. Ronald A. came into the clinic complaining of muscle pain all over his body but especially in the back. He moved well enough, but he was putting on weight, his skin was dry, his hair was brittle. We sent him to an internist, who confirmed our suspicion that Mr. A. had a low thyroid function. Mr. A. remained under the observation of his internist and has been fine since his physician has kept him on adequate thyroid medication.

A patient named Richard M. complained that he woke up with stiff muscles in the morning. Mr. M. was in his early twenties, and like many young persons, he never had had a complete medical checkup. I insisted that he have one in as much as his stiffness seemed out of proportion to his age and general appearance. The checkup by an internist disclosed that Mr. M. was suffering from rheumatoid arthritis of the spine. Therapy and exercises were an important adjunct to his treatment, but his basic problem was the concern of his internist.

Such cases are not in the majority. Most back pain, stiff neck, or tension headache are due to a muscular imbalance, overstrain and underexercise. If you should suffer an attack of back pain at home or at work, lie down on a hard surface. A hard mattress over a board is best. The painful muscles should be covered with a hot pack composed of a towel dipped in boiling water and then wrapped in a dry towel. To avoid scalding, make sure that the wet towel has been wrung out completely. What really counts is not how long the towel stays hot on your back but the fact that it is hot to begin with. The sudden heat of a very hot towel shocks the muscles, and this helps to relieve the pain. Continue to rest on a hard surface until a physician arrives.

If you do not have back pain and yet cannot pass all six K-W tests, you still need help. You are leaving yourself not only exposed to muscle pain but, in the long run, to the other hypokinetic diseases as well: obesity, ulcers, diabetes, heart trouble, and emotional instability.

Fortunately this can be prevented or remedied. You will have to take stock of yourself. You can learn how to combat tension. You can learn how to exercise properly to correct any faults you have.

chapter 6

Exercises for Sick Backs

IF YOU HAVE FAILED ONE OR MORE OF THE SIX KRAUS-WE-ber tests described in Chapter 1, you need help. You are underexercised and/or overtensed, and this may well be the breeding ground for future sickness. The K-W tests are designed to test the key muscle groups in your body, no matter what your age, height, or weight. These tests are self-correlating. They do not judge you by some outside arbitrary standard; they do not ask you to be as strong as a coal miner or as lithe as an acrobat. Instead, these tests simply reveal whether or not you have sufficient muscular strength to move your own body weight and the muscular flexibility to match your own size. By taking the K-W tests, you will know for certain whether you are muscularly below the minimum requirements for healthful living. You may have weak stomach muscles that need strengthening; you may have stiff back muscles, or you may find that you are tense. Then again you may have a combination of weaknesses. But once you know your deficiencies, you can do prescribed exercises designed to correct these specific difficulties. These are exercises with a purpose, to right what is wrong with you.

You may have been given exercises previously and they may not have helped. Do not let that discourage you. You may not have done the correct kind of exercise the right way for a long enough time. You might be able to decide this for yourself by answering the following questions: Have you been given a muscle test before exercises were prescribed? If not,

the chances are you were not given the correct exercises. Were these exercises just given to you without detailed descriptions of how they were to be performed? If so, the chances are you didn't do them properly. Were you supposed to do all exercises at once, or were you given a gradually increasing sequence? If you were given the whole program at once, the chances are it was not effective. Were you told to repeat each exercise many times, say five, ten, or more? If so, this may have been too much. Have you done your exercises every day, gradually increasing the number of minutes up to twenty or thirty minutes, slowly, relaxed, and consistently, for several months? If not, again, you may have missed the boat.

Giving a patient therapeutic exercise is a craft, even an art, and so is the prescribing of exercises. An exercise program should follow a rationale; it should be preceded by a thorough investigation of what has to be changed, and why, so as to give proper attention for your individual needs. An exercise prescription should be regarded as a potent medicine, which it is if properly given. You would not go to a drugstore with a prescription that simply said medicine or laxative. Instead, you would expect your prescription to be fully detailed as to what you were to get, how much, and when. The same thing is true for therapeutic exercise. You should get the proper type, in the proper dosage.

The exercises you will see in this chapter are not very spectacular or unusual. A number of them are prescribed by many physicians, by specialists in physical medicine and rehabilitation, and by therapists. You will select the exercises that fit your individual needs; you will do them the way they are prescribed, and you will build up your exercises gradually, day by day until you have reached the full program. If you do your exercises properly, you will find them surprisingly effective. Bear in mind, however, that there is no easy way to accomplish improvement. There is no such thing as a fast five minutes a day to develop strong and flexible muscles. If you really wish to improve yourself, you will have to work. Think of an athlete training to run the mile in competition. He may be a fast runner, but before he can hit the four-minute mile and get into national and international competition, he has to work unceasingly and systematically for weeks and months, even years. When he has reached his peak, he will still have to continue training to remain in condition. Now you are not trying to break a record, but you are trying to get from below par to par, and that is often harder than trying to set a record.

Before going any further, I want to give you the basic ground rules for proper exercise:

1. *Check with your physician to make certain that you do not have an ailment that could be made worse by exercising now.* Do not start exercising if you have back pain or have had it in the past without making sure that your condition does not require medical care.

2. It is imperative that, once you start exercising, you keep at it every day. It is better not to start exercising at all unless you do so regularly. This is an important point, and it cannot be stressed enough. To be sure, there will be days when travel, important business, or emergencies will cut into your time, but don't go looking for excuses to avoid exercising. If you start and then stop an exercise program, you quickly lose what you have gained.

3. Avoid fatigue, which might cause undue stiffness and soreness. Start with very gentle movements and gradually ease into your full program. If you are stiff and tense but strong, these exercises may seem "sissy stuff" to you, but you should still do them gradually. Do not try to accomplish everything in a short time. It is harder to learn how to relax, limber, and stretch than it is to develop strength.

4. Set aside a half hour a day for your daily exercises. Make that a "holy" half hour when you are not subjected to visitors, phone calls, or interferences or distractions of any kind. You owe this to yourself and your own peace of mind. It is immaterial whether you do the exercises in the morning, afternoon, or evening, but do not do them immediately after a meal. Perhaps you will want to do them in the morning because you feel that they prepare you for the day. The only danger here is that there may be mornings when you are rushed, and you should not do the exercises if you feel it necessary to do them quickly. Never rush through them. If you have to leave early in the morning, do the exercises later in the day when you can make the time and have privacy.

5. Never say that you are "too irritated" to do the exercises. The day that you feel too harried or put upon is the day you need the exercises most of all, particularly if you are exercising to release tension. A busy day will make you and your muscles tense, but if you do your exercises properly you will find the tension ebbing away. The tension that your muscles store up during a hectic day can be released through the exercises.

6. Get in a relaxed state of mind for the exercises. If you follow instructions, you will learn how to do this. In your half hour of exercise put the cares of the world behind you, no matter how pressing or urgent they may seem to be. In this half hour nothing is more important than the job at hand. If a problem is particularly pressing or vexing, ask yourself, what will it matter fifty years from now? Live one day at a time. Exercise one session at a time. At first you will need only five to ten minutes for these sessions. They will gradually increase in time to approximately a half hour as you add exercises. Do not do a full program the first day or even the first week. Do only three or four of the exercises the first day. Never add more than one new exercise every two or three days—add them less often if the last exercise seems hard to do. All these exercises are planned in logical sequence. You start with a warm-up, say the first three exercises, reach a peak with the fourth, then work your way back, doing the first three exercises *in reverse order* so that what were the warm-up exercises end as the cool-off exercises. You always repeat your exercises in reverse order.

7. *Never do more than two or three of the same exercises in succession.* If your program is complete, you may want to go through it twice in one day, if you feel the need for extra work. Never do the exercises more frequently than that. Repetition will make you stiff, and chances are that lack of flexibility is one of your problems.

8. Your exercises must be performed slowly and smoothly. Do not do jerky movements, do not strain, do not "goose-step." Be sure you stop after each exercise and rest for a second before starting the next one. That means a pause between each exercise, not only each set of exercises.

9. Always start with the first six exercises, regardless of how you did on the K-W tests. If you are tense they will make you relax, and if you are weak they will give you a very mild warm-up. If you are strong but need relaxing and stretching, they are doubly important. If you are strong but tense, remember that you are not trying to develop more powerful muscles. Instead, you are trying to relax. These first exercises are more important for you than they are for anyone else.

GENERAL EXERCISES

No matter which K-W test or tests you failed, here are the six general exercises that you will use at the beginning and end of every exercise session. When you end your daily session, do your exercises in reverse order so that you conclude with the exercise with which you began.

To begin, strip down to your underclothes, take off your shoes and stockings, and lie on your back on a rug or pad on the floor. Get in a comfortable position. Put a pillow under your knees, a pillow under each arm, and another pillow or a rolled-up towel under the back of your neck. Now you are ready to start with the first exercise. Remember, you do each exercise two or three times and rest in between each.

EXERCISE 1.

Loosen up by wobbling your neck, your shoulders, arms, thighs, legs, and feet. Raise your arms slowly, then let them drop. Do the same with your hands, legs, and feet. Let your head drop to the left, then to the right. Take a deep breath—do not strain—exhale slowly.

Now try to feel heavy—let your head, shoulders, arms, and legs rest on the floor. Do not keep them up even slightly by tensing your muscles.

Breathe again, close your eyes, let your jaw sag, try to exhale as slowly as possible, humming or hissing.

Tighten your arm muscles, then let go. Do the same with your thigh muscles and neck, then let go. The important part is the letting go—not the tightening. The tightening is important only to make you feel the difference between tenseness and relaxation.

Breathe again, slowly lift your shoulders to your ears, let them go, shrug. If the pillow interferes with the shoulder shrug, move it from under your head.

EXERCISE 2.

Get up, sit on chair, shrug your shoulders again.

EXERCISE 3.

Turn your head all the way to the left, then return it to normal front and center and relax. Turn all the way to the right as far as you can, return, and let go. If you have a stiff neck, do this while sitting as well as lying down.

EXERCISE 4.

Lie flat on your back with all pillows removed, this time with your knees flexed. Slowly draw your right knee up as close as possible to your chest. Slowly straighten your leg, let it fall to the floor limp and relaxed. Pull it up again to the flexed starting position. Now do the same thing with the other leg. Alternate legs.

EXERCISE 5.

Lie on your left side, place a pillow under your head so it rests comfortably and your neck can relax. Keep both knees flexed and hips slightly flexed. Slide your right knee as close to your head as is comfortably possible, then slowly extend the leg until it is completely straight. Let the leg drop to the floor relaxed. Do the exercise two or three times on one side, then turn over to the other side and do the same with the other leg.

EXERCISE 6.

Turn over on your stomach. Fold your hands under your head and let your head rest on your hands comfortably. Then tighten your seat muscles. Hold for two seconds, then relax.

To repeat, these six exercises should be done, no matter what your K-W rating. After you have done all of these six general exercises in proper sequence you are ready to start additional exercises to correct your particular deficiencies. Add to your program one by one the exercises that pertain to you.

However, before you begin adding individual corrective exercises to the general six, read through the rest of this chapter. The prescribing of therapeutic exercises requires not only care but special knowledge. For instance, you must never do two sets of different exercises on your back, or on your stomach, consecutively. You must alternate each stomach exercise with a back exercise and vice versa. If you do not, you can stiffen and strain your muscles. It is as important to keep your muscles flexible as it is to keep them strong.

Furthermore, depending on which K-W test or tests you failed, each exercise program varies. Here, then, are descriptions and illustrations of the numbered exercises, from 7 through to 27, to be used to correct deficiencies revealed by the K-W tests. Read through them, study them, and see how they are done. Then, beginning later on page 109, pick the prescribed program for you. Then you will refer back to the exercises enumerated here.

CORRECTIVE EXERCISES

EXERCISE 7.

Rotated Leg Raise. Lie on your back with both knees flexed. Straighten one leg, turn the toes outward, and gradually lift the leg as shown. To make this exercise more effective, you will have to add weights when they are prescribed. You may use sandbags or light weight-lifting shoes. Start with two pounds, and do not add more than half a pound at a time every second or third day. As soon as you have to jerk or strain, the weight is excessive. Reduce it to the point where you can do it with ease and only slight effort. Be extremely cautious when completing this exercise to avoid injury. (This and the next exercise are principally used to strengthen weak hip flexors.)

EXERCISE 8.

Heel Slide. Lie on your back, both knees flexed. Pull up both knees to your chest. When the knees have reached your chest, lower your legs gradually and straighten them at the same time until they finally reach the floor. Relax.

EXERCISE 9.

Abdominal Setting. Lie on your back, both knees flexed. Now tighten your stomach muscles. Try to tighten the seat muscles at the same time. If you do this correctly, the small of your back will be pressed against the floor. Do not do it by pressing with your legs. Let the tight muscles move your pelvis and bring your back against the floor. Do not push your back against the floor. You will not succeed at once. You may have to start by tightening your abdomen and later tightening your seat muscles separately before you can tighten them together. Once you succeed, hold muscles tight for two seconds, then let go.

EXERCISE 10.

Head Up Supine. (This and the next two exercises are principally used to strengthen weak stomach, or abdominal, muscles.) Lie on the floor, your knees flexed, hands loose by your side. Raise your head and shoulders off the floor, lower slowly and relax.

EXERCISE 11.

Knee Kiss. Lie on your back with knees flexed. Raise your head and your right knee at the same time and try to make them meet. Don't try too hard. You will probably not succeed. You will eventually. Return to your starting position and do the same with your head and left knee.

EXERCISE 12.

Sit-up, Knees Flexed. Lie on your back with your hands clasped behind your head, knees flexed. Tuck your feet under a chest of drawers, bed, or heavy chair. Be sure that the object is heavy enough so that it doesn't topple over. Sit up, then lower yourself slowly to lying position. You should sit up gradually, starting by raising your head, then your shoulders, and then your chest and lower end of the spine. Do not sit up by "hinging," that is, holding your trunk stiff and jerking your weight up. If you do not succeed in doing this exercise with your hands behind your neck, start by having them at your sides. Later, cross them over your stomach, and still later, when you are stronger, bring your crossed arms up to your chest and, finally, behind your neck and head. If you're unable to do this exercise at all, stick to earlier exercises until you have gained enough strength.

EXERCISE 13.

Single Arm Raise, Prone. Lie on the floor on your stomach with a pillow under your abdomen. Raise your right arm and shoulder, lower, relax. Alternate sides. (This and the next exercise are principally used to strengthen upper back muscles.)

EXERCISE 14.

Back Up, Prone. Lie on your stomach with a large pillow under your waist. Anchor your feet under a heavy piece of furniture. Watch that the furniture doesn't topple on you. Keep your hands at your side. Raise your back. Raise your back until it is straight in line with your legs, but *do not* arch backward. (Arching back exercises, so-called hyper-extension exercises, have been prescribed frequently in the past and still are, but we have found that they can cause discomfort and pain in many cases. Backward arching is not a normal movement of the spine unless you're an acrobat. Do not do it.)

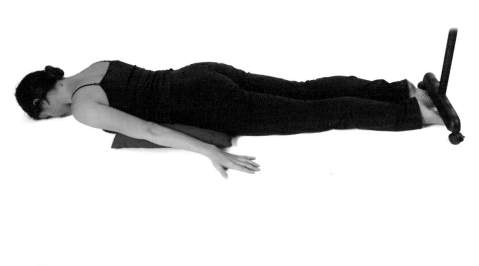

EXERCISE 15.

Single Leg Raise, Prone. Lie on your stomach with a large pillow under your waist. Raise one leg at a time, lower, rest. Alternate. (This and the next exercise are used principally to strengthen low-back and seat muscles. Note, however, that weakness of back muscles is very rare. If you cannot pass either of the back-muscle tests and fail other tests, too, you should definitely seek professional advice. Be sure to take the K-W tests with a sufficiently large pillow under your waist and be certain that your legs or upper back are respectively well anchored. If you don't anchor your legs and don't have a large enough pillow, you may not be able to pass, even though you are strong enough.)

EXERCISE 16.

Double Leg Raise, Prone. Lie prone with a pillow under your hips. Anchor your hands by holding on to heavy furniture. Watch that furniture does not topple on you. Raise both legs at a time, lower, rest.

EXERCISE 17.

Prone Stretch. Lie on stomach, stretch left arm and right leg as far as you can along the floor, relax. Then do same with right arm and left leg. Then stretch with all four limbs at the same time, relax. (This and the remaining exercises are principally used to stretch muscles, from your shoulders to your hamstrings.)

EXERCISE 18.

Bend Sitting. Sit on a chair, feet apart on the floor. Drop your neck, your shoulders, and your arms, then bend down between your knees, as far as you can. Return to upright position, straighten out, and relax.

EXERCISE 19.

Cat Back. Assume a kneeling position, resting on your hands and knees. Arch your back like a cat, drop your head at the same time, then reverse positions by bringing up your head and sway-backing your spine.

EXERCISE 20.

Bend Sitting Rotation. Sit on chair as in "Bend Sitting" (Exercise 18). Bend down, dropping your head and shoulders. Bend down to the left, then gradually straighten up, rest. Do the same to the right.

EXERCISE 21.

Hamstring Stretch. Lie on your back, both knees flexed, arms at sides. Bring one knee up to your face as close as possible, then raise your leg straight up in the air, then lower it slowly to the floor. As you do this you should feel a pull in your hamstrings. Return to starting position. Be sure that you relax before doing the same movement with the other knee. After completing this exercise with your toes pointed out as shown here, repeat with your heel pointed out.

EXERCISE 22.

Hamstring Stretch Standing. Stand up, clasp your hands behind your back, keeping your back and neck straight. Gradually lower your trunk, bending from the hips, and go down as far as you can until you feel a stretching of your hamstring muscles.

EXERCISE 23.

Pectoral Stretch. Sit in a chair, place your hands behind your neck, interlace fingers. Now bring your elbows as far back as you possibly can, return to starting position, then drop arms and relax. Repeat.

EXERCISE 24.

Kneeling Pectoral Stretch. Get on your knees and hands, then fore-arms, then gradually straighten out your back, sliding forward on your arms and keeping your back and head straight. This will stretch your pectoral muscles as you move away from your knees. Return to kneeling position, rest, repeat.

EXERCISE 25.

Upper Back Stretch. Sit on a chair with your hands on your shoulders. Try to cross your elbows by bringing your right arm as far left as possible and your left arm as far right as possible until you feel the stretch across your upper back. Return to starting position, drop hands, relax.

EXERCISE 26.

Shoulder Pull Prone. Lie on your stomach, pillow under hips. Pull your shoulder blades together and relax. This exercise can be helpful in combination with the "shrugging."

EXERCISE 27.

Floor Touch. This exercise is identical with the K-W test (No. 6) for flexibility. It is the peak exercise given in all programs. To do it, first relax by inhaling and exhaling deeply. Drop your neck gradually and

hang your trunk loosely from your hips. Drop your shoulders and then your back gradually. Let gravity help you. Do this two or three times. When you're completely relaxed, "hanging from the hips," try to touch the floor with your finger tips. Relax again, straighten up, then repeat.

Right

Wrong

Now that you have read through all the exercises, it is time for you to pick your prescribed program, a program prescribed to correct any deficiencies that have been revealed by the six K-W tests. Before you begin, however, remember that you should always take your time and that you should always start with general exercises 1 through 6 and conclude with them (and the rest of your program) in reverse order.

WEAK HIP FLEXORS

If you failed only K-W test 1 (shown here)—not being able to hold your heels ten inches above the floor for ten seconds—it is because you have weak hip flexors.

You will add the following exercises, one new one every two or three days, to the six general exercises: exercises 7 (without weight), 15, 7 (again, this time with weight), 19, 8, 18, and 27. Always do these exercises in this prescribed sequence, and when you have completed exercise 27, then return in reverse order to general exercise 1. Your full program, in order, will be exercises 1–6, 7, 15, 7, 19, 8, 18, 27, 18, 8, 19, 7, 15, 7, and 6–1.

WEAK HIP FLEXORS AND ABDOMINALS

If you failed K-W test 2 (shown here) you are unable to sit up because you have both weak hip flexors and weak abdominals.

Weak abdominals, or stomach muscles, are tested in K-W test 3, and test 2 is included in the K-W series to gauge the relative weakness of hip flexors and abdominals at the same time. If you are weak in *both* hip flexors *and* abdominals, and still pass the other tests, you will add the following exercises, one new one every two or three days, to the six general exercises: exercises 9, 15, 10, 13, 11, 19, 12, 18, 22, and 27. When you are doing this, full daily program, test yourself again. If you are able to pass K-W test 3 for weak abdominals, you probably will be able to pass K-W test 1 for weak hip flexors. But if you cannot pass K-W test 1, insert exercise 7 between exercises 18 and 22 and exercise 8 after exercise 27 in your program. You should always do all these exercises in this prescribed sequence and then return in reverse order to general exercise 1. Your full program, in order, will be exercises 1–6, 9, 15, 10, 13, 11, 19,18, (7), 22, 27, (8), 27, 22, (7), 18, 12, 19, 11, 10, 15, 9, and 6–1.

WEAK ABDOMINALS

If you failed only K-W test 3 (shown here) you are unable to sit up because you have weak abdominal, or stomach, muscles.

You will add the following exercises, one new one every two or three days, to the six general exercises: exercises 9, 15, 10, 13, 11, 19, 12, 18, 22, and 27. Always do these exercises in prescribed sequence, and when you have completed exercise 27, return in reverse order to general exercise 1. Your full program, in order, will be exercises 1–6, 9, 15, 10, 13, 11, 19, 12, 18, 22, 27, 22, 18, 12, 19, 11, 13, 10, 15, 9, and 6–1.

WEAK UPPER BACK

If you failed only K-W test 4 (shown here), you are unable to hold your trunk steady for ten seconds because you have weak upper back muscles and should seek professional help, as previously indicated.

   If your physician so advises, you will do the six general exercises and then the following exercises, one new one every two or three days: exercises 11, 13, 12, 17, 18, 14, 22, 24, and 27. Always do these exercises in prescribed sequence, and when you have completed exercise 27, return in reverse order to general exercise 1. Your full program, in order, will be exercises 1–6, 11, 13, 12, 17, 18, 14, 22, 24, 27, 24, 22, 14, 18, 17, 12, 13, 11, and 6–1.

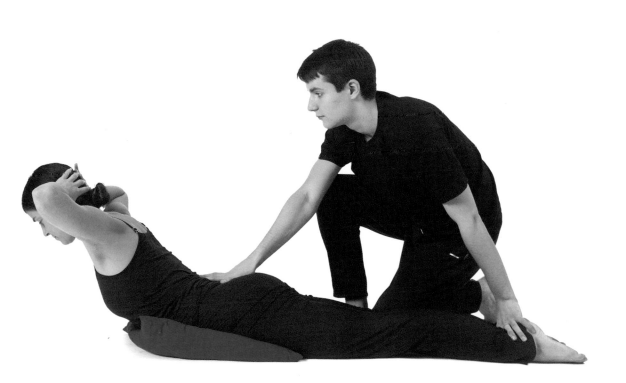

WEAK LOWER BACK

If you failed only K-W test 5 (shown here) and are unable to hold your legs up straight for ten seconds, you have weak lower back muscles and should seek professional help as previously indicated.

If your physician so advises, you will do the six general exercises and then the following exercises, one new one every two or three days: exercises 11, 15, 12, 18, 16, 22, 19, and 27. Always do these exercises in prescribed sequence, and when you have completed exercise 27, return in reverse order to general exercise 1. Your full program, in order, will be exercises 1–6, 11, 15, 12, 18, 16, 22, 19, 27, 19, 22, 16, 18, 12, 15, 11, and 6–1.

LACK OF FLEXIBILITY CAUSED BY TENSION AND STIFFNESS

If you failed only K-W test 6 (shown here)—inability to touch the floor with your finger tips—you are tense and lack flexibility.

You will add the following exercises, one new one every two or three days, to the six general exercises: exercises 12, 17, 18, 12 (again), 19, 11, 20, 21, 19, 22, 23, 24, and 27. Always do the exercises in this prescribed sequence, and when you have completed exercise 27, return in reverse order to general exercise 1. Your full program, in order, will be exercises 1–6, 12, 17, 18, 12, 19, 11, 20, 21, 19, 22, 23, 24, 27, 24, 23, 22, 19, 21, 20, 11, 19, 12, 18, 17, 12, and 6–1.

WEAK HIP FLEXORS AND LACK OF FLEXIBILITY

If you failed to pass both K-W tests 1 and 6 (shown here) but passed the other tests, you have both weak hip flexors and a lack of flexibility.

You will add the following exercises, one new one every two or three days, to the six general exercises: exercises 7 (without weight), 17, 18, 7 (again, this time with weight), 19, 20, 21, 22, 8, 23, 24, and 27. Always do these exercises in this prescribed sequence, and when you have completed exercise 27, return in reverse order to general exercise 1. Your full program, in order, will be exercises 1–6, 7, 17, 18, 7, 19, 20, 21, 22, 8, 23, 24, 27, 24, 23, 8, 22, 21, 20, 19, 7, 18, 17, 7, and 6–1.

WEAK ABDOMINALS AND LACK OF FLEXIBILITY

If you have failed *both* K-W tests 3 and 6 (shown here) but passed the other tests, you have both weak abdominal muscles and a lack of flexibility.

You will add the following exercises, one new one every two or three days, to the six general exercises: exercises 9, 15, 10, 17, 11, 18, 12, 19, 20, 21, 22, and 27. Always do these exercises in prescribed sequence, and when you have completed exercise 27, return in reverse order to exercise 1. Your full program, in order, will be exercises 1–6, 9, 15, 10, 17, 11, 18, 12, 19, 20, 21, 22, 27, 22, 21, 20, 19, 12, 18, 11, 17, 10, 15, 9, and 6–1.

WEAK HIP FLEXORS AND ABDOMINALS AND LACK OF FLEXIBILITY

If you failed K-W tests 2 and 6 (shown here), you have not only weak hip flexors and weak abdominals, but you lack flexibility as well.

You will add the following exercises, one new one every two or three days, to the six general exercises: exercises 9, 15, 10, 13, 11, 19, 12, 18, 22, and 27. When you have reached this program, test yourself again. If you are able to pass K-W test 3 for weak abdominals, you probably will be able to pass K-W test 1 for weak hip flexors. If you cannot pass K-W test 1, insert exercise 7 between exercises 18 and 22 and exercise 8 after exercise 27. Always do these exercises in this prescribed sequence, and then return in reverse order to general exercise 1. Your full program, in order, will be exercises 1–6, 9, 15, 10, 13, 11, 19, 12, 18, (7), 22, (8), 27, (8), 22, (7), 18, 12, 19, 11, 13, 10, 15, 9, 6–1.

WEAK UPPER BACK AND LACK OF FLEXIBILITY

If you failed both K-W tests 4 and 6 (shown here), you have weak upper-back muscles and lack of flexibility. You should seek professional help as previously indicated.

If your physician so advises, you will do the six general exercises and then add the following exercises, one new one every two or three days: exercises 10, 13, 11, 19, 18, 14, 20, 21, 23, 24, 22, 25, 26, and 27. Always do these exercises in this prescribed sequence, and when you have completed exercise 27, return in reverse order to general exercise 1. Your full program, in order, will then be exercises 1–6, 10, 13, 11, 19, 18, 14, 20, 21, 23, 24, 22, 25, 26, 27, 26, 25, 22, 24, 23, 21, 20, 14, 18, 19, 11, 13, 10, and 6–1.

WEAK LOWER BACK AND LACK OF FLEXIBILITY

If you failed *both* K-W tests 5 and 6 (shown here), you have weak lower back muscles and lack flexibility. You should seek professional help as previously indicated.

If your physician so advises, you will do the six general exercises and then add the following exercises, one new one every two or three days: exercises 10, 15, 11, 19, 18, 16, 20, 21, 22, and 27. Always do these exercises in the prescribed sequence, and then, after doing exercise 27, return in reverse order to exercise 1. Your full program, in order, will be exercises 1–6, 10, 15, 11, 19, 18, 16, 20, 21, 22, 27, 22, 21, 20, 16, 18, 19, 11, 15, 10, and 6–1.

SPECIAL ADDITIONAL EXERCISES

If you have been troubled by stiff neck or stiff shoulders, you may wish to add the following exercises to the end of your individual program (if they are not already included): exercises 23, 24, 25, and 26. In between each one of these exercises make sure that you shrug your shoulders and relax.

A NOTE OF CAUTION

If your K-W test failures do not fit any of the above combinations, you should again see your physician for a thorough review of your case. He will check on the possibility of pathology, trigger points, or fibrositis. If he excludes these as sources of trouble, he may compose a program for you, based on the exercises previously offered.

At long last, after consulting with your physician, you have embarked on your daily exercise program. Keep doing your prescribed exercises. Bear in mind, however, that although these exercises will bring you up to a level of "minimum muscular fitness," they will not make you fit for either heavy labor or demanding sports. These exercises do nothing whatever for your heart circulation. They will help get you in condition, but you must add two new exercises, given below, before your activity has any effect on your heart and circulation. In addition to these two cardiovascular exercises, you should also engage in sports, a number of which are discussed in the next chapter.

Before you start the two exercises designed to increase the strength of your heart and circulation, make sure that your heart is in good shape and that your physician approves these exercises. A weak heart can be gradually retrained by exercise, but you should not try to decide this without medical advice.

CARDIOVASCULAR EXERCISE

1. Run in place. Raise your knees only slightly in the beginning and do the place running only for one or two minutes.

2. Stand with feet parallel, slightly apart; spread and stretch arms while inhaling; exhale, crossing arms in front of chest. After two or three times, go into a knee bend while exhaling and crossing arms, and return to standing position, inhaling with arms spread.

3. Pulse rate and breathing must increase in order to help the cardiovascular system.

Stand with your feet parallel, go into a knee bend (a half knee bend at first), then straighten up, and jump an inch off the floor.

Gradually increase the knee bends and jump higher. If your neighbors complain, or the people under you hear your jumping, you may do this exercise without jumping, but you have to increase the speed to make it effective. Do these exercises after you have gone through half of your regular daily exercise program, and then return and do those exercises in reverse.

After running or doing strenuous exercise you should feel hot and tired but not exhausted. The day after you should not have any pain or real discomfort in your muscles.

chapter 7

Running, Yes; Golf, Maybe; Football, No

NOW THAT YOU HAVE STARTED YOUR EXERCISE PROGRAM, you must keep at it every day. When you are able to pass the K-W tests and are free from discomfort, you should also play sports or engage in some sort of vigorous physical activity to make sure that your muscles and heart get a good daily workout.

When you start playing sports, do so gradually. Do not rush yourself. Take it easy in the beginning, and build yourself up slowly. Above all, choose a sport or activity that will do you some definite good. Some sports are excellent, while others are harmful, even though they may seem pleasurable. When you take part in a sport, you should make certain that it is not only going to benefit you physically but emotionally as well. Some sports don't release tension. They add to it.

The basic sports, those that will put you in condition and give you good physical and emotional workouts, are swimming, calisthenics, gymnastics, hiking, running and bicycling. Each of these, however, presents its own problems unless properly approached.

By far and away the best thing you can do is a lot of running. There is nothing that can match running—hard running—as a conditioner. If you start to run on a regular basis, you will get into excellent shape in no time. When your muscles no longer get stiff and tense after a workout, you may substitute running for your formal exercises.

It is not hard to find a place to run. Perhaps you live near a track, a school, or a Y.M.C.A. You can use a city park, a dirt road in the country, or even your own back yard. A lawn, a beach, or an open field will do. If the ground is gently rolling, it will add to the value of the workout. If you have not done any running previously, start easy and jog a distance until you feel winded or tired. You may warm up by walking awhile, then jog gently and walk again. After accustoming yourself to easy running, you may add brief faster periods so that in a month or two you can run a mile with little difficulty. In fact, any forty-year-old who has a good heart should be able to run two or three miles at an average of eight minutes per mile. I know much older people whose speed is faster than that and they do not get winded. Clock yourself so you measure the improvement of your performance.

When you run, make certain that you warm up and cool off properly. Before and after you run, jog and walk. Work up a light sweat before you run; this is the sign that you are ready to go. When you have finished running, be sure to limber your back muscles and legs and then stretch them. Several years ago I treated a number of college runners at our clinic. Four or five of them came in with torn hamstrings. When another one showed up, I phoned the coach, Mr. G. "Five or ten minutes is not enough time for a sprinter to warm up," I said. "Your boys should be hot and sweating before they run."

The coach didn't say much. He just listened, and when I was finished, he hung up with a brief "Thanks." I thought he was angry, and I was sure of it when he didn't send us any more of his boys.

Some time later I spoke at a college track coaches' luncheon in New York, and I talked about proper warm-ups. When the questioning started, who stood up but Mr. G.! I thought he was going to give me the devil. "Gentlemen," he said, "I just want you to know that a couple of years ago I sent a number of boys to the doctor's clinic. He told me that they weren't warming up properly. After that I never sent another boy to that clinic. I didn't have to—because I saw to it that the boys worked up a sweat before they ran."

Swimming is another sport that will get you in good shape, provided you start slowly and increase your timing and distance by steps as you would in running. Swimming, of course, does nothing for you if you just take a dip and loaf in the sun. This is what many people do, and then they say they have had a workout.

Bicycling, too, is excellent for a vigorous workout. The same rules apply. Start gradually, don't overexert yourself, time yourself, and watch your distance if you're not used to it. You may be able to use a bicycle as transportation and so incorporate it into your daily activity. Be sure the handle bars and seat are properly adjusted so you don't crouch too much. When you pedal, you should straighten your knees completely, to stretch your hamstrings. Dr. Paul Dudley White, the heart specialist, is a great cycling enthusiast. He says he gets superb exercise from riding his bike, and at seventy-eight he should know.

Another basic sport is hiking. If you wish to do more than simply hiking over flat ground, look for hilly, rolling country or mountains. Hiking, especially with packs, can get you in shape if it is done regularly. If you hike at a brisk pace uphill or with a pack, it will do much for your cardiovascular system. Needless to say, any other activities involving hiking or running, such as hunting or chasing butterflies, are excellent too.

Gymnastics and calisthenics are excellent conditioners and should be taught in school. They do far more for overall development than do team sports, and they can keep you in good condition throughout life. They are true "carry-over sports." Unfortunately they have been dropped by many schools but there are still a few good teachers available. Without question, gymnastics and calisthenics should be revived and taught in every school.

Other sports and activities such as skiing, tennis, rowing, boxing, and chopping wood may help to keep you in condition, if you participate in them regularly. You have to be in shape to do these things. If .you are in poor condition and participate, you run the risk of injury.

Skiing, of course, is a seasonal sport. In recent years it has suffered from mechanization. Skiing is a good example of how we try to get the most pleasure from the least work. It has become mostly a chair-lift activity. No longer do you have to be able to hike up a slope before you can shoot down it. Unless you do warm-ups, you start your run cold (and often frozen after the trip in the lift), and so your first run down the mountain finds your body completely unprepared for any emergencies. If you like to ski, do some cross-country skiing, especially at the beginning of the season, and be sure to keep fit all year round.

Sad to say, skiing nowadays has become the sport of the non-athlete. A friend who leads a ski school in a resort near New York City told me that she had to refuse beginners who did not have enough strength to get up once they had fallen to the ground. I found it hard to believe her, but on my next visit to that resort I actually saw instructors reject several pupils who were completely unable to get up off the snow, even though the students were in the correct position to get up. This was true of a number of children as well.

Golf has lost much by mechanization. Golf carts have made walking unnecessary. One of the great fallacies about golf is the notion that it is a relaxing game. I am not overly sold on the game as a conditioner. Many patients say that they love the game because it "relaxes" them. It does not relax them, and it does not relax you. It *stimulates* you. Maybe golf does relax some people, for example, Arnold Palmer or Gary Player on a day when they've shot a 66 in the opening round of the Masters or the U. S. Open. But you are not Palmer or Player. A flubbed drive or a missed putt on one hole, and there goes your "relaxation." Do the same on the next hole, and you want to wrap your club around a tree. There can be no doubt that golf is an absorbing game, but it is absorbing because it is filled with mental tension from the first tee to the eighteenth green. I think the reason why golf is so popular with bankers, stockbrokers, and presidents of the United States is because depressions, recessions, and even wars seem like small stuff after a bad round.

One of our patients, Fred W., was an ardent golfer. Or at least he was before he came to see us. Fred is in his late forties, has a beefy-red complexion, and is an account executive for an ad agency. Now, as you undoubtedly know, advertising is a frantic business. A new client comes in, and joy reigns. A client leaves, and half the office gets fired. It's up and down, from the heights to the depths, all the time. Advertising is a profession built on anxiety and tension.

Fred had been in "the agency game" for twenty years, ever since he graduated from one of the Ivy League schools. Advertising was his life and soul. He liked excitement, and he got it. He "relaxed" weekends playing golf; otherwise, he got no exercise whatsoever, unless you count lifting a dry martini at lunch. If ever a man was designed for back pain, Fred was the man. He was tied up in knots with muscle tension, but he didn't think anything of it. Everyone he knew was in the same state. He thought tension was normal. In fact, he even thought he was in better shape than some of his colleagues because he didn't have ulcers.

One Friday, just as Fred was looking forward to a weekend of golf, there was a meeting with a client. The client was a pest, and the agency had thought of resigning the account. But inasmuch as business was not then at its best, the agency kept the client, and poor Fred was the executive who had to deal with him. This Friday meeting was particularly exasperating. The client was complaining worse than ever. The meeting started at ten in the morning; it dragged on through lunch and didn't end until four that afternoon. Nothing was solved by the meeting. It had just been one long aggravation, and when it was over, Fred felt like punching not only the client but his boss as well for keeping the account.

Instead of doing either, Fred left the office with his anger bottled up inside him. He seethed all the way home on the train. The fact that the train was late did not help. When he got to his station, he didn't drive home but headed for a nearby driving range to let off steam. He bought a bucket of balls, lined them up on tees, and tried to smack each one as far as he could. Whenever Fred topped a drive, he would swing even more viciously at the next ball. He had hit about fifty balls when he felt a sudden stab in his lower back. He tried to hit another ball, but when he raised his driver, his left side seemed to become one massive, writhing knot of pain. He was frightened. He put down the driver and dragged himself to the car, his hand holding his back. He got home, and his wife helped him to bed. That is where he stayed until Monday morning when he hobbled into the clinic for help.

We looked at his back. His muscles were in severe spasm. Ethyl chloride and gentle limbering movements relieved some of his pain,

and then we got his case history. We told him to go home and lie down and see us again on Wednesday. When he came back, we injected a trigger point in his low back with procaine. Fred had never heard of trigger points, so I told him about them. Then we discussed his case.

"I want you to do two things," I said. "When the pain eases, you must start on exercises to prevent it from coming back. This will make your back muscles flexible. As of now they are as stiff as a board. They are stiff with tension. You don't need any strengthening exercises. It's surprising, but you still have strength in your muscles. Your problem is tension. Now to help get rid of the tension, you should give up golf at least until I tell you it's all right to play."

"But I love golf," he protested. "It's my relaxation."

"It isn't," I said. "It's one of two sources of your tension. Your job is the other source. Would you rather give up your job?"

"No," Fred said.

"Then give up golf. When your back is in better shape, we'll see about golf. The chances are that you will be all right. Let's just see what happens."

Fred began his exercise program and kept faithfully at it. In two months' time he was coming along fine. He kept insisting that he wanted to start golfing again, and so after five months we let him go back to it. We were afraid that he would build up more tension from not being able to play. However, he now knows that he must exercise to keep tension down, and so he also swims three times a week at a health-club pool near his office.

Tennis is a good sport to keep you in condition. The important thing about tennis, or any other sport, is that you play regularly if you play at all. If you are overweight and forty and have just started one of the exercise programs described in the preceding chapter, do not rush out to play a hard game of singles or even doubles. Pace yourself. Be moderate. Then after you have gotten back into condition and have the knack of the game, start playing on a regular basis. By regular basis I mean once or twice a week at a minimum. Don't give up tennis for a month or two, and then suddenly get in a game on a Saturday morning and give it all you've got.

Fencing is another sport that will keep you in good condition, if done regularly. One drawback is that fencing is a "unilateral" activity; you use your body one-sidedly and thus you do not get an even workout. However, fencing does give you great tension release, and the activity is good for your cardiovascular system as well.

Much-maligned boxing can be a good carry-over sport, provided it is properly supervised and not done competitively. Boxing is often damned because professional boxing has been guilty of many ruthless practices. But that does not make boxing itself inherently bad. What I have in mind by boxing is a sparring session between partners of equal weight and skill. You can match opponents evenly, as you can in few other sports. You should make sure, of course, that the ring is sufficiently padded, that the gloves are of sufficient size to muffle the impact of the punches, and that head guards are worn.

The training required for boxing, such as punching the light and heavy bags, skipping rope, and running, is excellent for the system, and sparring in the ring, whereby you experience both tension ("Will he get me?") and release ("Ah, I got him!"), is most beneficial.

Many years ago, when I was still a young intern, a group of us used to exercise and box regularly with our friend and coach, Heinz Kowalski. At one time one of the boys was quite tense and more nervous than usual. He was getting ready to present his first paper to the local medical society. Obviously this was a great event, and he was tight and tense as can be. We all kidded him, but Kowalski took one look and said, "I'd like to spar a couple of rounds with you this afternoon before you start your great evening."

We had a good time watching Kowalski chase the young man around the ring, and pretty soon he seemed to have forgotten all about the impending ordeal. Only when he left the ring, warm, relaxed, and happy, did he notice that he had acquired a nice black shiner. The august members of the medical society might have wondered about this, but the young doctor's talk went off very well, with no hesitation or stumbling on his part.

Unfortunately our most popular sports are among the worst you can play. Football comes to mind at once, and I include touch football. Briefly put, football is legalized assault. A football game is not a contest between equals; a 150-pound halfback can be tackled by two or three 200-pound linemen. The chance for permanent injury is overwhelming. All too often a runner is clipped or hit from behind. Piling on is a common abuse. I have yet to treat one ex-football player as a back patient who was not also bothered by a bad knee or shoulder injury.

In many ways touch football is worse then tackle. It is now becoming the weekend game for suburban middle class males. More often than not, touch is played by men who are not in any sort of shape to start with, and as a result they are not prepared to withstand the sudden shocks and jars of the game. Touch football also builds tensions. Your neighbor gives you an extra hard block, and you retaliate. Before you know it, one of you is out of action with a broken wrist or arm and a bad temper. I know of one instance where a freelance photographer didn't get any more assignments after he broke the shoulder of a magazine editor in the opposing backfield. If you wanted to see that editor get angry and tense, all you had to do was mention that photographer's name for the next six months. Whether touch or tackle, football is a game that requires great fitness but does not give you a chance to develop it.

Baseball cannot be viewed as a good game either for a sufficient physical workout. Most of the time the players, with the exception of the pitcher and the catcher, simply stand around doing nothing at all. Then, all of sudden, the center fielder, the third baseman, or the shortstop has to rush into action to field a ball, then wheel and throw to a base. Coming after a period of inactivity, this sudden burst of action can bring about injury. This applies equally to a base runner. One second he is standing idly near first; the next second he's sprinting for third on a single, ready to slide to beat the throw.

Little League baseball does much more harm than good despite all the various excuses that have been made for it. Youngsters spend too much time playing baseball, time in which their bodies could be benefiting more profitably in far more vigorous pastimes. In addition, the intense competition can be harmful, particularly when the parents get emotionally involved and make the youngsters the pawns of their own egos. Go to a field and hear the parents carry on when a pinch hitter goes up in place of darling Junior or the umpire calls him out at home.

Intense baseball competition for youngsters is bad because it produces tensions, muscular and emotional, that cannot be relieved by the physical inactivity of the game. This holds true for the most talented youngster. He just cannot work off enough muscular steam in a ball game, and he may leave the field tense, no matter what the score or how many hits he got. Intense competition in any sport is bad for a growing child. It is especially bad for the youngster who, perhaps because of parental goading, has to push himself beyond his limits. When a child does this, he lays himself open to injury. He is playing under tension before the game even begins. This is true of some adults as well. Many of our patients are frustrated athletes. It is easy to spot them because they injure themselves repeatedly. We get skaters who cannot quite compete at the top level, but who push themselves nonetheless. We get the same skiers back time after time. They get hurt because they are not very adept at skiing, yet they constantly try to push themselves beyond their abilities.

Of course, baseball is the national game, and it is natural for a youngster to want to play it. Let him play, but make sure that he gets regular and vigorous physical exercise beforehand. Exercise is the main course, and baseball, or any other sport for that matter, can serve as the dessert.

Volleyball, in many ways, is similar to baseball. It does not release the tension it builds up in a participant. Basketball is better, but it has come to be a game for the very tall, which means that it is a game for the very few. Not long ago I heard of a college basketball coach whose office door is six feet, four inches high. Outside is a sign saying, "If you can enter without stooping, don't."

There are any number of marginal sports that are popular but do little to keep you in good shape. They remain important for their recreational value. Bowling, horseshoe pitching, archery, sailing, and fishing, for instance, do not do you any physical harm, but they do not do you any physical good either. We know a patient who is absolutely smitten with fishing. He fishes almost every day. There is an excellent bass pond about a mile through the woods from his house, and he is there any chance he can get. He fishes the pond by wading. Sometimes his children—a girl, seven, and a boy, five—go with him. One day I asked him what he did in the way of sports. He told me all about his fishing. Did he tell me! I thought he would never stop as he described one leaping bass after another. Finally, when he calmed down, I said, "But that doesn't do you any good."

He spluttered and fumed. "Why, Doctor," he exclaimed, "fishing is the greatest relaxation a man can have!"

I had to agree that fishing was a fine mental relaxation. "Now I'll agree with you that the mind influences the muscles," I said, "but your muscles do not get a decent workout when you fish. In fact, from what you tell me, you spend too much time standing in one spot in your waders waiting for a bass to come by. Let me make two suggestions.

"The first is to move around a little more. Don't stand in one spot or hold one position with your body for more than ten or fifteen minutes. Even though you are relaxing, holding a certain body position is likely to make you tense even though you don't sense it. The other suggestion—instead of walking through the woods to the pond, run in."

"But I can't run in waders," he said.

"Carry them," I said. "Change when you get there. If you run in to fish, and run when you're finished, that will do you wonders. That and your daily exercise program should keep you free of tension."

He said he would try it. Now when he goes he often runs, and his children run along with him. It's a great game to him and a great game to them. And I know that when those youngsters grow up, they'll have not only an appreciation for nature and the outdoors but healthy muscles and strong hearts as well.

chapter 8

Suggestions for Daily Living

MANY PERSONS ACTUALLY LEAD THE LIFE OF A CAGED ANI-
mal, often a tormented caged animal. They are plagued by irritations
which they cannot fight or from which they cannot run. They fall vic-
tim to hypokinetic disease, tension headaches, stiff neck, back pain,
ulcers, heart trouble, and obesity.

You may be such a person. But once you start daily exercising and
playing sports, you will have taken a giant step toward the prevention of
hypokinetic disease. For once you will be doing for yourself what you
usually expect others—the medical profession—to do for you: preventing disease. But this time it will be much harder than going to a doctor's
office and just getting a vaccination, because the disease prevention is
solely up to you. You are on your own with exercise. You have to do it
yourself; you have to take the time for it.

Since you will be making a personal effort to avoid
hypokinetic disease, you should also do all you can to
stop irritations before they start.

You must always remember that irritations
influence your mind and your mind then influences the muscles. Your mind and nerves
work hard, and they work overtime. You live
in a high-pressure society. Traffic lights, noise,
commuter schedules, jangling telephones,
missed appointments, a crying baby, a broken
appliance—all these things and more subject
your mind and then your muscles to repeated
tension. You can work out this tension with your
exercise program, but if you are smart, you will
avoid much of the tension to begin with.

183

First of all, you must realize that you have become used to constant irritations—so used to them, in fact, that you don't notice them. You must recognize these irritations, however minor they may seem, and you must put a stop to them. For instance, if you are home and forcibly subjected to irritations, you probably will turn on the radio. That radio noise in itself can be irritating. Then you may turn up the radio more, so as to drown out some vexatious street noise. That is doubly irritating. You probably keep the radio on even when you are talking to friends. Television will be going in one room and the radio in the next. You are so used to all this noise that you hardly concentrate on any of it. Yet this jumble of noise keeps diverting you, and you become used to drifting and being diverted. Your mind starts to feed on distractions and stimulants. You are eating the poison all the time without knowing it, and your mind and then your muscles become needlessly altered and tense. Sure, you are doing your exercises faithfully. Sure, you are running or swimming. Sure, you shed tension. But who let the tension get to you in the first place? You can stop it.

Take stock of your day. What external tensions bother you? Is it running to catch the train? Is it the children waking you up? Is it your teenage daughter's CD player blaring at odd hours? Make a list of these things, and rectify them. Don't run to catch the train. Get up earlier or catch a later train. Is it really that important that you catch that particular train? You must put things in perspective.

Take stock of situational tensions. Are you happy at work? Do you truly enjoy it? Do you get along with your boss or your employees? After you take stock you may find that some of these internal irritations are really not so annoying after all and that you can live with them peacefully. Look for the humor in a problem. Laughter breaks tension, and if you are able to laugh at yourself or smile to yourself at the foibles of your neighbors or fellow workers, you will do much to solve your problem. Then again, you may have to change what you are doing. You may have to let an employee go. You may want to ask for a transfer. You may have to change your job. The important thing is that you should be satisfied and happy in your life. If you are not, make a change. But if you cannot make a change, learn to accept. You are only hurting yourself by putting up with internal stress.

How is your home life? Here, too, changes can be made more easily than you may think, and they do not have to be drastic. You may wish to avoid visits from irritating friends or relatives or that annoying in-law. Your home is your castle, your place of rest. There is no reason why you should be disturbed if annoying visitors make you tense. You may have to give up living with your in-laws. You may have to stop forcing your son to become a lawyer when he really wants to be a teacher.

The most difficult task in dealing with sources of tension will be to solve inner emotional disturbances. All of us have problems, and for some of us they are serious. Exercise will ease tension, but exercise will not root out the cause of your tension. If you are willing to sit down with yourself and, instead of distracting yourself, concentrate on what irritates you, what upsets you, why a particular problem is hard to face, and what the alternatives are, you may be able to find the answer yourself. Then again, the source of your tension may be buried in some deep psychological disturbance, and you may need treatment for it.

That, of course, is up to you. Meanwhile you can avoid bad habits that we have noted over the years. They can contribute to muscle tension, back pain, stiff neck, and nagging headaches. Some of these habits are so bad, in fact, that they may lock your muscles into a set position for most of the day, thereby greatly diminishing the effect of your daily exercise program.

Start the day leisurely. Eat a leisurely breakfast. Don't bolt your food. Don't let the children upset you. A bad temper in the morning can set your mood for the day. Don't read the paper and listen to the radio and keep an eye on the clock at the same time.

Dress comfortably. Much of the clothing and apparel for men and women almost seems deliberately designed to contribute to stress and tension. Shoes, especially women's shoes, can have a very bad effect. High heels often cause poor posture, shorten the calf muscles and hamstrings (which contribute to tension), and put too much weight on the forward part of the foot. A shoe with narrow toes makes the foot muscles rigid and tense. In turn your leg muscles will become tense and then so will your back muscles. Similarly, if your feet do not rest on a flat support, the foot muscles will tighten. Your foot should fit your shoe like a grasping hand. It should never be forced to become a hoof.

The heels of your shoes should fit well. They should not chafe up and down, nor should they "bite" into the ankle. Heels that are too loose or too tight will cause your ankles to sway, and the knees, hip joints, and neck can be affected. Shop around for your shoes. Sandals, by the way, are excellent. They give your toes free movement and gripping action.

Check your stockings. They are often too tight around the toes and thus interfere with the relaxation of your toes and feet. Your toes should not be restricted. You should be able to wiggle them freely.

Girdles are a hindrance to stomach muscles. If a woman is in good condition, she does mot need to wear one. If she is not in good condition, she should try to build up her abdominal muscles so she can get along without support. A girdle is not only a concession to vanity; it is also a troublemaker. A tight girdle hinders natural trunk movements and turns the act of bending into a caricature.

Brassieres with narrow shoulder straps can cause painful shoulder aches and pain in the upper back, partly by the direct pressure of the straps and partly by forcing the wearer into an artificially rigid position that just invites tension attacks.

Collars should always be loose. A collar that is too tight or too high can cause stiff neck or prompt a tension headache. Perhaps you will want to get your collars a half size larger. It will still look perfectly all right, and it will give your neck moving room.

Pajamas and nightgowns should be loose fitting. Don't let them restrict your sleeping movements.

Sleep on a firm mattress. Bed manufacturers are always shouting the praises of their wonderful mattresses and the marvels they will do for your back. A good mattress should be firm, should not give or sag, and above all, it should not hold the body in a groove that prevents you from turning freely during sleep. Inspect your mattress now. Does it measure up to these standards? If it does not, get rid of it. Whenever a patient is in the clinic, I always ask, "Do you sleep on a firm mattress?" The inevitable reply is, "Of course." I then ask the patient to sit on my couch, which is really a very firm mattress. When they sit down and the couch doesn't yield, they usually jump up and exclaim how hard it is. "Well, that's how hard your mattress should be," I thereupon say.

If you have wide shoulders and sleep on your side, you should have big enough pillows. Avoid foam-rubber pillows; they tend to keep your neck in a rigid position.

One low-back-pain patient, a salesman in his mid-thirties, used to sleep on a soft mattress. Once he started exercising, he changed to a hard mattress with a board underneath. Now, he says, he cannot sleep on a soft mattress at all. When he goes away on trips, he makes it a practice to ask the hotel to supply a bedboard. Bedboards are readily available, and hotels are glad to supply one if you request it. But sometimes this salesman still finds the bed too yielding. When that happens, he strips the sheets off the bed, puts them on the floor, draws a blanket over himself, and goes off to sleep. He did this recently when

he was a house guest. His host thought it was rather strange, but the salesman says he had a wonderful rest on the floor.

Reading in an awkward position, be it peering closely at the print or holding the page at a distance, will bring on neck and back strain by forcing your muscles into an unnatural position. When you read, make certain that you are comfortable and that you have ample light.

Many persons get back or neck pain or stiffness from prolonged driving. If you are one of these persons, never drive more than one or two hours at a stretch. Pull over to the side of the road and walk around a bit. Relax. Shrug your shoulders frequently. You've been hunched over the wheel, and both you and your back muscles need a break. Look at the seat. It may be too small; it may also be too close or too far away from the foot pedals. Even if the seat is big enough and hard enough,

you may still get back pain, because long-distance driving is conducive to tension. Try to do your driving in easy stages. Don't rush. You'll get there.

Whether you are driving or staying still, sitting has its perils. Never sit in one position for more than an hour or two. If you have to do desk work, take an exercise break instead of a coffee break. Get up and move around. Keep your muscles limber. Don't let them get stiff. To take a quick breather, literally, inhale and exhale slowly three times. Shrug your shoulders a few times to loosen up tense neck and back muscles. Wobble your head from side to side. You may want to shift the posi-tion of your telephone. When it rings, your muscles go into alert. You get ready for fight or flight, and then you do neither. But you can react phys-ically if you make it a practice to shrug when the phone rings. Instead of keeping the telephone always on one side of your desk, move it to the other side. Move it back and forth 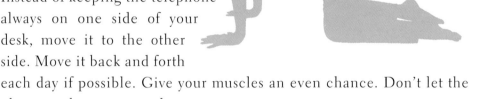 each day if possible. Give your muscles an even chance. Don't let the phone push your around.

Manual labor presents problems of its own. Usually there is not the mental tension that accompanies desk work, but in place of this are frequent and violent body movements. Carrying and lifting heavy loads are a frequent cause of back strain. Learn how to lift a heavy load cor-rectly. You are lifting incorrectly if you bend over from the waist. You should bend from the knees instead if the load is heavy. If you are used to physical effort, you will be able to decide when a load is heavy for you and needs to be lifted carefully.

The constant handling of elevator doors, turning of handles, or re-peated use of any instrument or machine may have telling effects on your muscles. Shoveling and using heavy hammers, especially when the blow strikes a hard surface, may cause all sorts of strain, especially in the upper extremities and in the shoulders. Vary your work routine. Break it up. Don't let it break you up. If you do not, detrimental effects are likely to occur, especially if you are not physically up to the job.

Whether day laborer, housewife, or executive, you should note what you are doing. Don't let yourself fall into a living pattern that invites tension. You can do a lot for yourself. Much tension is avoidable. By all means avoid it.

chapter 9

The Diet Fad: Eat but Exercise

THERE HAS BEEN MORE WRITTEN ABOUT EATING AND DI-eting than any single medical subject. No aspect of physical condition is of greater interest to the public than body weight. Obesity is discussed in innumerable books, pamphlets, magazines, newspapers, and on television. Overweight is a target for all sorts of commercial enterprises, whether they are special diets, reducing machines, or "gimmicks" to produce pinched waistlines.

Dieting has become a fad. You are told to start a crash diet, to start a gradual diet, to watch your calories, to eat fresh fruits and vegetables and cottage cheese, to avoid fried foods, to stay clear of starches, sweets, and fats. You are inundated with information and advice, much of it nonsensical.

There are exceptions to any rule, but there is one rule, solidly based on sound research, that applies to the great majority of people who are not bothered, say, by glandular disorder or hereditary obesity. That rule is: *Eat as much as you want, but work off what you eat.* Obesity is most often caused by physical inactivity, not only by how much or what you eat. As a matter of fact, numerous studies have revealed that trim people often have a larger caloric intake than do people afflicted with obesity. As an additional rule I would suggest that you go easy on starches, avoid animal fats (use vegetable fats instead), and cut down on alcohol.

The main reason for your concern with overweight is because fat is aesthetically unpleasing. A trim figure is a must for a man or woman who wants to be presentable or attractive. Amazingly enough, to

me, this desire for a trim figure is sometimes divorced from any wish for a physically fit and functional body. Such a desire is based on personal vanity. You do not think of losing weight and keeping trim through exercise to improve your health and have a well-functioning body. Instead, you think of losing weight through dieting because you want to "look nice." This is fallacious thinking. You should remember, instead, that obesity increases mortality and the incidence of many diseases, including high blood pressure, arteriosclerosis, diabetes, and back pain.

Unfortunately the diet fad has become ingrained in American life. Even nutritional experts contribute to this fallacious idea by stressing diet alone rather than exercise. Back in 1958 the Food and Nutrition Board of the National Academy of Sciences issued recommended daily caloric intakes for the average American man and woman, who were named, "reference man" and "reference woman." Reference man, according to the Board's calculations, was twenty-five years old and weighed 154 pounds and was five feet nine inches tall. Reference woman was also twenty-five, weighed 128, and was five feet four inches tall. The Board advised that reference man consume 3200 calories a day and that reference woman eat 2300 a day to stay lean and "healthy." But in May 1964 the Board ordered reductions for both. Reference man was told to reduce his caloric intake from 3200 to only 2900 calories a day, and reference man was told to reduce his caloric intake from 3200 to only 2900 calories a day, and reference woman was told to cut her calories from 2300 to 2100.

Why? Because the Food and Nutrition Board decided that the average American man and woman—that's you—were not exerting themselves as much physically as they had in the past. Why didn't the Board advise them to exercise more? As a prominent medical journal remarked in reporting the Board's orders to reduce, "With the spread of power mowers, golf carts, and electric toothbrushes, the American Way is fast becoming the Sedentary Way."

Instead of telling Americans to go on eating and exercise more, the Board told them to cut down on calories. This recommendation only adds to the problem. Underexercised people who diet often have the false and dangerous notion that they are in good condition. Furthermore, the Board's recommendations may be used as nutritional guides for hospitals, schools, and the Armed Forces, and many physicians will consult the Board's calorie counts for their patients, rather than advise increase of physical activity.

For twenty-five years exercise has been given no credit whatsoever by the diet faddists as having any role to play in weight control. In fact, exercise has been ridiculed and disparaged by the diet faddists, who have put forth a number of misconceptions to bolster their case. For instance, you often hear their argument that an increase in exercise leads to an increase of appetite and that exercise, therefore, is useless. This is false. Then again, you hear that you have to "split wood for seven hours" or "walk for thirty-six hours" to take off a pound of fat. This is true—but there is no rule saying that you have to split the wood in one session or do the walking at one clip. If you split the wood for fifteen minutes a day or walk an hour a day as a regular practice, you burn up calories and lose fat. As a matter of fact, if you split wood for fifteen minutes a day every day of the year, you would lose twenty-six pounds of fat in a year. If you also played tennis regularly, you would burn up an additional fifteen to twenty pounds a year. Add the wood splitting and tennis together, and that's more than forty pounds a year. Of course it is ridiculous to expect you to do all this in one stretch, as the diet faddists imply, but when you spread the exercise over the days of the year, you will keep your weight under control at the same time you keep your muscles healthy. But the diet faddists do not tell you this.

Diet faddists will also tell you that if you do a great deal of physical exercise you will eat more. True enough, but you will not put on fat because you will burn off the calories. That is why soldiers in the field, day laborers, and many athletes can consume more than 6,000 calories a day and still be in the best of shape. As Dr. Norman Jolliffe says in his excellent book, *Reduce and Stay Reduced*, "muscular activity increases the caloric expenditure more than any other single factor." I am sure you have seen table after table showing how many calories there are in a steak, a martini, or an ice-cream sundae. On pages 198 and 199, for your constant reference, is something different: a table of energy expenditure compiled by Dr. Jean Mayer of the Harvard University School of Public Health. Dr. Mayer is one of the country's foremost nutritionists, and the table will show you how many calories you use up in an hour in various activities. Check to see how you are doing and what you can do to burn off more.

There have been any number of interesting experiments on the effect of exercise on eating. A few years ago Harvard students were asked to double their daily food intake, from 3,000 to 6,000 calories. With all their classroom work the students were hard pressed to find the time to exercise, but they did exercise and they managed to "lose" the extra 3,000 calories per day.

Dr. Mayer conducted an extensive study on carefully paired groups of obese and trim suburban high-school girls. Particular attention was paid to a systematic comparison of caloric intake and physical activity in both groups. He found a marked difference between the fat girls and the trim girls. The trim girls were physically active; the fat girls were less than half as active. Even so, the trim girls generally ate more than did the fat girls, leading Dr. Mayer to the logical conclusion that being inactive contributed more to obesity than overeating. Ironically Dr. Mayer discovered that the fat girls were often excused from sports upon recommendation of physicians.

Similar findings have been made by other researchers. Dr. J. A. Greene studied more than two hundred overweight adult patients and found that the beginning of their weight problems was directly traceable to a sudden decrease in physical activity. Dr. Hilda Bruch studied 160 fat children, and inactivity was characteristic of the great majority; 88 percent of the girls and 76 percent of the boys were inactive. Danish researchers came up with much the same results in studies they made. I could cite one study after another, all by responsible scientists; they all show that it is not how much you eat but how much you exercise.

A diet may, of course, be essential in combination with exercise. Here is a sample case. One morning a salesman named Donald D. came into the clinic. I should say he waddled in. He was five foot nine, and he weighed 242 pounds. He was thirty-seven years old. His weight, for his build, should have been 170 pounds. Mr. D. was suffering from, chronic back pain. His muscles had become too weak to support his weight. Like most fat people, be they unhappy children, depressed housewives, or anxious executives, he tried to make up for his frustrations by eating and eating and eating. Since he did no exercise whatsoever, he became a balloon.

There was no point in seeing if Mr. D. could touch the floor. Even if he did not have tight back muscles and hamstrings, he never could have gotten past his bulging stomach. We started him on an exercise program, and to hasten recovery, he was also put on a strict diet. As it was, it took a solid year to get Mr. D. down to 170 pounds and his muscles in good shape. If he had not been put on a diet, he could have waited forever for his weight to reach normal. Once Mr. D. got his weight down, he took up swimming and tennis. Now he keeps up his physical activities, having learned that they are a need, not a luxury.

I would like to conclude by citing Dr. Mayer again. What he says is of the greatest significance for you. He writes:

"The author is convinced that inactivity is the most important factor explaining the frequency of 'creeping' overweight in modern Western societies. Natural selection, operating for hundreds of thousands of years, made

CALORIE REQUIREMENTS FOR VARIOUS ACTIVITIES*

Activities	Calories Per Hour
DOMESTIC OCCUPATIONS	
Sewing	10–30
Writing	20
Sitting at rest	15
Standing relaxed	20
Dressing and undressing	30–40
Ironing (with 5-lb. iron)	60
Dishwashing	60
Sweeping or dusting	80–130
Polishing	150–200
INDUSTRIAL OCCUPATIONS	
Tailoring	50–100
Shoemaking	80–100
Bookbinding	75–100
Locksmithing	150–200
Housepainting	150–200
Carpentering	150–200
Joinering	200
Cartwrighting	200
Smithing (light work)	250–300
Smithing (heavy work)	300–400
Riveting	300
Coal mining (avg. for shift)	200–400
Stone masoning	300–400
Sawing wood	400–600
PHYSICAL EXERCISE	
Walking	
2 mph	200
3 mph	270
4 mph	350
Running	800–1000

Activities	Calories Per Hour
CYCLING	
5 mph	250
10 mph	450
14 mph	700
Horseback riding	
Walking	150
Trotting	500
Galloping	600
Dancing	200–400
Gymnastics	200–500
Golfing	300
Playing tennis	400–500
Playing soccer	550
Canoeing	
2.5 mph	180
4.0 mph	420
Sculling	
50 strokes per minute	420
97 strokes per minute	670
Rowing (peak effort)	1200
Swimming	
Breast and back stroke	300–650
Crawl	700–900
Playing squash	600–700
Climbing	700–900
Skiing	600–700
Skating (fast)	300–700
Wrestling	900–1000

Figures obtained for 150-lb. subject.

* Modified from J. B. Orr and I. Leitch, "The Determination of the Caloric Requirements in Man," *Nutrition Abstr. & Rev.*, 7:509, 1938; and R. Passmore and J. V. G. A. Durnin, "Human Energy Expenditure," *Physiol. Rev.*, 35:801, 1955, by Dr. Jean Mayer.

men physically active, resourceful creatures, well prepared to be hunters, fishermen, or agriculturalists. The regulation of food intake was never designed to adapt to the highly mechanized sedentary conditions of modern life, any more than animals were made to be caged. Adaptation to these conditions without development of obesity means that either the individual will have to step up his activity or that he will be mildly or acutely hungry all his life. The first alternative is difficult, especially as present conditions in the United States, especially in cities, offer little inducement to walking and are often poorly organized as regards facilities for adult exercise. Even among the young, highly competitive sports for the few are emphasized at the expense of individual sports which all could learn and continue to enjoy after the high school and college years are over. But if the first alternative, stepping up activity, is difficult, it is well to remember that the second alternative, i.e., lifetime hunger, is so much more difficult that to rely on it for weight-control programs can only continue to lead to the fiascos of the past.

"Strenuous exercise on an irregular basis, in untrained individuals already obese, is obviously not what is advocated. But a reorganization of one's life to include regular exercise adapted to one's physical potentialities is a justified return to the wisdom of the ages."

chapter 10

What Can You Do for your Children?

ANY DISEASE PRODUCED BY LACK OF EXERCISE IS A DEFICIEN-cy disease. As such—like a vitamin deficiency—it hits hardest at the young.

Few mothers will forget to feed their children enough vitamins—but how many will see to it that they have enough exercise? Few parents will miss having their children vaccinated against smallpox, diphtheria, polio, and other contagious diseases, but how many even think of pre-venting hypokinetic disease? Still, lack of sufficient exercise and good exercise habits instilled in childhood is the main cause of tension pain, back pain, overweight, and heart disease in later life. Geriatrics starts in the cradle. It is up to the parent, then the school and the community, to do something about this. Yet they rarely do. The importance of this is not understood. Moreover, too many physicians and educators regard exercise and vigorous physical activity as a "frill" rather than a basic human need. Parents believe them and, if they are not active themselves, go along with this dangerous think-ing. If you are a parent, you must see to it that your children engage in vigorous physical activity not only at home but also at school, whether it be kindergarten or college.

Children are the first to suffer in our seden-tary society. Your children do not lead the com-paratively vigorous life that you led. Their muscles rarely get a workout, and their muscles do not develop properly. Instead of walking, today's youngsters ride. No-tice the next time your boy or girl wants to go somewhere. Even if it is just down the street, they'll ask you to give them a lift. And the bad part of this situation is that you don't think anything of it.

Think of the hours upon hours children spend staring at television. Studies reveal that high school teenagers spend up to thirty hours a week watching television and only two hours exercising. Even if every program were excellent—and I am sure you will agreee that often the opposite is the case—the time spent is harmful. Television and radio programs build up tension in a child at the same time that they keep him from having a physical outlet. You should no more let your child saturate himself with television or radio or similar sedentary distractions than you should expose him to a contagious disease without inoculation. This may sound harsh, but it is the truth. The muscular condition of the majority of American youngsters is appalling.

You can find out if your children have minimum strength and flexibility by giving them the K-W tests. If they do not pass all of them, this means they are not active enough, that they get more irritations than they can work off, that they watch more than they play, and that they are establishing a damaging lifelong pattern. You ought to change this. See to it that they run, that they swim, that they walk, and play games requiring lots of action. See to it that your child learns the feeling of physical effort and physical accomplishment. This—in our growing, hectic, urban society—can best be accomplished not only at home but in disciplined exercise classes. There the first roots of discipline—not regimentation—can grow; there the teacher can pay special attention to individual needs. If you have no classes available, band together with other families and hire a good exercise or ballet instructor for your group of children. Dance classes for even three-year-olds are excellent.

Children like to imitate their elders, and if you lead a physically active life, you will find that your children will want to do what you do. In this way physical activity will come naturally and easily for a child. It will be like breathing. When you go out to swim, hike, run, skate, or ski, let your child come along.

You can start with the baby. Instead of imprisoning him in a confining playpen, stick him out on the lawn and let him move around. Let him try out his muscles; let him develop them at a natural pace. If your baby does not walk as soon as the others in a neighborhood, don't worry. The crawling about does him a great deal of good; it gives him the opportunity to develop strong trunk muscles. As he grows older, let him climb trees and fences if he wants to. Too many parents—all too often the same parents who *push* their children into a sport—are afraid their children will hurt themselves. If a boy or girl breaks an arm, true, it may be in a cast for a while. That is not the worst catastrophe. The real danger is not letting the child learn about physical dangers. In point of fact, the child that does not have the chance to learn about danger is often the child who is likely to suffer severe injury.

Do not be overanxious. Of course, at the same time do not be reckless. There is a dividing line between the two. Let me give you am example. I know a couple, parents of a young daughter, who do a lot of skiing. When the girl was only three, she said she wanted to ski, too. Her parents neither pushed nor discouraged her. Instead, they simply gave her a pair of skis to use around the tack yard. Soon the little girl asked to accompany them skiing. Finally one weekend they gave in. They took her up the beginner's slope, then they let her loose. She schussed down, with her parents at her side to make sure that she did not hit a tree or rock. The little girl couldn't get enough, but her parents took her off the slope before she had a chance to get bored or tired. They did this for a number of weekends, always making her walk up the slope, and continued this routine the following winter. At the age of five she was ready for ski school. Later this little girl developed into an excellent skier. More important, she started to use her body. She learned to ski because her parents did, because she wanted to, and because she had parents who knew how to handle the problem. There is all the difference in the world between setting an example for children and pushing them into an activity for which they have no desire.

Children forced into a sport often rebel, especially if they are below par physically. I saw a twelve-year-old boy, whose parents brought him in to the clinic because they were alarmed about his "poor posture." There was nothing radically wrong with this boy—he had no organic diseases—but he hunched his shoulders and had what can only be described as a hangdog look, common in children and adults who are depressed or frustrated. When I tested the boy, I found that he had weak abdominal muscles and that his lower back muscles and hamstrings were stiff and rigid. All in all, he was extremely tense. You could see the prospective back pain developing right then and there. Obviously corrective measures were necessary.

I talked to both the boy and his parents, and the parents soon made it evident that while they were both active and athletic, the boy was listless. When he first went to school, he tried to make a class team but failed, even though he worked hard. This pattern kept up for the first few years in school, and he always competed unsuccessfully. By the fourth grade he hated anything connected with sports, and he used every possible excuse to avoid the merest hint of exercise. Of course, the more he balked the more his parents pushed him. He developed "poor posture" as a defense, and then his parents grew concerned.

I could tell that the boy was embarrassed at being seen by a doctor. It was bad enough that he was "no good" at sports, but now he had to see a doctor because something was "wrong" with him. To spare the boy further embarrassment that could only worsen the problem, I told the parents that I was going to send him to an exercise teacher. In the beginning he would do the exercises only with the teacher. Then, after he had learned the exercises thoroughly, he would do them in a compatible group. There would be no competition whatsoever, and I told the parents not to push him. As a result of working with an exercise teacher, the boy made excellent progress. His back and posture improved considerably, and his attitude changed. Now he plays sports, and although he is far from the best athlete in the world, he is a healthy youngster with a positive attitude toward vigorous exercise.

It really is easy to keep your children physically active at home; it becomes difficult when they start school. As long as they are infants and pre-schoolers, all you have to do is avoid suppressing their natural urge to move. But then comes school, and many school systems have very poor physical education programs. From an athletic point of view we have the most undemocratic schools in the world. A school can have as many as three to four thousand students, but the only ones who receive systematic muscular training are those who have won a place on one of the varsity athletic teams. This is contrary to common sense, which tells you that the children who are the least exercised are the ones who need it the most.

Instead of lavishing attention on the gifted athletes, schools should institute broad, non-competitive exercise programs that benefit all the students. This does not mean that competitive sports should be neglected. Sports have their place, but that place comes after the physical needs of the overall student body have been met. That should be the aim of physical education.

I consider this so important that I think it is worth repeating: instead of picking the most physically gifted and welding them into winning teams for the glory of the school (and the coaches), the emphasis should be on all the students. Then if, after years of systematic training, a few emerge with special talents, they should be encouraged to make their mark as competitive athletes.

Systematic physical training should start in kindergarten and continue through elementary school, high school, and college. Sports programs should be the icing on the cake, and they should be selective. Physical education for all should consist of one hour a day of for-

mal training, including calisthenics, gymnastics, running, and swim‐
ming. Parents should make sure that this period is really one full hour.
All too often school administrators skimp on this; it is often the first
time period they cut. Studies by Dr. Josephine L. Rathbone of Colum‐
bia University indicate that only twenty minutes of each school hour
assigned to physical education are actually utilized. Make sure this is
not happening in your school.

Exercise programs should be compulsory. I know exercise is all too
often taught without imagination. If taught properly and with a pur‐
pose, and if the participants are kept busy all the time, it is attractive
to youngsters. They love to play leapfrog, tumble, chin themselves, and
climb ropes. Exercise has to start early in life; if a child has become
sedentary and sluggish before the age of six, it will be hard for a teacher
to rouse his interest. And it is exactly this type of child that needs spe‐
cial attention and care.

The exercise class can be used to teach discipline, an area which
is neglected if not ignored in schools because it is usually confused
with regimentation. From easily understood and amusing exercises like
bunny hops and cat crawls children can be gradually brought to accom‐
plish more difficult movements. In short order they will be able to carry
out "difficult" exercises. As soon as possible, exercises should challenge
their strength, their endurance, and their coordination. The more chal‐
lenging they are, the more interesting they will be.

A young child should learn to improve his abilities without actual‐
ly competing with other children. He should measure his own improve‐
ment, not compare his performance with that of another. Children grow
at different rates, and competition should come in later childhood, say,
after twelve, and then competition should be encouraged only when it
buds spontaneously. To force a young child to compete when the con‐
test is hopeless and the child knows that he is destined to be a loser will
do the child no good. There is nothing more disheartening to a young‐
ster, and he falls into the lifelong habit of always doubting himself.

Above all, the teacher should set the example. He or she should
be fit, should come to class in gym clothes, and should work personally

with the children. He should not only be able to do what they do, but he should be able to do any exercise better than they can. When we administered the Kraus-Weber tests to children in Zurich, we talked to many local physical educators. I was impressed by their athletic appearance, and I was especially impressed by the oldest of them, a sixty-five-year-old man who was the chief of the local group. When I asked him whether he still worked actively with the children, he replied, "Yes, of course. I have to, because the moment I cannot chin myself better than the next youngster, and as soon as I cannot run and jump with them, I cannot function as a practical teacher, and I do not want to retire to theory at this stage."

By contrast, I remember an occasion when a friend, an excellent teacher in physical education, had to attend a dinner at a well-known

university. I went with him as a guest. The dining room was on the second floor of the physical education building, and the only elevator was very small. There was a great crowd of physical educators waiting on the first floor to crowd into the jammed elevator. Only a few of them decided to walk the flight of stairs to the dining room. As we walked up the stairs my friend said, "I am afraid that with so few using the stairs, physical education is still missing the first goal."

In the dining room I noticed that most of the physical educators were either overweight or stooped. There were a few with trim, athletic figures, but unfortunately very few. On the whole, the gathering did not look any different from any clambake of underexercised office workers. Why was this? Because in physical education there is more interest in methodology and theory than in actual doing. Since actual doing, actual moving, and actual exercising are only a small part of the curricula of the average physical education school, it is small wonder that the graduates do not look different from any other students who have spent four years sitting in a library. The basic need in physical education is a change of attitude. The basic need here is for acceptance of the physical as an important and essential base for the intellectual and not as a secondary afterthought. Because of efforts by dedicated physical educators such as Frederic R. Rogers, Harrison Clark and others, there are some schools with good programs; they stress the actual physical participation of the students.

Once, I was a speaker at the Physical Education Department at San Diego State College in California. When the morning program was over, I was asked to join the routine noon workout. The whole faculty, including the department head, Dr. Fred Kash, changed to gym clothes and joined the students for very active exercise programs. After a half hour of this everyone ran two miles on the campus lawn. The participants included graduates who had come back to see what was new, and I feel that they learned a lot. The afternoon session closed with a similar procedure, only this time swimming was added. The Physical Education Department works with schools and children in the growing

San Diego area, and it has performed a truly remarkable job in a short time.

Unfortunately, in contrast to San Diego's excellent programs, there are other schools where physical education is taken up by students because it is the "easiest" course and a degree gives a graduate an entree into the school systems as an "administrator." Such an administrator may have very little love for the actual physical improvement of his children.

Besides exercises, the daily school program should include healthy doses of calorie-burning activities, such as running, jumping, and swimming. Youngsters should get a well-rounded and vigorous workout every day at school. Intramural sports programs should not start until the fifth or sixth grade, and when they do start, the intramurals should be optional and held after school hours, as should be the case with varsity sports. In short, no sports activity should be allowed to replace or supplant the basic daily exercise program.

To those who claim that strong physical education programs and strong discipline smack of the totalitarian state, I would like to point out that Switzerland, the oldest existing democracy in the world, has a model program. The government sets the requirements to insure a basic national standard. Youngsters are graded and must pass annual tests, and the results of the tests are recorded in a booklet for each student. Upon graduating from high school a boy receives his booklet and then, in turn, presents it to the authorities in charge of military training. If his marks do not meet the minimum physical requirements, he receives special training before induction. Furthermore, a boy is not eligible for officer's candidate school unless his marks show that he can meet high standards. Girls are given similar physical-fitness tests in school, and although they do not have to serve in the army, the example set by the boys makes them adhere to the standards.

It is interesting to note that the Swiss have national standards. We do not have national standards for physical fitness. In his book *Swiss Education and Ours*, Admiral Hyman Rickover points out that this lack of minimum national standards is a great drawback. National or federal standards could be set without interfering with local school boards.

The minimum requirements set by Swiss schools and the government are not nearly as minimal as the word makes them sound. Besides their regular school training, children give over one afternoon a week, usually a Saturday afternoon, to an outing with the teacher. The whole class swims, hikes, and camps together. In addition, children are required to walk to school. Only those who live more than two miles from school are allowed to use streetcars or even bicycles. The Swiss authorities are very much aware of the influence of increasing mechanization, and they take every opportunity to offset it where it may harm or hinder the physical development of the young.

A specific instance of the careful Swiss attitude comes to mind. When we set out in 1952 to administer our tests to American and European school children, we had, of course, to secure permission from school authorities concerned. The receptions we got varied in different cities. When we asked for permission to test children in one very large American city, we were given evasive answers. A school official finally came out with the real reason for refusing us permission. "Why, we can't possibly let you do this," he said. "Suppose you find out our children are not as fit as they should be. Then what are we going to do?"

By comparison, in Zurich we got cooperation almost immediately. After we explained what we wanted to do, the medical officer in charge of the school system said he would be delighted to give us permission. He called in his aides and told them to give us all possible assistance. He saw to it that all the schools were notified. Then he gave us a breakdown of the school system, so that we could test a cross section of Zurich's children, from rich to poor. After he had done all this for us, he said that he only had one request, and that was that we were to inform him fully of our findings so that he could apply any corrective measures needed.

Without question, we need to revamp physical education in our schools. Physical education has never gotten the overhaul that the academic curriculum got when Sputnik went up. Indeed, when we all became aware that, an intensifying drive for quality education was necessary, this was frequently done at the expense of physical training. Not long ago the California legislature considered abolishing physical education as a requirement. In an attempt to prevent this, proponents of physical education stressed the point that physical education was needed to prevent an increase in hypokinetic disease. Much of the material that my associates and I had gathered, including our K-W test results, was offered as one of the arguments to prevent the change of law. The bill failed.

A revolution in physical education is crucially needed if youngsters are to be safeguarded from hypokinetic disease.

chapter 11

What Can Be Done for Our Country

Editor's note: The world has changed dramatically—in particular, the U.S.S.R. and many of its former satellites no longer exist as they once did—since Dr. Kraus first wrote this chapter. Nevertheless, the information and ideas remain valid even today, and thus, we have left it, for the most part, unchanged.

TREATMENT OF A BACK-PAIN AND TENSION PATIENT OFTEN lasts for months and sometimes a year or more. It is always pleasing when the patient recovers and returns to a full and active life, but the question always occurs to us, was all this effort, all this time, and all this suffering necessary? Could not all this have been prevented? The answer, for the vast majority of cases, is yes. Disease produced by lack of exercise is preventable. And yet we have no sooner finished with one patient than there are two more waiting for treatment. The flood seems never-ending.

Why does it continue? Because programs for adults are practically nonexistent. We can talk about what parents should do and what the schools should do, but so far very few have talked about what can be done for adults. Happily I believe that something—something positive—can be done, not merely to cure underexercise disease, but to prevent its occurrence in the first place. This we must do if we are to handle the problem intelligently.

The United States is a world leader in the prevention of contagious disease. It lags behind other advanced countries in the prevention of hypokinetic disease. Our medical scientists, philanthropic foundations, and social scientists have often seemed unaware of the fact that for many years countries around the globe have been carrying on programs to prevent hypokinetic disease. These programs are backed by private industry, labor unions, insurance companies, and governments. In country after country reconditioning centers have been established to offset the dangers brought about by mechanization in living.

Surprisingly, in the last century, one of the countries that was deeply committed to the prevention of hypokinetic disease was the Soviet Union. The results were impressive, so much so that the former Soviet Minister of Health, Madame Kovrigina, once boasted that for every death caused by heart disease in the U.S.S.R. there were more than two such deaths in the United States. I cannot evaluate the validity of this Soviet claim, but I do know for a fact that in the Soviet there were more than 2,500 reconditioning centers treating at least five million patients a year. These patients were put through reconditioning programs as part of the government's program of "physical culture." In addition, there were a great many "night sanitoria" attached to larger industrial plants, where overtired and tense workers were assigned for three weeks during off hours. When you consider the fact that the Soviet Union, which did not have anywhere near the prosperous (and underexercised) society that we had—and have—recognized and responded to the problem, you may well wonder why no action has been taken in this country.

The former Soviet satellites of Czechoslovakia and East Germany also maintained numerous reconditioning centers. East Germany instituted a seven-year plan for health preservation, with the goal of eventually reconditioning one million sedentary persons a year. By contrasts in the United States, prevention of disease through exercise has been practiced at an academic level at best. We need comprehensive reconditioning centers to combat hypokinetic disease at its onset.

Former West German centers might serve as logical models for institutions in this country. Socio-economic conditions and the incidence of hypokinetic disease were similar to our own, and there are years' worth of detailed reports on organization, methods, and experience that we can draw upon for study.

Dr. Peter Beckmann was the pioneer for the prevention of hypokinetic disease in West Germany. In 1953 he set up a reconditioning center in Ohlstadt, Upper Bavaria, for two hundred sedentary persons. The Ohlstadt center was so successful that others followed. They were supported by insurance companies and industrial enterprises, such as Opel Automobile, Mannesmann Steelworks, Siemens Halske Electric Works, and various Ruhr mining companies.

Treatment at the centers was free, and the patients received up to 80 percent of their regular salaries, depending upon family circumstances. The time spent in a reconditioning course did not count against vacation time. This might seem prohibitively expensive, but the centers more than paid for themselves, as work absenteeism through physical disability was cut in half.

Admission to a center was based upon the recommendation of an applicant's insurance physician and a statement from the applicant's supervisor, indicating that his work performance had regressed. Medical indications were liberal; the patient did not have to be in acute distress. He may have been admitted on the basis of minor problems, including subjective complaints concerning the cardiovascular and muscle systems, the digestive tract, insomnia, general fatigue, premature aging, and so on. Each patient had to present a complete pre-admission certificate and, in turn, when he left he received a report for his regular physician. If rejected for treatment, an insured worker had the right of appeal under West German law.

Although the centers put the primary emphasis on systematic and intensive exercise programs, they gave careful attention to psychological and emotional factors. The centers were intended to help tense, irritated, emotionally overstrained and fatigued patients from factories, shops, offices, and mines "get away from it all." The centers were situated in scenic areas, near mountains, forests, or sandy beaches. They offered plain but pleasant living quarters and were equipped with gyms, indoor and outdoor swimming pools, social halls, and sauna baths. In short, the atmosphere was congenial and mentally relaxing, and everyone had the chance to enjoy the beauty and invigorating influence of nature. To a good many patients this was an entirely new experience.

At Ohlstadt the daily program consisted of systematic calisthenics and breathing exercises, running, swimming, bathing, and ball games during the morning and an hour or two of relaxation after lunch. More games, hiking through the countryside, and climbing occupied the afternoon. The evening hours were given over to health discussions, lectures, lessons in crafts and hobbies, and cultural presentations. Radio and television were barred as irritants.

Competitive success in games was discouraged, but the prepatients were shifted from group to group according to their abilities. Those with orthopedic problems received special physiotherapy, therapeutic exercises, massage, and the like. Cold-water showers and steam baths were used extensively. Diets were generally low in animal-fat content.

Ohlstadt handled 125 patients at one time and had a staff of four doctors, several exercise instructors, three nurses, and ten administrative personnel. Sports clothing, bathrobes, and other items of equipment were supplied free.

Obviously Ohlstadt did not promise a complete "cure" for each patient, but the program generally broke the vicious circle of fatigue, tension, and loss of self-confidence, and it most certainly promoted the understanding for the need of healthy living habits. Each patient received instructions for a home exercise program and, if necessary, psychological advice was given to maintain the benefits of the program beyond the training period.

Humanitarian values aside, think of what similar centers, or even a pilot center, could do for the individual, for industry, and for labor in this country. As of now, fantastic sums are needlessly lost on absenteeism, medical care, and hospitalization.

Besides the humanitarian and economic values any American reconditioning center would have, a center would also open up new avenues of research in medicine, areas in which research is absolutely vital. In 1964 Dr. Wilhelm Raab of the University of Vermont College of Medicine held the First International Conference on Preventive Cardiology. Physicians and researchers from all over the world presented papers on exercise and heart disease. It was a magnificent gathering, yet Dr. Raab had to scrimp, scrounge, and beg funds to hold the conference. Many valuable papers were presented.

Dr. Herman K. Hellerstein of Western Reserve University reported on reconditioning programs he had started for heart patients in Cleveland. Among other things, Dr. Hellerstein discovered that recovered heart patients, who still had from 50 to 75 percent of their coronary artery flow shut off, could be restored to near normal function through exercise. One heart patient, who had suffered a very bad attack, was swimming a quarter of a mile a day.

Dr. M. E. Groover of the University of Oklahoma reported that he had found streaks of dead tissue in the heart muscles of Kenya baboons. Investigation then revealed that the damage had occurred when the baboons were trapped, when they were unable to respond to fight or flight. This condition, Dr. Groover said, may be "related to the mechanisms in the young executive who is caught in an emotional trap and cannot balance his nervous system by physical activity such as running or fighting."

Dr. Daniel Brunner of Tel Aviv reported on investigations of more than ten thousand men and women who were members of Israeli kibbutzim, collective settlements. The settlements were perfect laboratories in that they offered uniform environmental conditions. Each had one common dining room and no differences in living standards. And what did Dr. Brunner find? That heart attacks were two to four times more common among the sedentary kibbutzim workers than they were among the men and women who worked in the fields.

This was just one conference on heart disease and exercise. Think of the progress medicine could make if reconditioning centers and research facilities were established in this country. We could learn a great deal, and what we learned could then be applied to the public at large.

So far little progress has been made in aquainting the public with a real need, the imperative need for physical activity. The President's Council on Physical Fitness, the AMA, the Association for Health, Physical Education and Recreation have been talking, writing, and arranging meetings to that end. There have been public relations campaigns, too. But so far the main point has been missed. Physical activity is not a frill that you may indulge in, because it might be helpful and because it might make you more acceptable. **Physical activity is necessary for truly normal living and is an essential factor in disease prevention.** This must be emphasized.

But even when this has been done, we will still have more to do; we must answer the need for exercise. To do this best, we need a national organization, a national foundation, to supervise a country-wide program. Such a foundation would not be without precedent. Pehr Henrik Ling (see p. 32) organized the Royal Swedish Institute for Gymnastics in 1770. This institute has helped Sweden to become a leader in the development of physical training. Then again, it is not new in the United States to have a foundation to further national programs in health. There is the March of Dimes Foundation, which has had tremendous success. Before the discovery of the polio vaccine the foundation organized state and local chapters and trained members in exercise therapy for polio victims. The foundation introduced Sister Kenny's system of exercise and treatment, and although a number of physicians were opposed to this at the start, the system was widely taught and provided an excellent basis for the treatment of polio patients.

I would now hope to see a similar foundation for exercise created in this country. The honorary chairman should be the president, as was the case with the March of Dimes Foundation. This new foundation could establish an institute in which exercise would be the basic subject. This institute could call on all available talents, here and abroad; it might well establish student and teacher exchanges with the Scandinavian countries or others that are advanced in the field. This central institute could set up chapters in every state of the Union. These chapters, in turn, could cooperate with schools, hospitals, private groups, and any established reconditioning centers. The national foundation would have liaison with medical schools and departments of physical education. Within the foundation itself there would be departments to work on such diverse but important factors as liability laws, building codes, city school planning, home planning, city planning and, *of course*, outdoor recreation. The late President Kennedy was very aware of the fact that the President's Council on Physical Fitness did not and could not go much beyond public relations efforts. He was deeply interested in doing more, and shortly before his death a proposal for just such a national foundation was submitted to him. It is one of our losses that he did not have the time to act on it.

A new approach is essential. As of now, we are not doing the job.

Conclusion

WE HAVE DISCUSSED MANY THINGS: THE EFFECT OF OUR underexercised and stressful way of life on our health, how to determine whether or not we are underexercised and overstressed, and ways to contend with the problem. Intertwined with this physical and emotional problem is an unfulfilled spiritual need.

We have become far removed from the basic things: our bread comes processed, pre-sliced and packaged; pavements separate us from the earth; cars and planes give us exaggerated ideas of our power and ability to overcome space and time. Often our work is only a small part of a great organized effort, and laboring among the many we are deprived of the satisfaction of individual personal accomplishment.

We are shielded from the powers of nature—rain, storm, cold, heat and it takes floods and earthquakes to remind us of the humble place we occupy on this planet.

As we become more sheltered, we become all the more removed from the very forces that have formed and made us.

Since everything is so far removed, we rarely feel prompted to work on ourselves or our own improvement. We expect others and "things" to do for us what ultimately remains our very own responsibility.

Understanding our sickness and our weakness, and combating them by personal effort—by *doing*—may help reopen old avenues that we have forgotten in the rush of time.

Bibliography

BARZUN, JACQUES, *House of Intellect*, New York, Harper & Row, 1959.

BOYLE, ROBERT, "Report That Shocked the President." *Sports Illustrated*, August 15, 1955.

CANNON, WALTER B., *The Wisdom of the Body*. New York, W. W. Norton & Company, Inc., 1932.

EASTMAN, MAX, "Let's Close the Muscle Gap." *Reader's Digest*, November 1961.

GASTON, SAWNIE, AND SCHLESINGER, EDWARD B., "Injuries to the Low-Back Mechanism." *Trauma*, Philadelphia, London, Harrison L. McLaughlin, W. B. Saunders Company, 1959.

JACOBSON, EDMUND, *Tension Control for Businessmen*. New York, Toronto, London, McGraw-Hill, Inc., 1963.

JOLLIFFE, NORMAN, *Reduce and Stay Reduced on the Prudent Diet*. New York, Simon and Schuster, Inc., 1964

KENNEDY, JOHN F., "The Soft American." *Sports Illustrated*, December 26,1960.

KRAUS, HANS, *Principles and Practice of Therapeutic Exercises*. Springfield, Charles C Thomas, 1956.

KRAUS, HANS, AND RAAB, WILLIAM, *Hypokinetic Disease*. Springfield, Charles C Thomas, 1961.

SELYE, HANS, *The Stress of Life*. New York, McGraw-Hill, Inc, 1956.

STEINHAUS, ARTHUR H., *How to Keep Fit and Like It*. Chicago, The Dartnell Corporation, 1957.

STIMSON, B., "The Low-Back Problem." *Psychosomatic Medicine* G:210, May–June, 1947.